# THE MEANING OF THE CREATIVE ACT

NICOLAS BERDYAEV

# The Meaning of
# the Creative Act

$\oplus$

Foreword  *Boris Jakim*
Translator  *Donald A. Lowrie*

San Rafael CA

First Edition, Victor Gollancz, Ltd., London, 1955
Second, enlarged edition, Semantron Press 2009
Semantron is an imprint of Sophia Perennis LLC
Foreword and Biography © Boris Jakim 2008

For information, address:
Semantron Press, P.O. Box 151011
San Rafael, CA 94915
semantronpress.com

Library of Congress Cataloging-in-Publication Data

Berdiaev, Nikolai, 1874–1948.
[Smysl tvorchestva. English]
The meaning of the creative act / Nicolas Berdyaev;
[foreword by Boris Jakim].—Reprint ed.

p.   cm.
Originally published: New York: Charles Scribner's Sons, 1936.
Includes index.
ISBN 978 1 59731 262 2 (pbk: alk. paper)
1. Creation (Literary, artistic, etc.) I. Title.
BF408.B413 2009
128'.3—dc22            2009022495

Cover photograph by Dorlys Paris

# CONTENTS

# FOREWORD

Completed in 1914, and published in 1916, *The Meaning of the Creative Act* is a seminal work for Nikolai[1] Berdyaev. It adumbrates a number of crucially important themes that he develops in his later works, notably creative freedom as an essential element of human life and human creativeness as complementary to God's creativeness. Berdyaev says that his aim is to sketch out an "anthropodicy," a justification of man (as opposed to a theodicy, a justification of God); and man is to be justified on the basis of his creative acts, inasmuch as he is a creature who is also a co-creator in God's work of creation. Christianity had forgotten this truth, that man is a creative creature, but now a new religion of man as creator is being born. A transposition is taking place: humanity is being transposed from the material to the spiritual plane. It is in this crisis of humanity, in this new birth of man in the spirit, that Berdyaev sees the essence of his epoch (which is not too distant from our own). As he says, "the whole orientation of life must turn from without to within. And everything must be finally comprehended as a mystery of the spirit. . . . Everything external, material, everything of the object, is only a symbol of what is taking place in the depth of the spirit, in man" (p. 20, present volume).

A key element of Berdyaev's thinking is the idea of theurgy, of theurgic creativeness. Theurgy is artistic creation that goes beyond art, that goes beyond our world to create another world. Theurgy creates another being, another life; it creates beauty as essence, as being. Let us quote Berdyaev: "Theurgy

1. "Nikolai" is the more correct form of Berdyaev's first name. The original translations of Berdyaev's works into English used "Nicolas"; in order to avoid confusion this spelling is retained on the cover and title page.

overcomes the tragedy of creativeness, directs creative energy towards a new life. In theurgy, art becomes power. The beginning of theurgy is the end of literature, the end of all differentiated art, the end of culture, but an end which takes unto itself the world-meaning of culture and art, a super-cultural end. Theurgy is man working together with God; it is divine-human creativeness. In theurgic creativeness the tragic opposition of subject and object is removed, the tragic hiatus between the will to a new world and the attainment solely of cultural values. The theurge creates life in beauty. . . . The new art must lead us to theurgy. Theurgy is the banner of the art of the last times, the art of the end" (pp. 247–48, present volume). For Berdyaev, the final depths of all true art are religious. Theurgy is free creation. In theurgic action is revealed the religious-ontological, the religious meaning of being.

But to create, one needs freedom. Creativeness is nourished by freedom, grows in the soil of freedom, is impossible without freedom. Only those who are free can create. According to Berdyaev, when we are speaking of creativity "out of nothing," we are really speaking about creativity out of freedom: what is born of freedom does not derive from previously existing causes, from "something." Creativeness is something which proceeds from within, out of immeasurable and inexplicable depths, not from without, not from the world's necessity. "Freedom is the foundationless foundation of being: it is deeper than all being. . . . Freedom is a well of immeasurable depth—its bottom is the final mystery" (p. 145, present volume). Berdyaev talks about two freedoms: the negative, empty, formal freedom that is the result of the Fall of man and the creative freedom revealed by the Absolute Man, Christ. The falling away from God deprives freedom of its purpose, deprives it of power. In Adam, the active-creative calling of man had not yet been revealed. "The freedom of the all-man Adam had not yet been joined with the freedom of the Absolute Man, Christ, and in that earlier freedom were contained

4

the seeds of the Fall and of sin. . . .The cosmic mystery of the redemption overcomes formal and empty freedom. . . . Man, become son of God, rises to the consciousness of freedom full of creative purpose. . . . The freedom of the new Adam…is creative freedom, freedom which continues the work of God's creativeness. . . ." (pp. 147–48, present volume). "God expects from man the highest freedom, the freedom of the eighth day of creation" (p. 158, present volume).

In contemplating Russia's greatest saint, Seraphim of Sarov, and Russia's greatest creative genius, Pushkin, Berdyaev finds the two types to be complementary. Berdyaev proposes that the cult of saintliness be complemented by the cult of genius, inasmuch as the path of the genius involves sacrificial heroism and the creative ecstasy of the genius is no less religious that the ecstasy of sainthood. Just as the will to saintliness has been recognized as a religious imperative, so the will to genius will also be recognized as a religious imperative. The potentiality for both lies in every image and likeness of God. Berdyaev suggests that it is possible that a new type of monasticism might arise on the path of creative genius. Like conventional monasticism, the path of creative genius too demands a renunciation of the world and its goods. "The life of genius is a monastic life in the world." (p. 178, present volume)

One of the most fascinating parts of the book is the treatment of the relationship between creativeness and sex, and Berdyaev's opinions are unusual and controversial. According to Berdyaev, the human being must be liberated from the sexual act, which, being procreative, is not spiritually creative. A new, eternal sex is being prepared, and it is to be found in the androgynism of the new Adam-Christ. The revelation of the new sex is possible only in the revelation of the absolute human being in creative power and glory; this is being prepared in the new life of sex—the creative sex, i.e., sex that is rooted in Divine-human creativity. The Christian cult of eternal femininity (as manifested in the Virgin Mary) will be superseded, in the

5

new creative world-epoch, by the cult of the androgyne, the youth-maiden, of man as the image and likeness of God. There will result an eternal form of illuminated corporeality, freed of all weight and of the necessity of the sexual act.

To sum up, the problem of creativeness, the problem of the unfolding of man's creative powers (what Berdyaev calls "anthropological revelation"), is today the key problem of the world's life and of the world's culture. But Berdyaev points out that the world has not yet known true creativeness in the definitive and ultimate religious sense of the word. Our present life is only a transition to creative life, rather than creative life itself. The true nature of creativeness is something unknowable—it is something that must be lived. Berdyaev calls us to a grand initiative towards a full actualization of the creative life: this initiative must be audacious, and we must mercilessly clear the obstacles that block the path to its realization. If man refuses this creative initiative, he is not fulfilling his religious duty, he is not fulfilling the will of God. Berdyaev puts it in a single sentence: "God awaits from us a creative act."

BORIS JAKIM
2008

# TRANSLATOR'S PREFACE

ALTHOUGH HE WAS frequently asked to permit a reissue in Russian of *The Meaning of the Creative Act*, Berdyaev always refused, saying that he wished to revise it before it was republished. Completed in 1914, the book naturally reflects the atmosphere of the philosophy current at the time, and certain of its details would probably have been altered had Berdyaev been writing it in the later years of his life. But, as he has often said, the basic ideas in this book remained, to the end, the foundation of his philosophical convictions. It has therefore been decided to publish the present edition, despite the fact that the author never accomplished the revision he projected.

Berdyaev made one revision, however, for the German translation, published in 1927. Collation with that text has enabled the reproduction in the present version, of what Berdyaev authorized for publication at that time. In this connection, his Preface for the German edition deserves special attention.

I am indebted to Madame T. F. Klepinine and the late Miss Alissa A. Sezemann for generous counsel about this work. Special gratitude is due my wife for typing the manuscript.

D. A. L.

NEW YORK.
*May, 1954.*

# AUTHOR'S PREFACE FOR THE GERMAN EDITION

My book, *The Meaning of the Creative Act*, was written fifteen years ago. Since then mighty catastrophes have broken over Russia and the world. A new epoch in history has begun. The bases of my thinking remain unaltered. In my book I gave warning that the old world was going to pieces. But now the definiteness of my book appears to me as too optimistic. My faith in the imminent dawn of a creative religious epoch was too great. The book was written in one single movement, and it reflects the *Sturm und Drang* period of my life. To-day I am inclined to greater pessimism, and this is expressed in my *The Meaning of History*. But now as then, I still believe that God calls men to creative activity and to a creative answer to His love. Our creativeness should be the expression of our love toward God. But the crisis through which humanity is passing, which is expressed first of all in the bankruptcy of humanism, to-day seems to me more tragic, and offers no hope for the possibility of an immediate move into religious creativity. We shall have to pass through a period of darkness before the new light beams out. The world must look forward to a period of barbarization. Man is a creator not only in the name of God but in the name of the devil as well. This complicates the problem of creativity. But we must not be led astray into reaction against the creative spirit in general, by the power of Satanic creativity in the world of to-day. The Christian renaissance can be only a creative renaissance. Creativeness neither destroys nor diminishes the eternal truth of salvation: it merely reveals the other side of Christianity; it enlarges the Christian truth.

N. Berdyaev.

Paris.
*March, 1926.*

*Ich weiss, dass ohne mich Gott nicht ein Nu kann leben—*
*Werd ich zu nicht, er muss von Not den Geist aufgeben.*

ANGELUS SILESIUS.

# INTRODUCTION

THE HUMAN SPIRIT is in prison. Prison is what I call this
world, the given world of necessity. "This world" is not the
cosmos; it is a non-cosmic condition of divisions and enmity,
the atomization and falling apart of the living monads of the
cosmic hierarchy. And the true way is that of spiritual liberation from "the world", the liberation of man's spirit from
its bondage to necessity. The true way is not a movement to
right or left in the plane of "the world", but rather movement
upward and downward on lines of the ultra-worldly,
movement in spirit and not in "the world". Freedom from
the reactions of "the world" and from opportunistic adaptations to it is a great achievement of the spirit. This is a way
of great spiritual contemplation, spiritual collectedness and
concentration. The cosmos is true being, but the "given
world" is a phantom and so is the necessity of the given
world. This phantom "world" is born of our sin. The
teachers of the Church identified "the world" with evil
passions. Man's spiritual captivity to "the world" is his
fault, his sin, his fall. Liberation from the world is liberation
from sin, the redemption of faults committed, the uprising of
the fallen spirit. We are not "of this world" and should not
love the world and that which is in the world. But the very
doctrine of sin was born of slavery to illusory necessity. They
tell us: "You are a sinful, fallen being, and therefore do not
dare to enter upon the way of liberation from 'the world',
on the way of the creative life of the spirit; bear your burden

of meek acceptance of the results of sin." And the spirit of man remains shackled in a circle with no way out. For original sin is slavery, bondage of the spirit, subjection to diabolic necessity, the incapacity to affirm oneself as a free creative agent; man loses himself by his assertion in the necessity of the world and not in the freedom of God. The way of liberation from "the world" for the creation of a new life is at the same time the way of liberation from sin, the overcoming of evil, the gathering of spiritual forces for life which is divine. Slavery to the "given world", to necessity, is not only bondage but it is legitimizing and confirming the hated and divided non-cosmic condition of the world. Freedom is love. Slavery is hatred. But the escape from slavery into freedom, from the hatred of the world into cosmic love, is the way of victory over sin, over our lower nature. And we may not be refused entrance into this way on the ground that human nature is sinful and sunken in a lower sphere. It is a great falsehood, a terrible mistake of religious and moral judgement, to leave man in the lower depths of "the world", because he must be obedient to the results of his sin. On the soil of such judgement there grows a shameful indifference to good and evil, the refusal of manful resistance to wrong. The depressive concentration on man's own sinfulness gives birth to double thinking: the constant danger of confusing God with the devil, Christ with Antichrist. This fallen state of the spirit, shamefully in-different to good and evil, has now gone to the length of a mystic fascination with passivity and humility, to play with double-thinking. The fallen soul likes to flirt with Lucifer, likes not knowing which God she serves, enjoys feeling terror and danger everywhere. This fallen state, this palsy and cleavage of man's spirit, is an indirect result of the Christian doctrines of humility and obedience—it is a degeneration of these doctrines. Over against this decadent doubling of thought and this palsied indifference to good and evil we must firmly set the manful liberation of the spirit and creative action. But this requires a concentrated

12

resolution to be free from the false and illusory accretions of culture and its *scoriæ*, free from this refined captivity to "the world".

The creative act is always liberation and conquest. It is an experience of power. The revelation of this creative act is not a cry of pain, it is neither passive suffering nor lyric effusion. Terror, pain, palsy, destruction, must be conquered by creativity. In essence, creativity is a way out, an exodus; it is victory. The sacrifice of creativeness is neither terror nor destruction. The willingness to sacrifice is itself active rather than passive. Personal tragedy or crisis or fate is experienced as the tragedy or crisis or fate of the world. Concentration on one's own personal salvation and fear of one's own personal loss is monstrously selfish. Concentration on the crisis of one's own creativeness and the terror of one's own powerlessness is monstrously prideful. Egoistic and self-conceited concentration on oneself indicates a morbid separation between man and the world. Man was made by the Creator with qualities of genius (not always genius in the full sense of the word), and these qualities must express themselves in creative activity, must overcome everything personally-egoistic and personally self-conceited, conquer all fear of one's own loss, all concern for what others may think. In its ultimate base on the Absolute Man-Christ, human nature has already become the nature of the new Adam and is united with divine nature—it no longer has a right to feel itself cast-off and lonely. This sense of isolation and depression is itself a sin against man's divine calling, against the call of God, God's need of man. Only the man who lives the whole world within himself, experiences everything as being universal, only he who has conquered in himself the egoistic striving for self-salvation and prideful selfish reflection about his own powers, only he who has freed himself of anything that is torn away and separate— only such a man is strong enough to be a person and a creator. Nothing but man's liberation from himself will bring man to himself. The way of creativeness is a way of

13

sacrifice and suffering but it always means liberation from depression. The sacrificial suffering of creativeness is never depression. All such sense of depression is really man's being torn away from the true world, his being no longer a microcosm, his captivity to the "given world", his slavery to necessity. All pessimism and scepticism is egoistic and proud. Doubt of man's creative power is a self-conceited reflexion, a morbid egotism. Humility and doubting modesty in places where there should be daring confidence and decision are always disguised metaphysical pride, reflective retrospection and egotistic isolation, born of fear and terror. Times are coming in the life of humanity when it must help itself, conscious that the absence of transcendent aid is not helplessness; because man can discover limitless aid immanent within himself if he dares to reveal in himself, by the creative act, all the power of God and the world, the true world, freed from the illusory world. In our days there is too much unworthy and enfeebling self-abnegation, the reverse side of an equally unworthy and enfeebling self-assertion. You frequently hear: "We are not real men—in former days there were genuine people. Those men of other days dared to speak of religion. We do not venture to mention it." Such people are men of an illusory self-consciousness, atomized by "this world", who have lost the nucleus of their personality. This slavery to "the world" is really absorption with themselves and this absorption with themselves means the loss of themselves. Freedom from "the world" is union with the true world, the cosmos. Thus to go out of oneself is to find oneself, one's true centre. And we can and we must feel ourselves real people, with a real nucleus of personality, with an authentic, not an illusory, religious will.

We do not climb the stair of knowing in the dark. Scientific knowledge climbs a dark stairway—which it enlightens, step by step. It does not know what awaits it at the top of the stair; in it there is no light of the sun, of meaning, of the Logos, which lightens the path from above. But in the true higher gnosis there is an original revelation of meaning,

14

sunlight falling from above on the stairway of knowledge. Gnosis is an original comprehension of meaning: in it is the manly activity of the Logos. The modern spirit still suffers from fear of the light. By dark corridors the spirit has passed through lightless science and arrived at lightless mystic. The spirit has not yet reached the sunlight of consciousness. The mystic renaissance finds itself entering an epoch of darkness. This epoch of night is feminine and not masculine —it lacks sunlight. But, in a deeper sense, all modern history with its rationalism, its positivism, its belief in science, has been a period of night, rather than of day—the sun of the world has darkened, the light from above has gone out, all the light that was has been artificial and indirect. And we stand before a new dawn, a new sunrise. Once more we must come to recognize the intrinsic value of thought (in the Logos) as light-bringing human activity, as a creative act in being. The reaction against rationalism has taken on forms of hostility to thought and word. But we must liberate ourselves from this reaction, and in the freedom of the spirit, in an affirmation of thought and word which transcends all time, once more find meaning. Our consciousness is essentially something of the borderline, of transition. But on the threshold of the new world light is born which gives meaning to the world which is passing away. Only now we are able fully to recognize that which has been in the light of that which is to be. And we know that, in reality, the past will really be only in the future.

§

I know that I may be accused of a basic contradiction which tears apart all my sense of the world, all my world-outlook. I shall be accused of the contradiction of combining an extreme religious dualism with an extreme religious monism. I accept such attacks in advance. I confess an almost manichean dualism. So be it. "The world" is evil, it is without God and not created by Him. We must go out of the world, overcome it completely: the world must be

15

consumed, it is of the nature of Ariman. Freedom from the world is the *pathos* of this book. There is an objective source of evil, against which we must wage an heroic war. The necessity of the given world and the given world itself are of Ariman. Over against this stands freedom in the spirit, life in divine love, life in the Pleroma. And I also confess an almost pantheistic monism. The world is divine in its very nature. Man is, by his nature, divine. The world-process is self-revelation of Divinity, it is taking place within Divinity. God is immanent in the world and in man. The world and man are immanent in God. Everything which happens with man happens with God. There is no dualism of divine and extra-divine nature, of God's absolute transcendence of the world and of man. I am entirely conscious of this antinomy of dualism and monism, and I accept it as insurmountable in consciousness and inevitable in religious life. Religious consciousness is essentially antinomic. In our consciousness there is no escape from the eternal antinomy of transcendent and immanent, of dualism and monism. This antinomy cannot be abolished, neither in conscience nor in reason, but in religious life, in the depth of the religious experience itself. Religious consciousness experiences the world to the fullest extent, both as completely apart from God and as fully divine, experiences evil both as falling away from divine reason, and as having an immanent meaning in the process of the world's development. The mystic gnosis always found an antinomic solution for the problem of evil; in it dualism was mystically combined with monism. For the greatest of the mystics, Jakob Boehme, evil was in God—and it was falling-away from God; in God was the source of darkness— and God was not responsible for evil. Almost all the mystics have stood for the consciousness of an immanent experience of evil. The transcendent viewpoint is always the penultimate and not the final. And the experience of sin is something peripheral and exoteric, in religious life. Deeper, more exoteric, is the experience of an inner cleavage in divine life, resistance to God or the sense of being deserted by Him,

16

all as parts of the sacrificial way of mounting upward. A transcendent attitude towards God and a transcendent attitude towards evil are inevitable in religious experience. But equally inevitable in religious life is the attainment of immanent truth and the immanent experience of God and the world. And in the final depths, every mystic experience passes beyond all the opposition between the transcendent and the immanent. There is no given objectivity in religious life. Every objectivization, every exteriorization of God, of Christ, of the sacrament, is only a relative and conditional projection on one plane, a cultural-historic phenomenon. The paradox in religious life is astonishing: an extreme transcendentism gives birth to an opportunistic adjustment, an accommodation to the evil of the world—while a mature immanentism produces the will to a complete passage into the divine life of the spirit, to a radical overcoming of "the world". This world is captivity by evil, a falling away from divine life: "the world" must be overcome. But "the world" is only one of the moments of the inward, divine process of creating the cosmos, a movement in the Divine Trinity, man's birth in God. This antinomy is given in religious experience. Only a childishly-immature, simple, frightened consciousness is afraid of this antinomy: it is always dreaming of some idealization and justification of evil in the immanent-monistic thesis of the antinomy. But we may take a merciless attitude towards evil, towards "the world" and the slavery and ruin which it involves. The absolute is affirmed in the depths of spiritual life and not in the external conditional world, to which nothing absolute is applicable. The heroic struggle against the evil of the world is born in the liberating consciousness of immanentism, in which God is immanent in the human spirit and the world is transcendent to it. The desire may easily appear to interpret such a religious philosophy as "a-cosmism". In my consciousness "the world" is illusory—and not true. But for me "the world" is not cosmic, it is an a-cosmic condition of the spirit. The true, the cosmic world, means overcoming "the world", freedom

from "the world", victory over "the world". My consciousness accepts still another antinomy—the antinomy of the
"unique" and the "multiple". In distinction from all the
mystics of *the one* (India, Plotinus, Eckhardt) I confess a
monopluralism, i.e. I accept both metaphysically and
mystically not only the One, but a substantial plurality, the
revelation in One God of a permanent cosmic plurality, a
multitude of eternal individualities. The cosmic plurality is
an enriching revelation of God, God's development. This
consciousness leads to a metaphysical and mystical personalism, to the revelation of the "ego".

These introductory words will perhaps save me from being
too grossly misunderstood or accused in too elemental a
manner. I stand consciously on the antinomy and desire to
live it through rather than to eliminate it by logic or reason.
Hence, being a monist and an "immanentist" in the final
depth of mystic experience, believing in the divine quality
of the world, in the inward divinity of the world process, in
the heavenly quality of everything earthly, in the divinity
of the human person, I yet affirm the cleavage, the dualism
of freedom and necessity, of God, divine life and "the given
world", of good and evil, of the transcendent and the
immanent. This kind of radical, revolutionary, implacable
dualism leads to the final monism of divine life, to the
divinity of man. This is the whole mystery of Christianity.
Through this heroic dualism, through the contrast of the
divine and "the world" man enters into the monism of
Divine Life. Everything in the world must be "immanently"
lifted on the Cross. Thus the divine development is realized,
the divine creativity. Everything external becomes something inward. And the whole world is my way. We must
free ourselves from the Churchly Semitism which was an
expression of the immature period of Christianity. A
Semitic, Old Testament transcendentism deadens religious
life to-day; it has degenerated into police action against a
movement in spiritual experience; it encourages intolerance
and the judging of one's neighbour, produces anti-Christian

18

feelings. We already understand, we know the relativity of any ontological transcription of the moments of religious and mystic experience. Making absolute the dynamic moments of spiritual experience in Christian ontology and metaphysics may become a great falsehood of static, setting itself up against the eternal truth of the dynamic of absolute spiritual life. The dynamic transcription of religious experience must take precedence over the static transcription of religious ontology. Transcendentism is an inevitable moment of religious experience, but not the absolute truth of ontology. The final human mystery is the birth of God in man. The last mystery of God is the birth of man in God. And this mystery is the one and only mystery: for not only has man need of God, but God has need of man. In this lies the mystery of Christ, the mystery of the God-man.

In the vital source of this book and this religious philosophy there is a quite exceptional, imperial feeling of man, a religious comprehension of the Anthropos as a divine person. Up to now, religion, mystics and philosophy have been so inhuman and non-human that they led, with immanent necessity, to godless positivism. In German mysticism, it is true, there have been mysterious beginnings of an exceptional concept of man, of God's need for man, of anthropogony as continuing theogony. These depths are concealed in Paracelsus, J. Boehme and Angelus Silesius. And I feel a vital connection with them and find support in their dawning revelations. Many have written their justification of God, their theodicy. But the time has come to write a justification of man, an anthropodicy. Perhaps an anthropodicy is the only way to a theodicy, the only way not yet lived and used to the full. This book of mine is an essay on anthropodicy by means of creativeness. The religion of the race, material religion, is decaying and closing up in our world. Everything that is material, generic, ancient and organic, has a futurist-technical, mechanical end. A religion of man is being born. The human race is being re-born into humanity. This is a transfer from the material plane to another plane of being,

19

and in this crisis of the race and of matter, in the definitive birth of man and the life of the spirit—in these is the essence of our epoch. The whole orientation of life must turn from without to within. And everything must be finally comprehended as a mystery of the spirit, as one of its stages on the eternal way. Everything external, material, everything of the object, is only a symbol of what is taking place in the depth of the spirit, in man.

Moscow.
*February, 1914.*

# CHAPTER I

# PHILOSOPHY AS A CREATIVE ACT

THE DREAM OF MODERN philosophy is to become scientific, or something like the scientific. Not one of the official philosophers has any serious doubts as to the rightness and propriety of this effort to turn philosophy into a scientific discipline, no matter what the cost. In this they all agree— positivists and metaphysicists, materialists and "criticists", Kant and Hegel, Comte and Spencer, Cohen and Rickert, Wundt and Avenarius—all desire that philosophy should be either science or something shaped like science. Philosophy always envies science. Science is the eternal longing of the philosophers. The philosophers do not dare to be themselves —they are always trying to imitate men of science. The philosophers believe in science more than they do in philosophy; they have doubts about themselves and their work, and they raise these doubts to the place of a principle. The philosophers believe in knowledge only because the fact of science exists: and by analogy with science they are ready to believe in philosophical knowledge. This may be said not only of the positivists and the "criticists", but just as well of a great part of the metaphysicists of our time. Even metaphysics would like to become a science, to resemble science in every way, although in this it has little success. The modern philosophers consider that the liberation of philosophy from all dependence can be achieved by its final transformation into a special science. Modern consciousness is possessed with the idea of "scientific" philosophy, it is hypnotized by the forced idea of the scientific. But in this there is nothing really new: it is only a modernized expression of the old scholastic idea. Even metaphysical philosophy tried in its own way to be scientific, and for its time, and conditionally, so it was. Descartes and Leibnitz are no less scientific philosophers than Cohen and Husserl. When Haeckel, that naïve apologist for the scientific, wished to set up a scientific monism, he took for his model the old metaphysicist, Spinoza. Spinoza's geometric method was the same type of striving for the scientific in philosophy, as was the transcendental method of Kant. And the scholastic philosophy of the middle ages was all permeated with a stubborn, all-embracing desire to make into a formal, science-like discipline not only philosophy but theology as well. Of course, the concept of science in the middle ages was very different from the modern idea, but scholasticism adapted itself to the scientific conceptions of its time. Not in vain was Aristotle, the most apparently scientific philosopher of antiquity, the ruler of men's thoughts. In equal measure Thomas Aquinas and Cohen are "scientific" philosophers, each in his own time, according to the scientific criteria of his period. The scientific philosophy of Cohen is a direct inheritance from scholastic philosophy. Neokantism is neo-scholastic, but it has carried the problem of knowledge to tragic acuteness. For Thomas Aquinas metaphysics was a strict science of being and its principles. That was a purely rational science—its construction was severely logical. Thomas Aquinas did not know the critical doubts of modern philosophy; his science was dogmatic. Thomas Aquinas' science lorded it over both theology and the whole of life. Philosophy was the servant of theology—we may understand this to mean that philosophy made theology scientific. After all the critical doubts of modern philosophy, gnosseology now turns, in Cohen, into a new sort of metaphysics: the science of categories is transformed into the science of being and its principles, just as it was in Hegel. This scientific philosophy lays claim to lordship over life, just as did scholastic philosophy. The scholastic principle is one in which the school, science, science-like rationalism, dominate not only the philosophy but the whole culture of the time.

22

The content of this science-like rationalism changes but the principle remains the same: Aristotle, Thomas Aquinas, Descartes, Spinoza, Kant, Hegel, Spencer, Avenarius, Cohen, Husserl—all these differing philosophers convert philosophy into science-like scholastics. The desire of philosophy to be the universal science of its time is always scholastic. Philosophic consciousness is ever roiled and confused by false and illusory strivings towards the quality of science, towards ideals and criteria of a sphere alien to philosophy—in this age-old bondage of philosophy to a stranger.

*Philosophy is in no sense at all a science and in no way should it be scientific.* It is difficult to understand why philosophy has longed to resemble science, to become a science. Art, morals, religion, do not have to be sciences—why should philosophy? It would seem as clear as day that nothing in the world should be scientific except science itself. The scientific is an exclusive quality of science, and a criterion only for science. It would seem crystal clear that philosophy should be philosophical, solely philosophic and not scientific, just as morals should be moral, religion religious, and art artistic. Philosophy was born before science, it is nearer Sophia; it existed when there was still no science; from within itself it produced science. And the result was the expectation that science would produce philosophy! But this differentiation, which should have favoured philosophy by the liberation of its own independent sphere, gradually led to the enslavement of philosophy. If we were to recognize philosophy as a special science along with other sciences (for instance the science of principles of knowledge or principles of being) that would definitely abolish philosophy as an independent sphere of spiritual life. In that case we could not speak of philosophy as in a class by itself, along with science, art, morals, etc. We should have to speak of philosophy along with other sciences, mathematics, physics, chemistry, physiology, etc. But philosophy is an independent sphere of culture, and not an independent sphere of science. Many philosophers are

23

striving to make philosophy not so much a science as something scientific. What is meant by "scientific"?

No one seriously doubts the value of science. The fact is indubitable that man needs science. But one may doubt the value of and need for the "scientific". Science and the "scientific" are two quite different things. The scientific means carrying the criteria of science over into other spheres of spiritual life quite foreign to science. "The scientific" is based on the belief that science is the supreme criterion of the whole life of the spirit, that everything must be subject to the order established by science, that its permissions or prohibitions have decisive meaning, everywhere. It presupposes the existence of one single method for everything. No one will protest the employment of the "scientific" in science. But even here we may note a pluralism of scientific methods corresponding to the pluralism of the sciences. For instance, we cannot carry over the method of natural science into psychology or the social sciences. This has been shown, often, by the German gnosseologues. But these very gnosseologues have greatly forwarded the establishment of this ideal of "the scientific". There is a *pathos* of the "scientific" in German critical consciousness. The critical philosophers wanted to orient all culture towards "the scientific". The ideal of scientific philosophy is not so coarse in German criticism as in French and English positivism. The German idea is more refined and complex. But the German critical consciousness not only went so far as to insist that philosophy should be scientific, but it also recognized the authority of the scientific in the religious, moral, æsthetic and social spheres. There should be a scientific, critical differentiation of cultures: they should be scientifically arranged and ordered. This criterion of "the scientific" emprisons or liberates everything just as it wishes. Religion within the limits of reason, rational protestantism—this is clearly the domination of the scientific over religious life, this is a denial of its being outside such jurisdiction. But "the scientific" is not science and is not

24

derived from science. No science gives scientific directions for other spheres of thought. Astronomy, physics, geology, or physiology are not in the least interested in the scientific approach to philosophy or in the scientific ordering of culture. *"The scientific"—not science—is bondage of the spirit to the lower spheres of being, the constant and ubiquitous consciousness of the power of necessity, of dependence upon the things of this world.* It is only one of the ways of expressing the loss of freedom of the creative spirit. In this sense "the scientific" is deeply symptomatic. German criticism dreams of disciplining the spirit by means of "the scientific", of saving the spirit from chaos. This is the basic German idea, that everything must be justified by a scientific gnosseological consciousness, but this application of scientific discipline to everything which is, is only an expression of the spirit's bondage and its fractionization. German philosophers have even tried to make marriage something justified by the methodological and scientific. Science is a specific reaction of the human spirit to the world and, from an analysis of the nature of science and the scientific attitude towards the world, it should become clear that forcing the scientific upon man's other relations with the world can only mean a slavish dependence of the spirit.

In its specific essence, science is man's reaction for self-preservation: man, lost in the dark forest of the world's life. In order to live and develop, man must consciously orient himself in the given world which crowds upon him from every side. For this protective orientation man must bring himself into correspondence with the realities of the world, with the world's necessity which surrounds him. Science is a highly perfected means of adaptation to the given world and to the necessity forced upon it. Science is knowledge of necessity by means of adaptation to the given world, and knowledge out of necessity.

Again, science may be defined as a condensed economic description of the given world's necessity for the purpose of orientation and the reaction of self-preservation. Scientific thinking always corresponds profoundly with, and adjusts

25

itself to, the world's necessity: it is an instrument of orientation in the given world. And this mark of adaptation lies not only on scientific experiment but on that discursive thinking which science uses for its deductions. Scientific logic is an instrument for adaptation to necessity; in scientific logic there is submission to the world's necessity, and on it lies the mark of the limitations of such necessity, of the given world. All the limiting dilemmas of formal logic are only adjusted reflections of the limiting dilemmas of the world's necessity. A limited logic is the true reaction to the limited condition of the given world. Necessity in thinking is only its self-preservation in adaptation to the necessity of the world. The necessity of the world must be recognized, and a corresponding necessity in thinking must be elaborated. We may be critical of various expressions of pragmatism, but it is difficult to deny the pragmatic nature of science. Bacon had already revealed the practical-pragmatic nature of science. In E. Mach's theory of scientific knowledge there is an undeniable, factual truth. The science of true savants, not philosophers but scientific specialists who have greatly advanced science itself, justifies Mach and the pragmatists rather than Cohen and the criticists. Only philosophers have dreamed of a universal science: true scientists have always been more modest. They have separated the given world into distinct special spheres and under the name of the laws of nature have given an economically brief description of these various spheres. The value of scientific laws of nature has always lain in practical orientation to nature, in controlling nature by its own laws, i.e. by means of adaptation.

It is true that in science two souls have always lived and struggled, and one of them thirsted for knowledge of the secret of the world. But science was not created by this soul: this soul always inclined to philosophy, theosophy and magic. In order to make clearer the impossibility and the uselessness of scientific philosophy, it is important to emphasize the conclusion that *science is obedience to necessity*.

Science is not creativity but obedience; its element is not freedom but necessity. We shall see that science is Old Testament in its religious essence and bound up with sin. Science never was and never can be the liberation of the human spirit. Science has always been the expression of man's constraint under necessity. But it has been a valuable orientation in necessity and a sacred, knowing obedience to the results of the sin man has committed. In its essence, as well as in its purpose, science always perceived the world under the aspect of necessity, and the category of necessity is the fundamental category of scientific thinking as an orientative adaptation to the given conditions of being. Science has no vision of freedom in the world. Science does not know the final secrets because science is knowledge without danger. Hence science does not know Truth but knows only truths. The truth of science is significant only for partial conditions of being and for partial orientations within it. Science makes its own reality. But philosophy and religion set up quite other realities.

§

If science is an economic adaptation to the given world and obedience to the world's necessity, why and in what sense should philosophy be dependent upon science or be a science? First of all, and in every case, philosophy is a general orientation to the whole of being and not a partial orientation in partial conditions of being. Philosophy seeks the truth, not truths. Philosophy loves wisdom. Sophia moves all true philosophy. At the summit of philosophic consciousness, Sophia enters into man. In its bases and principles, in its roots and in its peaks, science may be dependent upon philosophy but never can the reverse be true. A philosophy of science may be admitted but scientific philosophy is inadmissible. By its essence and by its purpose philosophy has never been adapted to necessity. Real philosophers, true to their calling, have never been obedient to the given world because the philosophers sought the all-wise truth which surpasses the present world. The cherished purpose of philosophers was ever the knowledge of freedom and knowledge in freedom. The element of philosophy is freedom and not necessity. Philosophy has always striven to be the liberation of the human spirit from its bondage to necessity. Philosophy may investigate that logical apparatus, which is an adaptation of thinking to the world's necessity, but itself may never stand in slavish dependence upon that apparatus. The knowledge of wisdom is higher than the knowledge of logic. Philosophy is a knowing way out of the given world: it is vision which surpasses the necessity of the world. Philosophy is in principle a quality of reaction to the world other than science, and moves towards something other. And to subject philosophy to science is to subject freedom to necessity. Scientific philosophy is enslaved philosophy, which has surrendered its pristine freedom to the power of necessity. Subjection to the given world, something obligatory for science, is for philosophy a degradation and betrayal of the knowing will to freedom. We must state boldly and with full consciousness of what it means that the boundaries of the given world and the commands of the given world-necessity are not obligatory for philosophy. Philosophy is free from concern as to what sort of world is given us, since it seeks the truth of the world and the world's meaning rather than the given world. Even if the given world were exclusively material, philosophy would not have to be materialistic. And since the true *pathos* of philosophy has always lain in the heroic struggle of creative knowledge against all necessity and every given condition of being, since the aim of philosophy was ever the transcending, the passing of boundaries, philosophy never was science and never could be scientific. Knowledge is a marriage of male and female: in it there is both self-sacrificing receptivity and light-giving activity. Philosophy guards the knowledge of truth, as a masculine, sun-like activity in relation to that which is to be known. In the marriage of knowledge the knower is the man, i.e. the Logos. Only philosophy reveals this active-

28

masculine side of knowledge. *Philosophy is creativeness, and not adaptation or obedience.* The liberation of philosophy as a creative act is its liberation from all dependence upon science, i.e. heroic resistance to every sort of adaptation to necessity. In philosophy the self-liberation of the creative act of the human spirit in its reaction to the world takes place in the knowing resistance to necessity and to the given world, not in adaptation to it. Philosophy is art rather than science. Philosophy is a special art, differing in principle from poetry, music, or painting—it is the art of knowing. Philosophy is an art because it is creation. Philosophy is an art because it predicates a calling and a special gift from above, because the personality of its creator is impressed upon it, no less than on music or poetry. But philosophy creates existential ideas rather than images. Philosophy is the art of knowing in freedom by creating ideas which resist the given world and necessity and penetrate into the ultimate essence of the world. We cannot make art dependent upon science, creativeness upon adaptation, freedom upon necessity.

When philosophy becomes a science it fails in its prime purpose—passage beyond the given world, vision beyond its necessity. The human spirit conquers in philosophy, by active resistance, by creative mastery, while in science victory comes through adaptation, through bringing oneself into alignment with the world's data, forced upon us by necessity. Science represents man's bitter need; philosophy is luxury, a superfluity of spiritual forces. Philosophy is not less vital than science, but it is the vitality of creative knowledge which transcends the bounds of the given world rather than the vitality of adapting knowledge for self-preservation within it. The nature of philosophy is not at all economic. Philosophy is more often a squandering than an economy of thinking. There is something of the holiday in philosophy and for the utilitarians of every day, something just as idle as in art. Philosophy was never as necessary for preservation of life in this world as is science: it was needed for passing beyond the limits of the given world. Science leaves man in the senselessness of the given world of necessity but gives him weapons for his protection in this senseless world. Philosophy always strives to comprehend the meaning of the world, is ever resisting the senselessness of the world's necessity. The basic assumption of every true philosophy is that there is a meaning and that this meaning is attainable— the assumption that meaning can break through meaning-lessness. Kant recognized this, and one cannot deny that in the Kantian philosophy there is a creative urge which over-comes the passivity of the older metaphysicists. This urge is still stronger in Fichte. Adaptation to the meaningless, given world can only hinder us from comprehending meaning: but the partisans of scientific philosophy demand this adaptation, that is they deny the creative nature of philo-sophy. It is true that they are striving to lift the rank of science, to recognize it as a creative act and to see a higher meaning, the Logos, in the logical categories with which science operates. But this raising of the rank of science and its extension to higher spheres can be achieved only by bringing philosophy down into science, consciously or uncon-sciously. It cannot be denied that there are philosophic elements in science, that in scientific hypotheses there is sometimes a philosophical flight, and that scholars are not rarely philosophers. But we must distinguish in principle what is of science and what is of philosophy. We cannot demand of philosophy that it be scientific just because science sometimes has philosophical character. We cannot deny the relative importance of the logical categories on which scientific knowledge is based, but to assign them a higher and absolute ontological meaning is simply one of the false philosophies held captive by the given world, by being in a state of necessity.

§

The history of philosophy is dual; it is full of the deep drama of the thirst for knowledge. And the history of philo-sophy is so different from that of science, both in principle and in substance, that it would be impossible to write a history of scientific philosophy. There never have been and never can be elements of scientific progress in the history of philosophy. With the best will in the world it would be difficult to find in the history of the human spirit an increase in the scientific quality of philosophical knowledge. The history of philosophic consciousness has its own logic, which is not that of science. The historians of philosophy feel that their subject resembles the history of literature more than that of science; they convert it into a history of the spiritual development of mankind, tie it in with the history of culture. But in the final analysis the history of philosophy is the history of the human spirit's self-consciousness, the integral reaction of the spirit to the totality of being. Aristotle and Thomas Aquinas were far more scientific philosophers than many of the thinkers of the nineteenth century—more than Schelling and Schopenhauer, Franz Baader and Vladimir Solovieff, Nietzsche and Bergson. This leaning towards the scientific in philosophy is one of the permanent tendencies which have accompanied the history of philosophic self-consciousness in all ages. In Greece and in the middle ages, even in India, always and everywhere there have been attempts to give philosophy a scientific character, to adapt it to the science of the time, to make it agree with necessity. Cohen, Husserl or Avenarius are doing in the twentieth century just what Aristotle or the scholastic philosophers did in their time. There is neither anything essentially progressive nor anything essentially new in their philosophy. Philosophy has always struggled for the freedom of its creative act, has always been the art of knowing, and has always felt a slavish dependence on necessity, to which it attempted to adjust itself by means of a "scientific" attitude. Every age has known its heroes of philosophy, men who defended free philosophy as the art of creating essential ideas through which freedom might be glimpsed beyond necessity and meaning beyond meaninglessness. The history of philosophic self-consciousness is the arena of a struggle between two tendencies of the human spirit: towards freedom and towards necessity, towards creativeness and towards adaptation, towards the art of passing beyond the limit of the given world, and towards the science of bringing oneself into agreement with it. Plato was the great founder of the first of these. Materialism is the extreme expression of the second tendency, of submission, obedience to necessity, the lack of freedom. In philosophic creativeness the totality of man's spiritual forces has been active, the integral urge of the whole spirit to break through to the meaning of the world, to the world's freedom: and the individuality of its creators has left its mark on the history of philosophy, just as in the case of the history of art.

The philosophers would like to make philosophy scientifically universally valid, because truth ought to be universally binding and the scientific seems to them to be the only form of the universally valid. But a philosophy which on the surface appears to be subjective and unscientific may be far more true, may penetrate farther toward the world's meaning, than a philosophy which on the surface is objective and scientific. The final truth has no connection whatever with the scientific concept of universal validity. Truth may be attained by means of a break with the universally valid, by a refusal to appear scientific. We must admit that the truth may reveal itself through the art of Dante and Dostoevski, or through the gnostic mysticism of Jakob Boehme, in far greater degree than through Cohen and Husserl. In either Dante or Boehme there is another and not less universally valid truth than in Cohen. Truth is revealed in wisdom. The scientific universal validity of modern consciousness is the universal validity of a narrowed and impoverished spirit; it is a breaking of spiritual communion, its reduction to a minimum, just as much a surface phenomenon as are the relationships in the sphere of law. Scientific universal validity is analogous to the compulsions of law. This is the formalism of a humanity which is disunited within, lacking spiritual communion. Everything has been reduced to this scientific and legalistic communion—so

32

spiritually estranged are men one from another. Scientific universal validity, like that of law, is a mutual agreement among enemies to accept a minimal truth which maintains the unity of the human race. Men have lost their faculty of communion on the basis of truth which is not scientifically universally valid, not estranged from the depths of personality. Thus, truth in human intercourse is possible only if it is legally universally valid. Scientific philosophy is legal philosophy which has arisen out of the loss of freedom of communion, out of communion based only on the ground of bitter necessity. In the case of communion in liberty, the most true is the most universally valid. In creative intuition the œcumenical, universal truth is gained through freedom. But the recognition of a universally valid philosophy as a creative art predicates a higher degree of intercourse among men and a greater effort of the spirit than the recognition of universally valid scientific philosophy. Thus a moral universal validity presupposes a higher degree of communion than that of the law, and the universal validity of religion presupposes communion of a still higher degree. That is why philosophy viewed as an art is more all-human and œcumenical than philosophy considered as a science. The problem of universal validity is not a problem of logic— it is a problem of spiritual communion, of the œcumenicity (*sobornost*) of the collected spirit. For the disunited the truths of mathematics and physics are compulsory, while the truths about freedom and the meaning of the world are not. Strangers have to demonstrate to each other every single truth. The universal validity of science, as an adaptation to the given conditions of the world, expresses a lower, imperfect form of communion on the basis of the world's necessity. The universal validity of philosophy predicates a higher form of communion, since in philosophic creativeness there is an heroic overcoming of the world's necessity, accessible to a far smaller number of people. The intuition of the philosopher is verified by the œcumenical spirit.

In philosophical knowledge, creative intuition struggles

towards freedom. In philosophy, as in art, creative intuition is not arbitrariness or wilfulness. But we dare not trust every intuition. The intuition of philosophical knowledge is bound up with the truly-existent, with the meaning of being, and its creative nature does not mean that the existing is formed only in perception. In creative knowledge the existing only develops into higher forms, it only grows and increases. Can intuition be based on and justified by discursive thought? Can the intuition of philosophy be subject to the judgement of science? This would mean the grounding and justification of freedom by necessity, of creativeness by conformity, the limitless existence of the world by its limited condition. This would be seeking a safe shelter in the compulsoriness of discursive thought, in the necessary firmness of science—it would mean the withering of creative daring in knowledge. Men wish to assert themselves and their intercourse with one another on the basis of a minimum of the compulsory data which is necessary both in the material and in the form of knowledge. Whence has come this confidence that discursive thought is more universally valid than intuition? From reducing to a minimum the level of spiritual communion. Discursive thought is always the realm of the middle, never either the end or the beginning. The end and the beginning are always implicit in intuition. In discursive thought, taken by itself, there is always an inevitable necessity, a forcible compulsion, an inexorableness—a vicious circle. Left to itself, discursive thought falls into the power of an evil infinity, a bad plurality. Here there is no resolving end, as there was no beginning; the source is not visible. Discursive thought is a formal, automatic apparatus, brought into action by forces which lie outside it. In the final analysis, discursive thought is only an instrument of intuition; it is intuition which makes all beginnings and all endings. Discursive thought is an apparatus beautifully adapted to operations on the given world which is forced upon us; in it there is the necessity of adaptation to the necessity of the given world. Only by as much as men

34

have lowered their spiritual communion to a dull medium level do they seek exclusive support and the basis for their knowledge in the middle way of discursive thought; they see in necessity the justification of knowing. A more elevated spiritual communion, communion in freedom and from within freedom rather than in necessity and within necessity, should also recognize in philosophic knowledge the self-justification of creative intuition. This kind of commonality, this œcumenicity of consciousness, makes the philosopher less lonely in his intuitive creativity and helps to share responsibility for his courageous daring. When there is no spiritual communion responsibility is assumed only for the middle course of discursive thought, only for conformity to necessity in knowledge. Understanding it thus, it becomes clear that philosophical intuition seems less universally valid than scientific discursive thought, only because of the reduction to a minimum of spiritual community, of community in consciousness. In actuality, intuition is a sympathetic living-into the world, entering into the essence of the world, and hence it presupposes œcumenicity (*sobornost*)— being and acting together. For Christian communion, for the churches' consciousness, the truths about the Trinity and the divine-human nature of Christ are no less all-obligatory than the truths of mathematics and the laws of physics.

It is required of the philosopher that he justify his intuition by scientific, reasoned, compulsory criteria which lie quite outside philosophy and outside creative intuition; this only because in his vision he is left alone and estranged. But the philosopher is not obliged to lower himself and his work to some lesser degree of communion on the ground of necessity. The philosopher's intuition must remain at its high level and there justify itself, no matter how he may suffer from lack of communion with others and from the refusal to recognize the universal value of his creativeness, a refusal which grows out of this lack of common ground. Creativeness must not be lowered in quality for the sake of a larger common ground and general acceptance, i.e. a greater conformity to the lower forms of communion—this is a sin against the Holy Ghost. The philosopher may have deeper communion than anyone else with the œcumenical, universal reason, but he may be lonely and not understood by his fellow men who have not this communion with eternal reason and hence reject the universal value of his work. The criterion of *"sobornost"*, of communality, of œcumenicity, is not a quantitative criterion, a criterion of the majority. Œcumenicity is a quality of consciousness. The demand that science provide the base and set the limits for philosophical intuition is only a decision of the majority of those who have conformed themselves to necessity. For the philosopher, obedient only to the voice of œcumenic reason, such human demands do not have to be accepted: they appear to him only as some unpleasant kind of noise. He who is called to philosophy cannot agree to lower the quality of his work in this world: he waits until the level of spiritual community shall rise and the criteria of universal value shall change accordingly. It would be criminal for pristine freedom to yield place to the demands of necessity. A minority may be more fully in communion with œcumenical reason than the majority, and hence philosophy does not have to be something for all men who lack such communion; it should not stoop to that minimum which is called "scientific". In every age, in various forms, philosophers have defended their own independence and their resistance to the given world, saying that the aim of their knowing was freedom and not nature, spirit and not matter, value and not actuality, meaning and not necessity, essence and not appearance. Philosophy, like every creative act, strives towards the transcendent, towards passing beyond the borders of the given world. Philosophy does not believe that the world is really like that which is forced upon us by necessity.

§

A sharpening of consciousness, and a crisis of consciousness in all spheres, characterizes our time. We cannot fail to note a serious crisis of scientific, obligatory and object-ivized philosophy. Never before has there been such a desire to make philosophy scientific to the last degree. Now even idealism, which once was metaphysical, has either become scientific-minded or thinks of itself in such terms. On the other hand, never has there been such disillusionment in the scientific, such a thirst for the irrational. Now even positivism is considered as a poor sort of metaphysics and the "scienti-ficalness" of science itself is almost doubted. Everywhere there is a profound dissatisfaction with rationalism and a tendency to set free the irrational in life. In modern Neokan-tianism there is this profound duality of extreme rationalism and extreme irrationalism. The criticists of the new type are inspired both by the scientific and by irrationality. The scientific gnosseologues are flirting with mysticism and love to refer now to Plotinus, now to Eckhardt. They are trying scientifically to liberate and to justify the sphere of the mystic-irrational without noticing that, by doing this, they put the sphere of the irrational into slavish dependence. Philosophy itself is transformed into a science of values, of what, as the German has it, "*gilt*" (Windelband, Rickert, Lask). Thus an object of science is set up which is essentially outside and above science, and values are studied by methods to which they cannot be subject. In the last analysis, the science of values is one of the kinds of metaphysic of the existent, the metaphysic of the meaning of the world, and least of all scientific. Not only is it true that value cannot be investigated, it cannot even be grasped. The philosophy of Rickert, like every philosophy, strives out beyond the limits of the given world, of the world's necessity, towards the world's meaning and its liberation. But this halfway philo-sophy cannot break with the power of necessity, with its captivity by the "scientific". Philosophy, as a science of values, is always caught in a vicious circle and an evil infinity. If gnosseology is a science of values, then the principle of criticism demands a preliminary gnosseology of this science of values, i.e. a gnosseology of gnosseology and so on, ad infinitum. A critical gnosseology would have to demand not the form of knowledge but the form of the form of the form. Lask very ingeniously demands a logic of philosophy itself, reminding us that, besides the logic of scientific knowledge with which for some reason the philosophers have exclusively concerned themselves, there ought to be a logic of philosophic knowledge itself and a corresponding doctrine of categories. But I go further and demand a logic of that very logic of philosophy, of the very doctrine of categories of categories, and of the forms of the forms of philosophic knowledge. It is clear that this way of thinking is caught in the power of necessity, shackled to an inescapable and evil plurality. This will always be the case if philosophy is held to be a necessary science, rather than a free art of knowing. The knowledge of values, i.e. of that which lies beyond the limits of the given world and the actuality forced upon us, is the task of philosophy as a creative act and not as a science, and hence does not require a logic of the knowledge of values. There may be a logic of science—but there neither could nor should be a logic of philosophy. Philosophy may concern itself with categories of scientific knowledge but categories of scientific knowledge may not concern themselves with philosophy. In philosophy intuition is the ultimate—logic is the penultimate. In the philosopher's intuition there is its own justification and sanction and no foregoing knowledge is required. This is the way out of the evil infinity of the logical series. Philosophic intuition, being primeval, precedes every logic and every teaching of categories; it uses logic only as an instrument which it controls. But this means that philosophy does not need, neither does it permit, any sort of scientific logical foundation or justification. Science and its logic are always on a lower level than philosophy and always follow rather than lead. Logic is only a ladder by which intuitive philosophy descends to the given world; it is only an instrument. Philosophy has to explain logic—logic is incapable of explaining philosophy. And the philosophic relation to the world lies quite outside the

38

sphere in which the logical apparatus of the scientific relation to the world is set up. The perception of the world as value or as meaning is essentially not a scientific perception of the world: it is a creative act and not an adaptation to necessity. The philosophy of values breaks with the scientific. We must remember that philosophy is the love of wisdom. And in the *pathos* of the love of wisdom there is the right of primogeniture.

§

Pragmatism is a symptom of the crisis of scientific philosophy. But pragmatism is very strong in science and in the theory of scientific knowledge and has long since been accepted by scientists themselves. They are straining in an attempt to transfer scientific pragmatism to philosophy and thus in a new way to make philosophy like science; so a non-rationalistic conception of science leads to a non-rationalistic conception of philosophy. But in the last analysis Anglo-Saxon pragmatism is really demanding only more various forms of adaptation to the given world, to necessity. The sort of philosophy thus created is very shaky—its creative character is denied. We must make an exception for Bergson; his pragmatism is essentially different from that of the Anglo-Saxons, who always lean towards the positive and the utilitarian. The philosophy of Bergson is the most significant phenomenon in the crisis of scientific rationalist philosophy. In Bergson's consciousness philosophy strives creatively to escape the grip of scientific necessity and the shackles of rationalism. In reality, Bergson defends philosophy as a creative act and attempts to bring it nearer to art. Bergson sees in philosophy a vital impulse towards creative upsurge, to passing out beyond the limits of necessity. Bergson admits that philosophy as a creative act is not a science and does not resemble science. But he goes only halfway, like all other modern philosophers. He too, is afraid of science and dependent upon it. His *L'Evolution Creatrice* gives a brilliant criticism of all scientific theories of development and puts a foundation

39

under creativity, but it is constructed in a scientific manner and is slavishly dependent on biology. Bergson's biologism is a scandal in philosophy. Metaphysics fall into dependence upon a special science. And to intuition he ties the weight of necessity, with the whole material of analytic science. Bergson recognizes the vital irrationality of actuality and strives to bring into line with it the irrational in knowledge. This, after all, is still a form of adaptation to the given world. The philosophy of Bergson is a philosophy which is in the course of making itself free but it is not yet free. Philosophy becomes an art but still casts a frightened glance back towards science. Bergson's irrationalism is too biological, i.e. drawn from the science of life. His creative philosophic talent smooths over the formal sin of his biologism, his "halfway-ness". Bergson does not hold himself to the boundary line between philosophy and science and hence his philosophy is more a crisis than a way out, but he has understood that philosophic knowing rests upon intuition, i.e. upon a sympathetic, loving penetration into the essence of things, rather than upon scientific analysis which leaves us outside things, merely on their surface. Is the creative mobility of the real, into which, according to Bergson, the metaphysical intuition penetrates—is this the true reality of the world? One might think that for Bergson the immovable world of necessity is set up only by scientific concepts, is only a useful adaptation of scientific knowledge.

But the duality of freedom and necessity, of creativeness and immobility, lies in being itself, rather than in the methods of knowing it. Metaphysical intuition is not only a true penetration into the real actuality that is scientific analysis with its concepts—it is also an active, creative resistance to the given condition of reality for the sake of an upsurge towards the higher meaning of being. Scientific concepts are economically the most useful and logically the most sure penetration into the world of necessity, while metaphysical intuition is penetration into another world which lies beyond the borders of the given, and comprehension of

40

the given world only as a partial and unsound condition of another world. A further reason why philosophy is not a science but an art is that the philosopher's intuition presupposes genius, which is a universal perception of things. A philosopher may not be a genius, but philosophic intuition always has something genial, it always implies participation in the element of genius. Bergson arrives at this conclusion and hence he should have broken completely with philosophy as a science, should have definitely admitted that philosophy orients itself more by artistic vision than by scientific concepts. Scientific philosophy is academic philosophy: it is confirmed by the academic instinct of self-preservation. But knowledge is life and dynamic in being: the world blossoms in knowledge.

§

The best men now begin to recognize the fact that the old passive philosophy of necessity, in whatever form it was presented—metaphysical, critical or positivist—is approaching its end. Materialism and positivism are just as much philosophies of obedience to necessity as are the scholastic or rationalist metaphysics. But Kant's philosophy, probably the most perfect and refined philosophy of obedience, is a philosophy of sin. All these philosophies have the common characteristic of an obedient passivity of the spirit before the threatening face of the world's necessity, the spirit's diffidence in asserting its own freedom. This obedience to necessity, this spiritual passivity, may receive various philosophical formulations: the power of matter and the power of ideas, the power of sensations and the power of categories, the power of sensuality and the power of reason, the power of nature with its implacable laws and the power of reason with its norms. Critical philosophy is an obedient consciousness of the necessity, not of nature, but of the consciousness itself, not of matter but of reason, it is obedience to necessity by way of obedience to categories. The creative, active nature of philosophic knowledge has been felt in the flight of genius, but has been held down by general obedience to necessity, connected as we shall see, with the most profound religious causes. Philosophic knowledge cannot be only a passive, obedient reflection of being, of the world, of actuality—it must be an active, creative overcoming of actuality and a transfiguration of the world. Only a spirit under some deep oppression, crushed by its own sin, could understand its knowledge as passive obedience to the world. Both the rationalists and the empiricists saw in knowledge the expression of the world's actuality. The criticists endeavoured to recognize the creative nature of knowledge, but in reality they transferred the whole necessity of nature to the categories of reason and thus became obedient to necessity from the other end. The philosophy of the future will recognize the creative overcoming and transfiguring nature of knowledge, for in knowledge it will see the dawn and the flowering of being, itself. Philosophy will recognize its spiritually revolutionary nature, will recognize that it is in conscious rebellion against the captivity of necessity and against the slavery which conceals the secret and the meaning of being. In the creative, knowing act of philosophy there is an upsurge towards another being, another world, daring to approach the ultimate mystery. Philosophic knowledge does not stand over against being as something opposite to it and outside itself. This is an error of abstract rationalism. Philosophic knowledge is in being itself, since the knower is in being—it is a special quality of being and a special function of universal life. Knowledge is a function of the growth of being. It is the sun's ray which penetrates to the inner depth of being. A passive, obedient philosophy of necessity always considers necessity as truth and, with a certain moral *pathos*, demands humility before it.

Obedience to necessity (of nature or of categories) is understood as intellectual honesty and conscientiousness. Men believe that the criteria of truth are intellectual and that truth is accepted positively by the intellect, that knowledge of truth is honest and conscientious obedience. They doubt everything else but believe firmly in this. If truth lies in this, that the world is necessity and not freedom, that there is no meaning in the world, then it is dishonest and conscienceless to turn away from this truth and invent non-existent freedom and meaning, to recognize as truth whatever you will. And all the efforts of our spirit along the line of least resistance, the line of the given world, all the passive obedience of the spirit, speak for the assumption that there is neither freedom nor meaning in the world, that that towards which the spirit strives is non-existent. The *pathos* of obedience to necessity, to the world as it is, is transformed into the *pathos* of truth. The passive philosophy of necessity may be a sad and hopeless, but yet a true, philosophy, not thought out according to our desire. This customary opinion, proclaimed with a false *pathos* of nobility, puts more acutely the question whether the knowledge of truth is passivity, obedience of the intellect, or activity, the creativeness of the spirit? Is not the "truth" of the passive intellect with its purely intellectual conscience only a spectre, the self-hypnosis of a spirit oppressed and divided within itself? The obedience to "truth" of the passive intellect is slavery and palsy, not honesty and conscientiousness. The "truth" of a passive intellect simply does not exist—it is merely an intellectual expression of spiritual depression and dependence. Truth is revealed only by the creative activity of the spirit; outside this, truth is incomprehensible and unattainable. The absolute reply of the Gospel: "I am the Truth" has also absolute philosophical and gnosseological meaning. The Absolute Man is Truth. Truth is not that which is, that which is forced upon us as a given condition, as necessity. Truth is not the duplication, the repetition of being in the knower. *Truth is comprehension and liberation of being, it presupposes the creative act of the knower within being; Truth is meaning and may not deny meaning. To deny meaning in the world means to deny truth, to recognize nothing but darkness. Truth makes us free. To deny freedom is to deny truth.* There cannot be truth in the idea that the world is merely a meaningless necessity,

43

for the exclusive power of necessity is the power of darkness in which there is neither truth nor any way to liberation. Either truth does not exist at all, and then we should cease all philosophic assertions, or truth is a creative light giving meaning and liberation to being. Truth is light and one cannot acknowledge truth and deny all the light in the world. Truth is the enlightenment of darkness and hence there cannot be a truth about the meaningless and utter darkness of being. Truth presupposes the Sun, the Logos; and He who was the Sun and Logos of the world could say: "I am the Truth." The passive, intellectual, abstract "truth" must be sacrificed and by this sacrifice must be purchased victory over a slavish oppression of the spirit. The passive slavery to this "truth" is a great hindrance in the way of knowing the genuine truth. Dostoevski has a moving word about how, if truth were on one side and Christ on the other, it would be better to refuse truth and to go with Christ, that is to sacrifice the dead truth of a passive intellect for the sake of the living truth of the integral spirit. And to-day all philosophy must pass through the heroic act of denying the "truth". Then philosophy will become a creative act of knowing, i.e. active knowledge. What is, what is given and forced upon the intellect, this is not at all the truth; neither is it obligatory, for it may be that it is given and forced upon us only because of the slavish oppression of the spirit and will disappear like a mirage with the spirit's liberation. Knowledge of the truth means the provision of a reasoned meaning for being, its bright liberation from the dark power of necessity. Truth itself resists the world as it is, as it is given, otherwise truth would not be value, meaning; otherwise the Logos would not be living in it. Lowering truth to those scientific concepts which were a result of adaptation to necessity is a fall of the spirit, its renunciation of creative activity. Therefore creative philosophy cannot be scientific philosophy. There is a gnosis which goes beyond science and is independent of it. But creative gnostic philosophy is not a sentimental philosophy either, not a philosophy of the feeling,

44

of the heart. A philosophy of feeling is also passive, obedient and not creatively active. Philosophy is not dreaming but action.

§

Philosophy is palsied by a frightful disease—the disease of reflection and dissociation. Philosophers have tried to raise this reflection, this Hamletism, to the level of a methodical principle. In the rationalism of Descartes, in the empiricism of Hume and the criticism of Kant, reflection and doubt are lifted to the rank of a virtue of philosophic knowledge. Reflection and doubt, however, deprive philosophy of its active-creative character, make it passive. He who stops to reflect or he who doubts cannot be active in the world, he cannot be a warrior—he is plunged in his own enfeebling self-division; he does not believe in the active creative force with which he might act upon the world. The creative act of knowledge which overcomes all boundaries and all obstacles can be achieved only by one firmly convinced of his own power of knowing, only by one who is integral and not divided against himself. Doubt and division make the knower dependent upon the given world with its evil multiplicity, make him the slave of necessity. Creative philosophy is dogmatic philosophy, not critical and not sceptical; it is integral and not divided. The man of modern times has had to pass through critical doubt, through solitude in knowing, through times when he felt deserted by all his fellows. The transition from the comfortable knowledge and well-being of Thomas Aquinas to the tragedy of knowledge in Kant was fruitful. There can be no return to the old, childish dogmatism—we must turn to a new, mature, creative dogmatism.

The dogmatic philosophy of the future is a philosophy which dares to make a choice, to fix the consciousness upon that which has been chosen. Dogmatic philosophy is a philosophy which dares, which creates. He who creates is always dogmatic: he always dares to make a choice and then asserts it. Dogmatic philosophy is free philosophy; in it is completed the creative act of spiritual force. Critical philosophy is dependent: in it the spirit is incapable of accomplishing the creative act; it is characterized by a reflective, divided condition of the spirit. Dogmatism is integrity of the spirit, its creative confidence in its own power. Criticism is a divided state of the spirit, lack of confidence in its own power, which paralyses creativity. Creative knowledge, like every creative act, is the self-revelation of a power which cuts and chooses and casts away. Reflection, divided opinion and doubt are a palsied adaptation to the evil multiplicity of the world of necessity. A condition of doubt is an un-free condition, a state of dependence and oppression. He who doubts is incapable of choosing among the bad infinity, the evil multiplicity, of truths thrust upon him by the given world of necessity. He who doubts is in the situation of Buridan's ass. Doubt is metaphysical lack of character, a lack of the will and the power to put an end to forced multiplicity by one incisive, creative act. Dogmatism is an expression of metaphysical character, of a will which cuts asunder this evil multiplicity. Dogmatism is the expression of a steadfast consciousness which chooses and decides— a consciousness which dares to act creatively. Doubt is slavery to an evil infinity, obedience to an evil multiplicity. Creative dogmatism overcomes the power of evil infinity for the sake of eternity; it cuts short the evil multiplicity for the sake of choosing the one.

The creative act of knowledge is an act of loving choice, selecting the one good from among an evil multiplicity. Selective love is the necessary predicate of philosophic knowing. The true philosopher is a man in love, he who has chosen the object of his knowing love. Creative philosophic knowledge means ceasing to doubt that which one has chosen, with which one has fallen in love. The man in love chooses by a creative act which one he loves among an evil multiplicity of women. And you cannot tell the man in love that, besides the one he has chosen and whom he loves, there are many other women no less good or even better. And you

46

cannot tell the philosopher who is in love with a truth that besides the one he has chosen to love there is a multitude of other truths no less probable. Philosophic knowledge is impossible without Eros. And the *pathos* of philosophy is an erotic *pathos*. A critical, divided, doubting philosophy does not know the philosophic Eros, lacks the *pathos* of knowing love. For this very reason philosophy is an art and not a science—that it presupposes Eros, selective love. The erotic, marital tone of philosophical comprehension and vision radically distinguishes philosophy from science. Philosophy is an erotic art. The most creative philosophers were erotic philosophers, as, for instance, Plato. Those philosophers who lack the erotic are perhaps more like a type of scientists, but in their philosophy the creative vision is lacking. Philosophy yearns towards the marital secret of knowing. This marital secret of knowledge is denied by critical philosophy; in this lies its sin against the age-old expectations of philosophy. Philosophic knowledge, as a creative act, is a marriage for love. Critical, scientific philosophy would transform philosophy into a marriage of reasonableness; it does not want to be dangerously in love but prefers a safe family comfort—and hence it denies the marital mystery, the mystery of love itself. Creative philosophy is an act of knowing love and not a science of knowing family comfort and order.

Scientific philosophy would gladly put proof in the place of knowing love. Always and in everything it demands proof that the truth of knowing love is the best and the only truth. But proof is only one of the expressions of the power of necessity over the freedom of the human spirit. What is proved is forced upon us, inevitable, necessary. "Scientific" philosophy would like to have everything proved and nothing selected, would like to have necessity and not freedom in everything. Proof is a necessity in discursive thinking—adaptation to the necessity in the given world. In a proof there is no break-through of the creative act. Proof is obedience and not creativity. And dependence upon proof is a slavish dependence. The eternal demand for proof is the

demand of lowered spiritual communion, of inner dissociation, a state in which everything is sensed as necessity rather
than as freedom. Whence came this firm conviction that the
truth is that which is most completely proven? Who knows
but that proof is an obstacle of necessity encountered in the
way of knowing the truth? Creative philosophy must free
itself from the tempting power of proof, must fulfil the act of
renouncing this safe adaptation to necessity. In science that
which is most completely proved is the most completely
adapted to the world's necessity, for better orientation in it.
Hence the force of demonstration in the logic of the sciences.
In philosophy, the most true, the most creative, that which
bursts out through necessity to freedom, out of meaninglessness to meaning, may be the least provable. There is no logic
of proof in philosophy, just as in general there is no logic of
philosophy, nothing logical which precedes the intuition of
the philosopher. In philosophy, what had been proved would
not be creative knowledge: it would only be adaptation. In
philosophic knowledge it is the creative intuition which is
convincing, not the demonstrable evidence of discursive
thought. In philosophy truth is shown and formulated, not
proven nor grounded in reason. The task of philosophy is to
find the most perfect formulation for truth, perceived in
intuition, and to synthesize formulæ. These carry conviction
by the light which shines out from them, rather than by
demonstration or conclusions. Demonstration lies always in
the middle, neither at the beginning nor at the end, and
hence there can be no proof of initial or final truths. In
essence, demonstration never proves any truth, since it
presupposes the acceptance of certain truths by intuition. In
the middle you may prove any sort of lie. Proof is only the
technique of the logical apparatus and has no relation to
truth. All of which again leads us to the acute realization
that philosophic knowledge predicates a higher degree of
spiritual communion, and that only then it is convincing,
only then it is not arbitrary. Philosophy presupposes communion on the basis of initial and final intuitions rather than

48

the median proofs of discursive thinking. Only then can an elevated dogmatic philosophy be compelling and convincing rather than a philosophy lowered to the critical level. One can accept and understand the truth of philosophic knowledge only when there are present rudiments of that intuition of being which has attained its highest expression in the creative knowing act of the philosopher. Communion in philosophic knowledge presupposes a certain maximum of living contact, unity, the communion of selective love. And the final criterion of the truth of philosophic intuition may be only the universal communal spirit. Œcumenicity of consciousness is the only knowing love. Proof is not needed in œcumenic (*sobornoe*) consciousness. Proof is necessary only for those who love differences, who have differing intuitions. You offer proof only to the enemies of your beloved truth, not to its friends.

§

In defining the nature of philosophy and its tasks, a central question to be solved is that of anthropologism in philosophy. Philosophy cannot get away from the primal consciousness that man philosophizes and that man philosophizes for man. There is no way of denying that philosophic knowledge takes place in an anthropological milieu. No matter how hard Cohen and Husserl try to assign to knowledge a nature which transcends man and to liberate knowledge from all anthropologism, their efforts will always be like lifting oneself by one's bootstraps. Man precedes philosophy; man is the prerequisite of all philosophic knowledge. This fact not infrequently seems to hamper and shame the philosophers: they would like to derive man from philosophy, and not philosophy from man. It seems to such philosophers that this fatal anthropologism in philosophy is a lowering of the quality of philosophic knowledge, its inevitable relativization. And the majority of philosophers, in the final analysis practise a sort of half-conscious, partial anthropologism, hesitant and somewhat ashamed. It is awkward for the philosophers that man, who is still a problem for philosophy,

49

so evidently precedes philosophy and commands it. Critical philosophy subjects to doubt even being itself—for it everything is only a problem. But behind this very critical philosophy stands man; man is the doubter, man puts the problems. And critical philosophy makes the instructive experiment of trying to free itself, to cleanse itself from man. We find this murderous tendency in Husserl, Cohen and others. They would like to create a philosophy in which philosophy itself would philosophize rather than man. By this they desire to raise the rank of philosophy, to make it not relative but absolute. The critical gnosseologues nowadays like to say that scientific knowledge is the most genuine reality, the very absolute. Science is the very existent; science is existent in a higher degree than man; science is more ontological than man. Hegel also thought, though in another way, that philosophy was more real and more absolute than man. This murderous philosophy is an expression of the titanic pride of the philosopher—not of man, but of the philosopher, and not even of the philosopher but of philosophy itself, of philosophic knowledge itself. This is panlogism, i.e. raising logic and its categories to the rank of absolute being. And still in Hegel we must perceive a truth which will not die: for Hegel knowledge was a development of being, knowledge was ontological. In Hegel idealism is transformed into realism. Hegel's great merit is in his break with formal logic. In Hegel's titanic effort philosophy attains its culminating point, and after him it begins to slide, to fall; it suffers catastrophe. Man rises against philosophy and demands that he be recognized as something more real, more truly being, than philosophy. An extra-anthropological or a sub-anthropological philosophy cannot be called creative philosophy: in it there is no creator, no creative mastering of the world's necessity by creative man; in such a philosophy man is brought into the condition of absolute obedience to the categories of philosophic knowledge: such a philosophy would endeavour to eliminate man, to put itself in his place: *only that Logos does not destroy man, who is Himself*

50

*the Absolute Man.* Hence only in Christological consciousness (Christ the Logos) is man redeemed and confirmed.

Another way has been opened of liberation from the relativist results of anthropologism, results which are destructive for the work of philosophy. This is the way of raising the rank of man, of absolutizing man, recognizing man as the supreme centre of the universe, the image and likeness of Absolute Being, a little cosmos, who includes everything in himself. Then man becomes not a comparative, relativistic predicate to philosophic knowledge, but its absolute prerequisite, giving to knowledge firmness and solidity. *In this case philosophy will be understood as the creative, knowing power of man dominating the world.* Philosophy is the power of man by means of creativeness; science is his power by means of obedience. Creative philosophy is anthropologic philosophy, presupposing a creator and his purpose. But then the anthropologism of philosophy becomes conscious and absolute, instead of relative and half-conscious. Such anthropologism must reveal its universal ontological nature. The source of philosophic knowing cannot be a condition of man as a closed individual being—cannot be psychologism. The struggle against psychologism is fully justified: psychologism means the death of philosophy. Man is not a psychological prerequisite of philosophic knowledge—he is a universal, ontological, cosmic prerequisite. Only cosmic, universal conditions of man may be the source of philosophical knowledge—not man's psychological, individual condition. Pythagoras taught that "Man is the measure of things" and this became the source of relativism, scepticism and positivism. Disunited from the cosmos, closed within himself, having lost his connection with the absolute being, man can least of all be the measure of things. The sophists, the relativists and positivists do not know man as a microcosm, as the image and likeness of absolute being. With them, man is lowered in rank, de-absolutized, transformed into a relative condition, a bunch of sensations, a drop in the sea of the world's necessity—a grain of sand in the desert of

51

being. But man must be recognized in quite another, higher, sense as the measure of things. In man and only in man is there a concrete and creative apprehension of cosmic conditions, since in him there is a relationship with the whole cosmos, of which he represents the highest hierarchical degree. Philosophy is man's self-consciousness of his imperial and creative role in the cosmos. Philosophy is knowing liberation from oppression. Science is a consciousness of dependence.

§

Psychologism and human relativism in philosophical knowledge may be overcome only by those philosophers who recognize the existence of a world Logos and Œcumenical Reason, and recognize man as participant in the Logos, as akin to Reason, capable of taking possession of this Reason. He who sees in man no trace of the world's Logos is fated to remain in the grip of psychologism and relativity. Philosophy is not, like religion, a revelation of God—it is the revelation of man, but of man as participant in the Logos, part of the absolute man, the all-man, and not a closed individual being. Philosophy is the revelation of all-wisdom in man himself, by his own creative effort. In genuine philosophic intuitions and visions man is joined with the universe, anthropologism with cosmism (the cosmic). In the small cosmos, man, there is the great cosmos, the universe. The submergence of the human microcosm in its own depths by means of intimate intuition seems to be only subjective and non-obligatory. In reality we have here an immersion in the secret of the macrocosm. The secret of the macrocosm is revealed only to those who reject obtrusive necessity—the necessity which seems to be thrust upon them, that which seems like necessity—and approach the macrocosm through the microcosm, through the freedom of the absolute man.

Philosophic knowledge cannot have its source in books or in schools. The source of philosophy is not Aristotle or Kant, but being itself, the intuition of being. The only true philosopher is he who has an intuition of being, whose philosophy has its source in life. Genuine philosophy has immediate connection with being. A school-philosophy, scholastic, academic, is a mediate philosophy. The creation of academic philosophy predicates stopping the vital nourishment of philosophy and substituting for this the nourishment of books. The purpose of philosophy is not the construction of a system, but a creative knowing act in the world. Philosophy should not be systematic. In system there is always an economic adaptation to necessity: system is opposite to creative intuition. We must not identify synthesis with system. Philosophy lives on religious-vital nourishment. Philosophy may be oriented towards religious revelation. But philosophy is not religion and cannot be externally subject to religion, still less to theology. Subjecting philosophy to theology created one kind of scholasticism, subjecting philosophy to science created another. Philosophy must be free of any authority outside itself, of all methods of knowledge outside itself. It must be much more free than modern critical and scientific philosophers will admit. But philosophy cannot be drawn away and separated from the profoundest sources of being, from that living-religious sap which the philosophizing man finds in his own microcosm. Philosophy demands free access to the living, immediate sources of being, and considers itself enslaved when this access to first sources is denied. Religion is integral life. The truth of religion is revealed to man by divinity. Philosophy is knowledge. The truth of philosophy is revealed by man. And the union of divine and human, religious and philosophic knowing in the final knowledge of one Truth, is accomplished not by external authority and submission but by an inner, free, creative act. The final religious significance of philosophy, like that of art, is immanently expressed in the free development of philosophy. For philosophy, religious revelation is the intuition of the philosopher. The gracious help of God in philosophic knowledge, without which integral and final truth cannot be attained, cannot be a method of

53

philosophy: it can be only a gift sent in recompense for the creative deed of knowing. But philosophy must re-establish the original truth of the mythological nature of human consciousness. Even philosophy freely recognizes that the world is knowable only mythologically. Plato considered myth the highest form of knowledge.

The free philosophy of the creative epoch will begin with the conscious sacrifice of scientific obligatory philosophy, adapted to the given world. This sacrifice is not at all an easy thing: it presupposes great freedom of the spirit and the renunciation of bourgeois attitudes and bourgeois communion, for the sake of another world and another communion. It means leaving philosophical safety, and consenting to commit oneself to the dangerous in knowledge, it means pushing off from a firm shore and renouncing the bourgeois spirit, refusal to occupy a definite situation of knowing in the given world. A philosophy of creativeness can be the philosophy only of these who create, i.e. those who in a creative act pass beyond the boundaries of the given world. A philosophy of creativeness predicates, as well, a philosophy of freedom—it is a philosophy of liberated men. Creative philosophy cannot be academic, or state or bourgeois philosophy. The philosopher is a free man, independent of the world, a man who refuses to adapt himself. The philosopher cannot serve the nation or political parties, he cannot serve academic or professional aims. The philosopher cannot serve the good of mankind; he cannot be in service to anyone or any personal human purposes. I speak here of philosophy as a creative act, not as a system of adaptation.

The philosophy of recent times has been too much absorbed with the problem of science which has struck men's imagination, and philosophy has been transformed into a theory of scientific knowing, into a logic of science. It has wished to "orient" itself on science. Philosophic knowledge itself as an independent action has been covered over by the problem of scientific knowledge. The object of philosophy has been science rather than being. The method

54

of philosophizing has striven to be scientific, in correspondence with its object. But philosophy must finally free itself from this exclusive absorption by the problem of science. Kant was completely under the influence of the fact of mathematical natural science, the work of Newton, and burdened philosophy with this problem. Nowadays the very existence of an ideal mathematical natural science is brought under doubt, there is a crisis of mathematism and mechanicism in science itself. Philosophy will now have to deal with the problem of pragmatic science, and this will free it from the nightmare of mathematical science. Scientific pragmatism is definitely undermining the idea of scientific philosophy which was nourished by the phantom fact of the existence of an ideal mathematical science, of an absolute natural science. The future belongs not to Cohen—that last attempt to absolutize and mathematize scientific knowledge—but more likely to Bergson, with his profound and revolutionary refusal of mathematism. The crisis of scientific philosophy is being prepared by science itself.

§

The striving for the scientific, for scientific form, has captured not only philosophy but theosophy as well. The modern theosophic movement is penetrated by the unfortunate idea that religion and mysticism are a sort of scientific knowledge. The old gnosticism is reborn in a science-like form. The most noteworthy and significant of present-day theosophists, Rudolf Steiner, builds his theosophy like a science, a strict and dry science. His theosophy is like some sort of a natural science of other planes of being—it is like transferring Haeckel to other worlds. Steiner intentionally writes his books in the style of text-books of mineralogy or geology. His method is purely descriptive, purely scientific, not philosophic. It is as if he remained in the sphere of science-like naturalism, and wished only to extend and widen that naturalism but not at all to overcome it. For Steiner the fact of science is the basic fact in the life of mankind. But he struggles against the materialistic results of that fact. He writes of the mystical in a scientific rather than in a mystical manner. In his writings you will not find the personal experiences, inspirations and visions which charm us in all the mystics. Quite drily and descriptively he lays down the object itself, the map of being. Theosophy seems to adapt itself to the world's necessity and thus makes itself more accessible to the level of the average man. But creative philosophy cannot admit this science-like theosophy. If philosophy cannot be scientific, still less can its highest sphere, theosophy, the knowledge of God, be scientific. Steiner's methodological dependence upon naturalism is further evidenced by the fact that his is not theosophy in the exact meaning of the word, as was the case with Jakob Boehme or Franz von Baader. The occult science of Steiner still remains in the sphere of created nature and does not provide the Knowledge of God, does not speak of God as did the gnostic mystics before him. One may speak of scientific magic, as De Presle tries to do, but not of scientific theosophy. Magic is dependent upon nature—theosophy must be free from nature. The knowledge of God and of the ultimate mystery of the world differs essentially from scientific knowledge and contains as little naturalism as mathematicism. Neither Haeckel nor Cohen can be admitted to the sphere of theosophic and metaphysical knowledge. Philosophy, as a creative act, has nothing in common with either naturalistic or mathematical knowledge—it is an art. But mystic theosophy is the highest art. And Steiner himself finally comes to this, in so far as he sees in knowledge an upsurge of being, the development of man himself. When I say that philosophy is an art, I do not mean to say that it is "the poesy of concepts" as Lange does, obligatory for no one, individually arbitrary. The art of philosophy is firmer and more obligatory than science; it comes before science, but it presupposes the highest exertion of the spirit and the highest form of communion. The mystery of man is the initial problem of a philosophy of creativity.

# CHAPTER II

# MAN, MICROCOSM AND MACROCOSM

THE PHILOSOPHERS HAVE constantly returned to the
idea that to solve the mystery of man would mean solving
the mystery of being. Know thyself, and through this know
the world. All attempts at external perception of the world,
without immersion in the depths of man, have produced only
a knowledge of the surface of things. If one proceeds from
man outward, one can never reach the meaning of things,
since the solution of the riddle of meaning is hidden within
man himself. Positivism was the extreme expression of this
tendency, not only to attain the world by an exterior way,
which lies as far away as possible from the inner man, but
even to place man in the rank of the external things of the
world. But in truth a philosophy which exerts itself to deny
the exceptional significance of man in the world and to
refuse to recognize man as the exclusive source of knowing
the secret and the meaning of the world suffers from internal
contradictions and from an error which destroys that
philosophy itself. The act of man's exclusive self-consciousness of his significance precedes every philosophic perception. This exclusive self-consciousness of man cannot be one
of the truths of a philosophic knowledge of the world: like
an absolute *a priori* it precedes every philosophic perception
of the world, which becomes possible only through this
selfconsciousness. If man were to consider himself as one of
the external, objectivized things of the world, then he could
not be an active perceiving subject; by this fact philosophy
has become impossible for him. Anthropology, or more
exactly the anthropological consciousness, precedes not only
ontology and cosmology, gnosseology and even the philosophy of consciousness—it precedes all philosophy, all

57

knowledge. Man's *consciousness of himself as the centre of the world, bearing within himself the secret of the world, and rising above all the things of the world, is a prerequisite of all philosophy: without it one could not dare to philosophize.* He who knows the world philosophically must rise above all the things of the world: he cannot be one of the things of the world, on a level with other things—he must himself be the world. The daring idea of an effort to attain knowledge of the universe could never occur to a fractional part of it: for such a fraction the problem of knowledge or of philosophy could never arise. The very statement of the daring task of knowing the universe is possible only for him who is himself the universe, who is capable of standing up against it as against an equal, capable of including the universe within himself. The knowledge of man rests upon the supposition that man is cosmic in his nature, that he is the centre of being. Man existing as a closed-off individual would have no means of knowing the universe. Such a being would not be of higher order than other separate things in the world, would not overcome this separate condition. The way of anthropology is the only way of knowing the universe, and this way presupposes man's exceptional consciousness of himself. Only in man's sense of himself and in his self-consciousness, are the divine mysteries revealed. Philosophers have always accepted this, sometimes consciously, sometimes unconsciously.

But there have been tendencies, in two directions, to move away from this exceptional self-consciousness of man. Man has tried to philosophize, as it were, now lower, now higher, than himself, depending on what personal conditions and powers he laid down as the basis for his philosophizing. Empiricism and positivism take personal and lower spheres of sensation and external experience as the basis for their philosophizing, thus fractionizing the human spirit. Rationalism and criticism also base their philosophizing on particular, although higher, spheres of the categories of reason, in another way dividing the human spirit and attempting to make knowledge non-human. But empiricists and positivists, rationalists and "criticists", each in their own way, proceed from the presupposition that in man there must be some exceptional sources for knowing the world. In the last analysis even the most extreme sensualist must recognize in man's sensations his microcosmic nature. And the most extreme rationalist of the type of Cohen must recognize in his categories the microanthropic nature of being. *Man is a small universe—that is the basic truth for knowing man, and the basic truth which precedes the very possibility of knowing.* The universe may enter into man, be assimilated by him, be attained and known by him only because in man there is the whole component of the universe, all its qualities and forces—because man is not a fractional part of the universe but an entire small universe himself. Perceptive endosmosis and exosmosis are possible only between the microcosm and the macrocosm. Man penetrates into the meaning of the universe as into a larger man, into a mac-anthropos. And the universe enters into man, submitting to his creative effort, as into a small universe, a microcosm. Man and the cosmos measure their forces against each other, as equals. Knowing is a conflict between equal forces, rather than between a dwarf and a giant. And I repeat: this exclusive self-consciousness of man is not one of many truths acquired as the result of philosophizing; this is a truth which precedes every creative act of philosophic perception. This predicate and prerequisite of all philosophy is often unconscious, but it must become conscious. Man is capable of knowing the world only because he is not merely in the world as one of its parts but outside and above the world, surpassing all the things of the world—he is a being equal in quality with the world. As Lotze well says: "of all the errors of the human spirit, the strangest has always seemed to me to be how man arrived at doubting his own existence, which he alone experiences directly, or how he came upon the idea of giving this existence back to himself like a gift from an external nature, which we know only secondhand, that is by means of that very spirit which we have denied." Man knows himself

59

earlier, and more fully, than he knows the world, and hence he perceives the world after himself and through himself. Philosophy is the inner perception of the world through man, while science is the external knowledge of the world outside man. In man is revealed absolute being: outside him, only the relative.

§

Man is the meeting-point of two worlds. This is attested by the duality in man's consciousness of himself, a duality evident throughout his whole history. Man recognizes that he belongs to two worlds: his nature is dual, and, in his consciousness of himself, now one of these natures now the other seems to prevail. With equal firmness man founds the most contradictory ideas of himself, equally justified by facts of his nature. Man is conscious at once of his greatness and power and of his worthlessness and weakness, of his imperial freedom and his slavish dependence: he knows himself as the image and likeness of God and as a drop in the ocean of the necessities of nature. With almost equal right we may speak of man's divine origin, and of his development from the lowest forms of nature. With almost equal force of argument the philosophers defend man's original freedom and a complete determinism which leads man into the chain of fateful, natural necessity. Man is one of the phenomena of this world, one of the things caught in the mælstrom of all things of nature: and man passes beyond this world, as the image and likeness of absolute being transcends all things of the order of nature. What a strange being— divided and of double meaning, having the form of a king and that of a slave, a being at once free and in chains, powerful and weak, uniting in one being glory and worthlessness, the eternal with the corruptible! All deep thinkers have felt this. Pascal, who had a remarkably clear sense of the antinomic quality of religious life, understood that the whole of Christianity is related to this duality of man's nature: "*Nulle autre religion que la chrétienne n'a connu que l'homme est la plus excellente créature, et en même la plus misérable.*"

60

Jakob Boehme says: *"Nun siehe, Mensch, wie du bist irdisch und dann auch himmlisch, in einer Person vermischt, und trägest das irdische, und dann auch das himmlische Bild in einer Person: und dann bist du aus der grimmigen Qual, und trägest das höllische Bild an dir, welches grünet in Gottes Zorn aus der Qual der Ewigkeit."*

It is almost incomprehensible, how a tiny bit of nature, completely dependent upon its irresistible round, should dare to rise against nature and demand his rights as a descendant of another world, as a being with another destiny. *Man's highest consciousness of himself is not explicable by the world of nature and remains a mystery to that world.* The natural world would never be able to outgrow itself into man's highest consciousness of himself. No such possibility is inherent in the natural forces of "this world". The higher could never have been born of the lower. And yet man presents a documentation proving his aristocratic descent. Man is not only of this world but of another world; not only of necessity, but of freedom; not only out of nature, but from God. Man may know himself as a necessary part of nature and may be crushed by this knowledge. But knowing himself as part of the natural world is a secondary factor in man's consciousness of himself: man is first given for himself, and experiences himself as man, as a spiritual fact outside nature, outside this world. Man is prior to, and deeper than, his psychological and biological aspects. Man, the all-man, the bearer of absolute humanity, regaining consciousness after his eclipse in the world of nature, after his fall into the necessity of nature, becomes conscious of his infinite nature, a nature which cannot be satisfied or fully nourished by temporary realizations. And yet everything in man's life is corruptible, everything seems to deny eternity. The duality of man's nature is so striking that the naturalists and positivists teach of man with real conviction and so do the supranaturalists and the mystics with no less assurance. The fact of man's being and the fact of his consciousness of himself offer a powerful and indeed the only refutation to the apparent truth that the world of nature is the only and final world.

61

*In his essence, man is a break in the world of nature, he cannot be contained within it.* The learned rationalists are compelled to stand in bewilderment before the fact of Christ's self-consciousness, before the inexplicable fact of His divine consciousness of himself. And the learned rationalists should also stand in bewilderment before the fact of man's consciousness of himself, since this consciousness transcends the natural world and cannot be explained by it. There is a deep and very significant analogy between Christ's consciousness of Himself and man's consciousness of his own nature. Only the revelation about Christ gives a key to solving the problem of man's consciousness of himself. The supreme human self-consciousness sets an absolute limit to all scientific knowledge. Science rightly knows man only as a part of the natural world and insists upon the duality of human self-consciousness as the limit of its knowing. But a philosophy of man's higher consciousness of himself is possible only when it is consciously oriented to the fact of the religious revelation concerning man. Anthropological philosophy accepts this religious revelation as its free intuition, rather than as the authority of dogma. Anthropological philosophy has to deal with the fact of man, not as an object of natural knowledge (biological, psychological or sociological) but as subject of a higher self-consciousness, a fact outside nature and beyond this world. Hence this philosophy proclaims that man's nature is the image and likeness of absolute being, a microcosm, the supreme centre of being, and so throws light on the mysterious duality of the nature of man. Philosophical anthropology is in no way whatever dependent upon scientific anthropology, since it sees man not as an object of nature but as a super-natural subject. Philosophical anthropology is wholly based upon that higher consciousness which man has of himself, which transcends the limits of the natural world.

The official rational philosophy, recognized as universally valid, has never revealed a true anthropology, a doctrine of man as microcosm. This philosophy was more or less restricted by the dependent situation of man in the world of nature. The utmost which can be drawn from officially recognized philosophy is the timid and modest doctrine of man in Herman Lotze's *Microcosm*. With Schelling, who drew upon the mystics, philosophical anthropology was submerged under his *Naturphilosophie*. For Schelling the basic fact is a concept of nature, rather than of man. In a philosophy which in reality presupposes the exclusiveness of man, one can find only fragments of a doctrine of man. Man's consciousness moves upward only hesitantly and fearfully in philosophy and is stopped completely in scientific philosophy. The ardently-atheistic philosophy of L. Feuerbach is of greater importance only because of its making more acute an anthropological consciousness. Feuerbach's genial *The Essence of Christianity* is the truth of religious anthropology turned inside out. For Feuerbach the riddle of man remained a religious riddle.

Only in mystic or occult philosophy, which the official and obligatory philosophers do not want to recognize, has there been a revelation of the true doctrine of man as a microcosm. This philosophy began the initiation of man into the mystery of himself. In mysticism, man is freed from his subjection to the natural world. The strongest element in most occult doctrines is the doctrine of cosmic man, the knowledge of the great man. Only the mystics have correctly understood that everything which takes place in man has world-significance, and is reflected in the cosmos. They have known that man's spiritual elements were cosmic, that in man may be discovered all the different layers of the world, the whole make-up of the world-status. Mysticism was always deeply antagonistic to that psychologism which sees in man a closed and individual being, a fractional part of the world. Man is not a fractional part of the universe, a fragment of it, but a whole small universe including in himself all the qualities of the great universe, imprinting himself upon it and receiving its imprint upon himself. The psychology of the mystics was always cosmic. For instance, anger for them is not only an element in man but an element of the cosmos. The subject is visible in the object, and the object in the subject. A spiritual materialism characterizes the mystics. In the mystical teachings of Jakob Boehme there is so much water, fire and sulphur, spiritual material and material spirituality! The undying truth of astrology was deeply convinced that all the layers of the cosmos, all spheres of heaven, leave their imprint on man and on his fate; that man is cosmic in his nature. Although astrology cannot be reborn in a naïvely-naturalistic form, just as the pre-Copernican naturalistic anthropocentrism cannot be restored, the supra-naturalistic truth of astrology which sees other planes of being in the cosmos may be and is being resurrected: you may say that it never died. There is the same sort of eternal truth in alchemy and magic. Astrology guessed the inseparable connection between man and the cosmos and thus broke through to the truth, which was hidden from the science of man which did not know the heavens and from a science of the heavens which knew not man. Occult and mystic doctrines have always taught that man was a complex being, made up of many elements, including within himself all the planes of the cosmos, experiencing within himself the whole universe. That philosophy which sees in man only a special phenomenon of the natural world, fails completely to see him as the cosmos, as a small universe. Only that philosophy is capable of glimpsing the cosmos in man which sees that man surpasses all the phenomena of the natural world and is himself the supreme centre of being. There are hidden in man mysterious occult and cosmic powers, unknown to official science and to the ordinary everyday consciousness of man—of this it is scarcely possible longer to doubt. This consciousness is growing, rather than decreasing: it is crowding in upon the official scientific and "healthy-thinking" consciousness. The central truth of the mystics must soon become an open and obligatory truth from which one can hide only in non-being. St. Paul has a doctrine which brings Adam and Christ together. We find the doctrine of man as a microcosm in the cabbalistic philosophy of that greatest of mystics, Jakob

64

Boehme, in Franz von Baader, who continued his teaching, and in the remarkable modern popularizer of occult teaching, Rudolf Steiner.

In the Kabbala, man's consciousness of himself reaches a high point. In the usual Christian consciousness, the truth of man the microcosm is obscured by the sense of sin and of man's fall. In official Christian consciousness anthropology is still that of the Old Testament. In the basic book of the Kabbala, the Zohar and in Boehme's *Mysterium Magnum* (a commentary on the Book of Genesis) the fetters of limitation and subjection of the ancient consciousness are removed from the Bible and the truth of man's cosmic nature begins to be visible. The Kabbala teaches about the Heavenly Adam. The Zohar says: "Man is the reason, the sum and the highest point of creation. For this reason he was created on the seventh day. Once man had appeared, everything was finished, both the higher and the lower world, because everything is included in man: in himself he unites all forms." "He is not only an image of the world, a universal being, which includes Absolute Being as well: he is also, and principally, an image of God, with the inclusion of all His infinite attributes. He is divine presence on the earth: he is the Heavenly Man who, emerging from the original darkness, creates the earthly Adam." "Within is the mystery of the heavenly man. Like the earthly man, the Heavenly Adam is inward, and everything takes place in both directions, upward and downward." The Kabbala contains the profound doctrine of the Androgyne. The Zohar says: "No form which does not contain both the masculine and the feminine principle is a complete or a higher form. The holy finds its place only where these two elements are completely united. The name person (man) may be given only to man and woman united in one being." Man serves as a mediator and a uniting force between God and nature. And both God and nature are reflected in his dual being. As the Zohar says, "when the lower world is inspired by desire, by burning thirst for the higher world, the latter descends to it. In man this desire attains its highest consciousness and power, and in man the two worlds meet and penetrate more and more into each other." In the Kabbala there is hidden a profound anthropology, in thorough agreement with Christian truth. The truth about man was never fully revealed in the Christian Church, which has maintained the ancient biblical anthropology for the sake of redemption. A greater truth about man began to be revealed in mysticism, and first of all in the cabbalistic mysticism, truth connected with man's very origins. The Kabbala reveals the truth about man as the image and likeness of God. But in the Kabbala this truth about man has not yet become dynamic or creative. In the book of Hermes, also, we find a very high doctrine of man. "Let us dare to say," writes Hermes Trismegistus, "that man is a mortal God and the heavenly God is an immortal man. Thus everything is directed by the world and by man." Or again: "The Lord of eternity is the first God, the world the second, and man the third. God, Creator of the world and of everything that is included in it, directs and rules all this as one whole, and brings it under man's authority. And this makes everything an object of his activity."

But it is in Jakob Boehme, the greatest mystic-gnostic of all time, that anthropological visions are revealed which rise above and beyond time itself. For Boehme anthropology is inseparably connected with Christology. The doctrine on Adam is inseparable from that about Christ. Following St. Paul, Boehme daringly brings Christ and Adam together. And Boehme's first Adam is the same as the Heavenly Adam of the Kabbala. And Christ, the Absolute Man, is the Heavenly Adam. The whole of Boehme's anthropology is related to his doctrine of the androgyne, to which we shall frequently return. All the astounding *Naturphilosophie* of Boehme, although not fully comprehensible to us, pre-supposes that man is a microcosm and that everything which takes place in man takes place in the cosmos. Spirit and nature are one. Boehme ought to form a permanent part of our spiritual life, for never has human gnosis reached a

66

greater superhuman height. "I have no need of your approaches and your methods, neither of your formulas, for I did not learn this from them," says Boehme. "I have another teacher and that teacher is the whole of Nature. Not from man nor by man, but from Nature itself I have learned my philosophy, astrology, and theology." Here the superhuman, natural-divine source of Boehme's knowledge makes itself felt. "In my own power, I am just as blind as any other man, and just as feeble, but in the spirit of God my inborn spirit sees through everything: this is not always true, however, but only when the spirit of the Love of God breaks through my spirit, and then animal nature and Divinity become one Being, one understanding and one light. And I am not the only person like this: all men are like this." Sophia, the Divine Wisdom, may be revealed in any man, and then the true gnosis is born. What idea of man is revealed in Boehme's gnosis? The first man is androgynous. Only that man is the image and likeness of God "who has in Himself the immaculate Virgin of the Divine Wisdom—man first received his name 'man' as a mixed being". Only a virgin-boy, a man-androgyne, is the image and likeness of God. Without the youth-virgin it would be impossible. "Before he had Eve, Adam himself was an immaculate Virgin, neither man nor woman; he had in himself both natures, that which is in fire, and that which is in the spirit of humility—and if only he had withstood all the testing, he might himself have given birth in the heavenly order, without a break with it. And has a man been born of another, anywhere, and at any time, in that order in which Adam by virtue of his virginity became the image and likeness of God? His being had wholly to proceed from eternity, else nothing of eternity would remain." In Boehme there is an astonishingly mystic *rapprochement* of heaven with earth, God with man, Christ with Adam. "God must become man, and man, God: heaven must become one with earth, the earth must become heaven." "Adam was created by the Word of God, but he fell from God's Word of Love into God's Word

67

of Wrath: then in His mercy God again awoke in Adam's image of Wrath His beloved Word of the profoundest humility, love and mercy, and introduced the great entity (*ens*) of love into the entity (*ens*) of aroused wrath, and in Christ transfigured the wrathful into the holy Man." "So Christ became the God-man, and Adam and Abraham in Christ became God-man: henceforth God and man are one indivisible Person by all three principles and out of all three, in time and in eternity, in flesh and in spirit, in all the nature of man and all the Divine nature, except that serpent nature imprinted on Adam from without, and accepted by him, although he should not have taken it unto himself. But by entity (*ens*) I mean human being (*ens*) in which the devil sowed his seed; this, man had to take upon himself and in this nature crush the head of the serpent and the devil, in it break the chains of death which hold enslaved the heavenly nature and then blossom out, as did the rod of Aaron with almond blossoms." "Adam was also the natural son of God, created by Him of his own nature, but Adam lost his sonship and his heritage, was driven out, and with him all his sons." "For Christ died of man's self-hood in the wrath of the Father and in the will to self-hood was buried in eternal death, but he rose again in his Father's will, and lives and reigns eternally in the will of his Father." Here is Boehme's most essential word on Christ and Adam: "Understand that human nature must be preserved, and that God did not cast it out entirely, so that a new and strange man should rise from the old; rather he must rise from the nature and qualities of Adam and from the nature and qualities of God in Christ, *so that man should become Adam-Christ—Christ a Christ-Adam, God-man and man-God*" [italics mine]. This is what I call man's birth in God, his entry into Divine life. Christ is the Man Absolute, the Heavenly man, man born in God, as a hypostasis of God. "So the Adamic man, who was destined to become an apostle or Christ, was already born before Christ suffered in him; but first Christ had to rise from the dead in this man's nature, and Judas, as the will of

68

the serpent, had to be crushed and die in the death of Christ, together with his evil will—*only then the man-Adam became a Christ.*" [Italics mine.] The train of Boehme's thought is quite irrational not logical, and can be heard only by a special listening faculty, as a harmony of the heavenly spheres.

The uncomprehended and forgotten mystic of Boehme was revived in the nineteenth century by Franz von Baader. In the essentials Baader follows Boehme, but he adds something of his own. In Boehme there is an extraordinary preponderance of *Naturphilosophie*; in Baader we find both a philosophy of history and social philosophy. Here his philosophy of history is connected with the Church. At this moment we find Baader's anthropology interesting—"Man is a mediator between God and the world, hence he is neither a mortal being of the world, nor a finished process of creation. Only in man is God revealed in his integrity: hence, at the creation, God could not observe His sabbath until man was created." "Man is the pinnacle of creation, and hence stands above the angels. God is God even to the Devil. He is the creator of everything that is. But only in man is He a Father, or wishes to be a Father. God became man and not an angel in order to save man from his fallen state. He sent his heart, Jesus, to men, stretching out His hand to them, in order that they should become participators in sonship. Only through Christ is power given to man to realize his true destiny as the pinnacle of all creation." "Man, who should have become God in miniature (*microtheos*) became the world in miniature (microcosm), but still has not lost his predestination and his duty to become a microtheos." "Man is the centre, the extract, the ideal, the focus of the universe. Outside him everything is only the shattered members of creation; in him everything fits into a beautiful harmony—the microcosm. Man is a sort of general centre of feeling, touching everything, enjoying everything, making everything his own. In each of man's separate capacities there is a whole world, and a generating centre which from time to time expresses itself in disharmony." "In so far as man by his dual nature is a mirror of Truth itsélf, in the sense that all the laws of everything that is spiritual and everything that is feeling are rooted in his own law, by so far man is divine nature." "The truly good will in man is Christ in him."

The great mystic doctrine of man in our time is recognized and revived in a too-scientific form by Rudolf Steiner, the founder of the anthroposophic society. Steiner, also, reveals the microcosmic nature of man, sees in man all the various planes of being, all of planetary evolution. With Steiner man is only a passing moment of the cosmic evolution: he rises and disappears. Anthropo-sophy has not justified its name.

§

While in official philosophy, from Descartes on, the mechanistic conception of nature triumphed and, with rare exceptions, philosophy could not overcome the spectre of a dead mechanism of nature, for mystic philosophy nature always remained something alive, a living organism. Nature was alive for Paracelsus, for Jakob Boehme, and for the naturalist philosophers of the Renaissance. Science obediently adapts itself to the mechanism of nature, but philosophy should look beyond this and see organism. Even the element of death in nature, which cannot be denied, must be understood as coming from a falsely-directed freedom of the living being. The deadly mechanism of necessity began with the sinful freedom of living beings. Nature is the organic hierarchy of living beings. The material element in nature is only an incarnation, an objectivization of living beings, of spirits of various hierarchic degrees. And the material element which science so carefully investigates, is not only an incarnation of a living spirit, it is a fettering and enslaving spirit—it bears the stamp of the Fall, of degradation to a lower sphere. Man, the microcosm, belongs to a higher, royal degree in the hierarchy of nature, as a living organism. Man, the microcosm is responsible for the whole structure of nature and whatever takes place in man affects the whole of nature. Man gives life and spirit to nature,

70

through his creative freedom, and he kills or fetters it through his own servitude and his fall into material necessity. The fall of the highest hierarchical centre of nature carries with it the fall of all nature, of all its lower ranks. The whole of creation groans and weeps and awaits its liberation. The element of death in nature and that evil materialization, into the power of which all the beings of this world have fallen by the force of necessity and can find no way out of their limited condition—all this is the result of man's fall, of an evil shifting of the hierarchical centre of nature. The degree of responsibility for this death-bound condition of nature depends upon the degree of freedom and upon the hierarchic place in the cosmos. Man is most responsible and stones the least responsible. The tsar is more responsible than the lowest of his subjects. Man's fall, and the consequent loss of his royal freedom and his being plunged into lower spheres of necessity, deprived man of his place in nature and placed him in slavish dependence on the lower spheres of the hierarchy of nature. Having by his fall and enslavement brought death and mechanization into nature, man encountered everywhere the resistance of nature's dead mechanism and became a slave of natural necessity. Stones, plants and animals control man as though they were taking revenge for their own lack of freedom. This resistance, this power of the petrified parts of nature, finally lost in the material necessity of the lower ranks of the hierarchy of nature, is the source of man's sorrow and his need—man, the dethroned king of nature. The poison from the dead bodies of those ranks of nature which have been done to death have caused death to man himself, forced him to share the fate of the stones and the dust. Man becomes a part of the natural world, one of the phenomena of nature, subject to nature's necessity. "This world", the world of natural necessity, fell with the fall of man, and man will have to renounce the temptations of "this world" to regain his regnant place in it. Man must free himself from the lower ranks of the hierarchy of nature, must become ashamed of

71

the fact that he is slavishly dependent upon that which is lower than himself and which should rightly depend upon him. Nature must be humanized, liberated, made alive and inspired by man. Only man can take the spell off nature and give it life, since it was man who bound nature and condemned it to death. Man's fate depends upon the fate of nature and of the cosmos, and he cannot separate himself from this. Man must give back spirit to the stones, reveal the living nature of stones, in order to free himself from their stony, oppressing power. There is a heavy layer of dead stone in man, and there is no other way of escaping from it than by liberating the stone itself. By his whole material nature man is fettered to the material in nature and must share its fate. And yet fallen man remains a microcosm and contains within himself all the ranks and all the powers of the world. But it was not individual man who fell, it was the all-man, the first Adam, and so not the individual man may rise, but the all-man. The all-man is inseparable from the cosmos and its fate. The liberation and creative upsurge of the all-man is the liberation and creation of the cosmos. The destinies of the microcosm and the macrocosm are inseparable— they rise or fall together. The condition of the one is imprinted upon the other; they mutually penetrate each other. Man cannot escape the cosmos—he can only change or transform it. The cosmos shares the fate of man and hence man shares the fate of the cosmos. Only the man who takes the place in the cosmos prepared for him by his Creator, has the power to transform the cosmos into a new heaven and a new earth. One of the great mystics of the orthodox east, St. Simeon the New Theologian, puts it beautifully: "When it saw that Adam was driven out of paradise, the whole of creation would have refused to save him: the moon and the stars did not want to give him light; the springs did not wish to give water or the rivers to continue their flow; the wind thought it would blow no more, so that Adam, having sinned, would not have air to breathe; all the animals of the earth, when they saw that he was deprived

72

of his pristine glory, began to despise him and were ready to attack him; the sky would have fallen upon him and the earth did not wish to carry him any longer. But, having created everything, including man, what did God do? He restrained all these creatures by His power, and by His kindness and His grace did not permit them to fall upon man, and commanded that all creatures should continue in subjection to him, and having become mortal, should serve mortal man for whom they were created, in order that when man should once more become renewed and again a spiritual being, incorruptible and immortal, the whole of creation, also subjected by God to man's service, would be liberated from this work and would be renewed together with man and also become incorruptible and as it were spiritual." This is a wonderful statement of man's connection with the cosmos and his loss of his royal glory.

The restoration of man to his former dignity could be accomplished only by the appearance of the absolute Son of God, in the Incarnation. Man is not only higher than all the hierarchical grades of nature, he is higher than the angels. For angels are only the accompaniments of God's glory: theirs is a static role. Man is dynamic. The Son of God became a man and not an angel, and man is called to a royal and creative role in the world to the continuation of creation. Man is created in the image and likeness of God: the beast in the image and likeness of the angels. Hence we find in the world a dynamic-creative, divine-human hierarchy, and the uncreative, static, angel-animal hierarchy.

*The prevalence of static over dynamic in the Church, the dulling of its creative spirit, is the result of the prevalence in its spiritual structure of the angel-animal hierarchy over the hierarchy of the divine-human.* Clericalism is the domination of the angelic element in the world, instead of the human. And as a result we have the animalization of man. The clergy are of the angelic, rather than the human order and hence they cannot be actively creative in our world: the clergy is only a medium for the divine; when the attempt is made to place an angel

73

instead of man in the centre of the universal hierarchy, a pope, a bishop or a priest instead of man, in this case the static overcomes the dynamic and humanity easily falls into the animal state. For the animal is like the angels, while man is like God. And the animal world is called to become the setting for the glory of man, just as the angelic world is the setting for the glory of God. Displacing man from his hierarchical position in the world always gives rise to evil and slavery. The angelic are not the highest degree in cosmic hierarchy—the highest is man the centre, like unto God his Creator. The angels are a hierarchic appurtenance of the divine organism and, as intermediaries or mediums of divine energy, the protectors of man. The angel who desired to become the emperor of the cosmos became the devil. Boehme says: "For Lucifer left the repose of his hierarchy and entered eternal unrest." And this arrogant act of the angel was caused by the fact that the beast, like the angel, desired to reign in the cosmos. On earth, in the pope or any priest, any angelic order which desires to rule or dominate, we see reflected the fall of the angel, his diabolic falling-away from divine repose, from his pristine glory. Man was created the dynamic and creative centre of the universe but, in using his freedom, he followed the fallen angel who had desired to become the centre of the world and lost his royal position, weakened his creative power and fell into an animal-like condition. Instead of bravely asserting himself as a free creator, man subjected himself to the fallen angel. The devil has no creative, dynamic power, because the angels have not got it and are not destined to use it. The fallen angel lives by falsehood and deceit, hiding his powerlessness. But man, even in his fallen state, does not completely lose his creative power. His falling-away from God is a poor exchange of the divine-human for the angelic-animal hierarchy. The divine-human is restored by the incarnation of God's Son, by the appearance in our world of the Absolute Divine Man. Man's kingly position in the world is confirmed by the God-man, and the principle of the fallen angel is overcome. The

74

new Adam represents a higher degree of cosmic-creative development than did the First Adam in Eden. The old consciousness that man was supposed to be only a static adjunct to the glory of God, a passive being deprived of knowledge, reflected the fallen state of the fallen angel who wanted to become the ruler of the cosmos. Not man but the fallen angel himself was called to be the adjunct of God's glory. Man, on the contrary, is called to glorify his Creator by creative dynamic in the cosmos. He must leave a state of repose. Adam, reborn through Christ into a new spiritual man, is no longer passive and oppressed and blind, but a clear-seeing creator, the son of God who continues his Father's work.

§

Naturalistic anthropocentrism cannot stand against criticism. Copernicus and Darwin evidently did away with that concept and made the idea of man's central position unacceptable to scientific consciousness. The closed universe of antiquity and of the middle ages was suddenly opened out and an infinity of worlds was revealed in which man, with his pretensions of being the centre of the universe, was completely lost. Copernicus demonstrated that the earth is not the centre of the universe and that the other worlds do not revolve round it as a centre. The earth is one of the planets, a very modest one. Darwin showed that man is not the absolute centre of this modest planet, the earth: he is one of the forms of organic life on the earth, of the same nature as other forms—one of the moments of evolution. Thus science taught modesty to both the earth and to man, lowering their natural self-consciousness. In the world of nature man does not hold an exceptional place. He is part of the circulation of nature, one of its phenomena, one of its things: he is a tiny, infinitely small, part of the universe. Now, when man contemplates the star-strewn sky at night, he feels himself lost in that infinity of worlds, oppressed by this terrible infinity; the vast multitude of solar systems, the vast multitude of microorganisms or, in modern terms, supra-worlds and infra-worlds,

75

rob man of his consciousness of himself as dominant and exclusive. As a purely natural being man is not the centre of the universe and not its king: he is only one among many and is forced to struggle for his place with an infinite number of beings and powers which are also striving to rise.

But the collapse of naturalistic anthropocentrism which had naïvely tied man's significance to the natural world does not mean the collapse of man's highest consciousness of himself as a microcosm, as the centre and ruler of the universe. It is only the childish science of the Bible, the naïve biblical astronomy, geology and biology which have collapsed: the Bible's religious truth about man remains valid. Man claims something immeasurably greater than the self-consciousness which naturalistic anthropocentrism can offer him. For us, the efforts of man in the middle ages to base their significance on the naïve scientific ideas of humanity's childhood seem laughable. *Man's infinite spirit claims an absolute supernatural anthropocentrism: he knows himself to be the absolute centre—not of a given, closed planetary system, but of the whole of being, of all planes of being, of all worlds.* Man is not only a natural being, but a supernatural being as well, a being of divine origin and divine destination, a being which although he lives in "this world" is not of it. This absolute anthropocentrism, which by the eternal element in man overcomes the evil infinity of the stellar system, cannot be overthrown by any science, just as it cannot be confirmed by any science; it is beyond the reach of science. Of this absolute anthropocentrism what can the science of Copernicus, Lowell or Darwin have to say? Their science is only an adaptation to the present limited condition of the world of nature. And this limited condition of the world of nature, so carefully described by Copernicus, Lowell and Darwin, is due to man's fall, shifting the hierarchic centre of the universe. The inferior position taken by man in the present condition of the natural world and our given planetary system by no means argues against man's central position in being or against the absolute truth that man is the focal centre of all planes of being; for the earth fell with the fall of man and so came into the circle of natural necessity. However, the earth's metaphysical meaning is revealed not by astronomy or geology but rather by anthropological philosophy, a philosophy which is mystical rather than scientific. The truth, that the value and significance of the earth and of man surpassed the whole world of nature, would naturally be hidden from science which is adapted only to the necessity of this given world. This truth is a break-through of all barriers and all boundaries into another world. In the teaching of the mystics there is implicit the truth of man's relation to other planes of being, other planetary systems (not in the natural-astronomic, but the supernatural, astrological sense of the word) a truth hidden from official science and official philosophy. The reason for man's occupying a subordinate place in the natural world and in the solar system is revealed only mystically.

The fact that man receives light from the sun and that his life turns round the sun is an important sign of man's subjection. The fact that the sun lighted man from without is an eternal reminder that man, like all things of this world, is by himself in everlasting darkness, having in himself no source of light. The sun should be in man, the centre of the cosmos: man himself should be the sun of the world, round which everything else revolved. The Logos-Sun within man should be giving light. But the sun is outside man and man is in darkness. In the world of nature the light of life depends upon an external and distant source. If the sun should cease to shine, all the objects of the world of nature would be plunged into impenetrable darkness and life would cease, since life without light is impossible. The magic of our "white nights" with their extraordinary beauty is explained by the fact that no visible source of light appears (sun, moon, lamps or candles) that everything seems to shine with an inner light. The white nights are a romantic reminder of the normal and inner light of all things and beings on the earth. The sun's central place outside man and man's

dependence upon the light is a degradation of man. Man's
fall, before the world was, meant his removal as a hierarchical
centre. In the world of nature, in the metaphysical formation of our planetary system, this resulted in the sun's
transferring itself from within to a place outside. Man fell,
and the sun went out of him. The earth with man living upon
it began to revolve round the sun, when the whole universe
should have revolved round man and his world and should
have received light from man by virtue of the Logos living
within him. Having lost the sun within him, man fell into
sun- or fire-worship, made a god of the external sun. The
apocalyptic image of the woman clothed with the sun is an
image of the sun's return into man. The right hierarchical
order of the cosmos is restored. Angelus Silesius says:
"*Ich selbst muss Sonne sein, ich muss mit meinem Strahlen das
fabulose Meer der ganzen Gottheit malen.*" But the sun can return
into man only through the incarnation in the world of the
Absolute Man-Logos. The Logos is the Absolute Sun-Man
who restores to man and to the earth their absolutely central
situation which was lost in the world of nature. Man's higher
consciousness of himself as a microcosm is a Christological
consciousness. And the christological consciousness of the
new Adam surpasses the self-consciousness of the First Adam:
it marks a new phase in the creation of the world.

§

The true anthropology can be founded only upon the
revelation of Christ. The fact of Christ's appearance in the
world is the basic fact of anthropology. A higher anthropological consciousness is possible only after Christ. The
world-act of man's consciousness of his divinity could be
accomplished only in Christ and through Christ. Only man's
son-ship to God, accomplished in Christ, Christ's restoration
of human nature so damaged by man's sin and his fall,
reveals the secret of man and his primogeniture, the mystery
of man's person. In Christ God becomes a person, and man
becomes a person. Boehme says: "*Gott ist keine Person als nur*

78

*in Christo.*" The mystery of Christ is the mystery of the Absolute Man, the God-man. Christ, the Son of God, is the divine man "before all worlds". From all eternity the Son is born of God, the Absolute Man, the Divine Man, the God-Man. The Divine Son and Man is born in heaven and on earth, in time and in eternity, above and below. Hence what is accomplished in heaven is also accomplished on earth. The drama of earthly man is also the drama of heavenly humanity. Through the Son of Man nature participates in Divine nature and the human person is comprised in the Divine. The self-consciousness of Christ, as perfect God and perfect Man, lifts man to a dizzying height, lifts Him to the Holy Trinity. *Through Christ, man becomes a participant in the nature of the Holy Trinity, for the second hypostasis of the Holy Trinity is the Absolute Man.* Oh, certainly, man is not God, he is the son of God but not in the unique sense that Christ is the Son of God; but man is a participant in the mystery of the nature of the Holy Trinity and is a mediator between God and the cosmos. Through Christ every human person is a part not of the mortal world alone but of the Divine as well. Man's nature is God-worldly, and not simply worldly. Man is not only a natural-mortal being, but a divine-mortal being. There is a natural divinity in man; hidden within him is a natural-divine element. Christ restores man's lost right of primogeniture, his right to claim a divine descent and a divine calling. The documentary proofs were lost after man's fall into the order of natural necessity. Fallen man, now become a natural being, fettered by necessity, is powerless to free himself from his captivity and slavery, to return to his divine origins. Only the absolute divine Man, through whom every man participates in divine power and the divine nature, has power to do this. The Absolute Man in God retains his human personality as it was made by God the Creator. In the Absolute Man human nature remains in the higher, divine spheres of being, while at the same time in fallen "natural" man it is plunged into lower spheres of being in order to lift fallen man to higher spheres. The

Absolute Man, the God-man is the Logos, the Sun of Creation. Through Him man becomes the sun, the Logos of creation, for which he was predestined by his Creator.

The relationship between man and nature, between anthropos and cosmos, should correspond to the mystical relationship between Christ the Logos and the world's mortal spirit. Mystic symbolism has always envisaged in the relationship between Logos and the world-spirit the relationship between male and female. The same relationship between male and female may be discerned in the relationship between man and nature. The male is of the sun, the female of the moon; the female gives light only by reflecting it from the sun. Through the male element man partakes of the natural spirit of the world. In the one aspect, Christ the Logos is man rather than woman—Absolute Man in His masculine nature. In another of His aspects Christ is androgyne. The prevalence of the female over the male means the prevalence of the natural element of the world over the Logos. Mystical vision and religious consciousness have always understood that man's fall was concurrent with his subjection to the female element, that the fallen angel worked through the female element.

Christianity has always taught of the weakness and fall of man, of the sinfulness and weakness of human nature. At the same time Christian anthropology recognizes the absolute and royal significance of man, since it teaches of the incarnation of God and the divine possibilities in man, the mutual inter-penetration of divine and human natures. *But for some deep reason, hidden in the secret of times and seasons, Christianity never revealed in its fullness what one might dare to call a Christology of man, that is the secret of man's divine nature, a dogma of man, analogous to the dogma of Christ.* Christianity has revealed the nature of the Holy Trinity and the nature of Christ, but very little of the nature of man. In the Christianity of the early Fathers there was a monophysite tendency, a hesitancy about the revelation of Christ's human nature and hence of the divine nature of man, his oppression under

80

sin and his thirst for redemption from sin. This tangential tendency is evident in the whole of Christianity and is not at all the result of chance. *And yet in Christian revelation the truth about man's divine nature is really only the reverse side of the medal of the truth about Christ's human nature.* The Christology of man is inseparable from that of the Son of God: Christ's self-consciousness is inseparable from that of man. The Christological revelation is also an anthropological revelation. And the task of humanity's religious consciousness is to reveal the Christological consciousness of man. Only the mystics, transcending all times and seasons, have glimpsed the truth of the Christology of man. Man is a microcosm; his is rightly a central and royal place in the world, because human nature mystically resembles the nature of the Absolute Man, Christ, and thus participates in the nature of the Holy Trinity. *Man is not a simple creature, together with other created things, because the only-begotten Son of God, begotten before all worlds and of equal worth with His Father, is not only absolute God but Absolute Man.* Christology is the only true anthropology. Christ, the Absolute Man, appeared on earth and in humanity and hence for ever confirmed a central significance in the universe for man and for the earth. Neither Copernicus's astronomy nor Darwin's biology can overthrow Christological anthropology, which surpasses this world, a truth which is truly before all worlds. Before the world was created the image of man was already in the Son of God, born of the Father before all time. Only the Christology of man, the reverse side of the anthropology of Christ, reveals in man the genuine image and likeness of God, the Creator.

The anthropology of the Church Fathers revealed only very partially the Christological truth about man. The religious anthropology of the Fathers and teachers of the Church is limited: it has no room for the creative mystery of human nature. This anthropology is still too much burdened by the consciousness of man's fall: it teaches about human passions and man's deliverance from sin. In reality the

Church Fathers' theory of man is still dependent on ancient pagan anthropology. In the patristic concept the absolute and vertiginous truth about man does not correspond to the absolute and vertiginous Christological truth about the redemption. The mystery of the redemption has, as it were, veiled-over the creative mystery of man. The infinite distance between man and God still remains. Even in the dogmas of the œcumenical councils, which reveal only the Christological mystery, the mystery of redemption, there is no final anthropological revelation. And neither in the Christtianity of the early Fathers, nor in that of the œcumenical councils could there be a truly Christian religious anthropology. This whole historical epoch stood under the sign of the consciousness of sin, and of redemption through Christ as the only way to deliverance from sin. Religious consciousness had to be oriented wholly towards Christ rather than towards man. To know the truth of redemption man must be conscious of his weakness and helplessness. Only rarely in patristic literature does the consciousness of man's royal calling break through, which sings in the words of St. Gregory of Nyssa: "Just as in this life an artist is given tools suited to his needs, so the greatest Artist created our nature as a vessel useful for royal purposes and both by its spiritual advantages and its bodily appearance created it as something which could play a kingly role. For the spirit proves its royal qualities, its superiority, its great distance from vulgar baseness by the very fact that, freely without demeaning itself, it harbours wishes and desires. Who, other than a king, could have such qualities? And beyond this—to be the image and likeness of a Being which rules over everything means nothing other than that from his very creation man had a royal nature." Or St. Simeon the New Theologian: "When Christ came, from that moment man became a light through union with that first and unfading light of God, and had no further need of the written law." Or St. Macarius of Egypt: "Know thy nobility: that thou art called to royal dignity: that thou art 'a chosen race, a holy tongue—a holiness'. The mystery of Christianity is something incomprehensible for this world, the visible riches and glory of an emperor are earthly, passing, mortal: but divine kingliness and riches are heavenly glories which will never pass away and never end. For in the heavenly Church they co-reign with the Heavenly King. And since He is the 'first-born from the dead' so those who reign with Him are also firstborn." But in Patristic Christianity in general the consciousness of man's loss of freedom in his fall prevails over that of man's royal liberty.

In the Fathers and in the most valuable ascetic literature only a doctrine of the passions and liberation from them, i.e. a negative anthropology, is well worked out. The Fathers' positive anthropology still remains that of the old paganism: the doctrines of the natural man and the old Adam. The doctrine of the heavenly Adam, of man as a supernatural microcosm is scarcely revealed at all, or rather it is revealed only in Christology and not in anthropology. Only some of the mystics have broken through the boundaries of times and seasons. That man is a creator, like God the Creator— about this, nothing at all is evident in the consciousness of the Fathers and teachers of the Church. And up to now Christian consciousness has been that of the Church Fathers. The patristic consciousness could not see the microcosm in man since it was not oriented towards the macrocosm. The question of man's positive, creative calling in the world was never even raised by the teachers and Fathers of the Church. That most ardent and radical of the Fathers, St. Isaac the Syrian, says: "In this is virtue, that man should not occupy his mind with the world. The heart cannot remain in quiet and be undisturbed by dreaming, so long as man's feelings are active." "The beginning of real life in a man, is the fear of God. But God will not consent to live in any man's soul together with the vaporizings of his mind." "The world is a collective noun, comprising all the passions we count over." "By nature the soul is passionless." "A being is able to become a spectator of the truth rather than the wishful contemplator, only when a man has first, by suffering, self-activity and sorrow, slipped off the old man of passion just as a new-born babe slips out of the covering he has worn in his mother's womb. Then the mind is capable of being born again, spiritually, to become visible in the spiritual world and to accept the contemplation of his fatherhood." And here is a word which as it were reveals all the fullness of the divine and cosmic in man: "He who subjects himself to God is near the point when everything else will be subject to him. To him who knows himself is given the knowledge of everything: hence to know oneself is to have full knowledge of everything and in the subjection of thy spirit, everything is subject to thee." But for St. Isaac the Syrian the world consists only of passions, and man becomes strong and receives knowledge not by revealing his human nature, but by its final suppression in order to give place to God. Man becomes divine, but only by suppressing all that is human, by the disappearance of man and the appearance of Divinity in his place. The teachers of the Church had a doctrine of the δεωσις of man, but in this δεωσις there is no man at all. The very problem of man is not even put. But man is godlike not alone because he is capable of suppressing his own nature and thus freeing a place for divinity. There is godlikeness in human nature itself, in the very human voice of that nature. Silencing the world and the passions liberates man. God desires that not only God should exist, but man as well. In this is the meaning of the world. For the Church Fathers man's task was to return to his pristine state before the Fall. St. Simeon the New Theologian says: "God became man in order by his incarnation to bring human nature again into a state of grace. Hence we must learn by what means through the incarnation of Christ man is brought again into a state of Grace." "Men are born into the world to glorify God, since they are thinking and reasonable beings. They alone among all visible creatures are able to know, to magnify and to thank God. Contemplating creation, they are amazed at the

84

Creator, and having recognized his greatness, unthinkable and limitless, they honour Him and sing praise before Him." Man is born "in order to become worthy to live in the heavenly mansions and be counted among the multitude of the holy angels", that is, man's calling to be angelic: to be passive rather than creative. The whole significance of the patristic consciousness lay in heroic struggle against the old Adam and against worldly passions.

§

The result in daily living of this limited horizon of patristic anthropology was felt throughout the whole of the middle ages, in both west and east. The Fathers' consciousness, occupied exclusively with the mystery of redemption, resulted in a non-heroic period, in demeaning man and suppressing his creative power. The conception of St. Isaac the Syrian can be only the heroic act of a personality, but as a guide for organizing the life of mankind which has not known the saint's personal experience, it can become a source of fatal difficulty for man. The mystic experience must be personal, and its results cannot be observed from the outside. In the middle ages the whole of anthropology was pagan rather than Christian. In the east the anthropological was completely suppressed: in the west it had a certain development and expression, but this western anthropologism gave to Catholicism a clearly expressed form of pagan-Christianity. The Christian element in Catholicism contains no anthropological revelation: only in its pagan element was there an anthropology, but this was Roman or barbarian, something outside Christianity. The idea of knightly honour contained within itself a great anthropological truth about personality, but a truth quite foreign to the patristic consciousness. The whole structure of papal theocracy and the feudal hierarchy was a pagan and barbarian anthropologism.

This failure to reveal anthropological truth in Christianity led to the rise of humanistic anthropology, set up by the wilfulness of man himself in a formal reaction against the religious consciousness of the middle ages. The anthropological concept of humanism arises in the period of the Renaissance and developed in modern times down to the twentieth century when it reaches its climax and reveals its limitations. Humanism put the anthropological problem, and gave free rein to man and his powers. But in the period of the Renaissance it was only the mystics like Pico Della Mirandola who were conscious of man's being a microcosm. Pico says: "Man is the connection which joins all nature together and as it were, an essence made up of all its juices. Hence he who knows himself, knows in himself everything." The prevailing and conquering humanistic consciousness liberated and established the natural man, who has lost his royal and microcosmic qualities. Humanism confirms a subjective-psychological, rather than an objective-cosmic anthropocentrism. Man is left to himself, with his limited human powers, connected only with natural necessity. Man had to pass through the experience of being forsaken by God. Humanism was a necessary experience for mankind. Man had to be set free in the natural world, and human life had to be secularized. Man, as an essential part of the natural world, desired freedom and independence and wilfully and subjectively made himself the central purpose in nature. Humanism is an ideal of the natural, dependent man. The humanistic consciousness does not wish to recognize man's high origins or his high calling. The humanistic consciousness lacks all sense of son-ship to God. Humanism is obedient to the fact of man's enslavement to the world of nature. But in this world of nature humanism desires to make man as free and independent as possible and to give him the utmost possible happiness. Humanism gradually loses all consciousness of God and deifies man and the human.

But humanism does not know man as the image and likeness of God, since it does not wish to know God: it does not know man as a free spirit, because it is in the grasp of natural necessity. Hence humanism can deify only the

86

natural man, only man as an empirical fact, as a drop in the sea of nature which has subjectively set itself up as a final purpose. If the patristic consciousness, while having a Christology, lacks a corresponding anthropology, humanistic consciousness has no Christology to correspond with its anthropology. Humanism does not know the heavenly Adam, the Absolute Man, and hence cannot know man's true dignity. The mystery of human nature is unknown to humanism and therefore humanistic anthropology is false from its roots up. Humanism knows man only as a natural object, and does not know man as a supernatural subject. Humanistic consciousness is oppressed by Copernicus' discovery. And it transfers anthropocentrism to a subjective and wilful condition of man, confirming a psychological anthropocentrism. Man is of a low origin and has no calling whatever, but by his own powers he rises through various degrees of the natural world and makes himself the end and object, the final goal. Fatefully and inevitably, humanism in the nineteenth century leads to positivism, to the forced installation of man in the limited territory of the given, natural world. Humanistic positivism would like to put an end to man's consciousness of belonging to two worlds. There is no other world; man belongs wholly to this one and in it he must seek happiness. But in this world man is a slave of necessity, an infinitely tiny part of the gigantic mechanism of nature. Naturalism and positivism definitely degrade man. They even deny man, for man is more than a bunch of impressions, changing sensations, a fractional part of the circular eddy of nature. In positivism that truth of the humanism of the Renaissance disappears, which was connected with the revival of antiquity as human value. And humanism is reborn as anti-humanism: it denies man. Without God and the God-man, the real man, man the microcosm, the king of nature, cannot exist. Either man is the image and likeness of Absolute Divine Being, and then he is a free spirit, the king and the centre of nature, or else he is the image and likeness of our given natural world, and in this case man does not exist—he is only one of the passing expressions of nature. We must choose: either man's freedom in God, or the necessity of a passing phenomenon in the natural world. In its positivistic limitation, humanism chose the latter and thus committed murder in thought; it refused man's higher consciousness of himself, transcending the given natural world, and thus denied man's primogeniture, betrayed man for the sake of adjustment to the given world of nature and for happiness within it. The fate of humanism is a great tragedy of man who seeks an anthropological revelation. The lack of anthropological revelation moves into the way of humanism. The Patristic consciousness leaves man helpless in the revelation of his creative nature. And the criticism of humanism must be immanent, just as living it out must be immanent.

In the nineteenth century, humanism took the form of a religion of humanity. L. Feuerbach's anthropology and August Comte's positivism are the philosophic climaxes of humanistic consciousness. The style of the humanism of the Renaissance bears little resemblance to that of the nineteenth century; but the first contained the seed of the second. The humanism of the nineteenth century was much more monistic; in it the rational and positivistic spirit finally prevails. The *pathos* of all humanism lies in its affirmation of man as the highest and the final, as God, and in its denial of the superhuman. But once you have denied God and deified man, man falls to a level lower than the human, since man remains at the height of his dignity only as image and likeness of a higher divine being; he is true man only when he has sonship with God. Man cannot be only a father, the father of his children, of future human generations; he must also be a son, he must be a descendant —must have roots which go down into absolute being and eternity. Humanism denied man this sonship, renounced his descendence, renounced man's freedom and his guilt, renounced man's dignity. Humanism undertook to abolish everything difficult or problematic or tragic in man, in order

88

to establish man better on the earth and make him happy. But man's well-being and happiness on the earth, if it turns away from the ineluctable tragedy of human life, is a denial of man as belonging to two worlds, as participating not only in the natural kingdom of necessity, but also in the supernatural kingdom of freedom.

Feuerbach had scarcely proclaimed the religion of humanity when Karl Marx, in his materialistic socialism, carried humanism to a final denial of man, to man's final enslavement to necessity, making man into an instrument of material productive forces. Marx finally denies the intrinsic value of human personality; he sees in man only a function of the material social process, and sacrifices every man and every human generation to the idol of the future state and of the proletariat which will be blissfully happy in it. Here humanistic anthropology arrives at a crisis: man is wiped out for the sake of something vague and visionary and superhuman, for the sake of socialism and the proletariat. The proletariat is higher than man: it is not merely the sum of all men, but a new god. Thus the superhuman must inevitably rise out of the ruins of humanism. Marxism is one of the ultimate products of the anthropological consciousness of humanism, annihilating humanism and finally killing man. Positivism in theory and socialism in practice—these are the ultimate fruits of humanism disclosing the falsity of humanistic anthropology. For that anthropology is false, which kills man himself, which does not answer to man's limitless nature, does not know the secrets of human nature— the key to the mystery of being. Nevertheless man had to pass through the humanistic consciousness in order to arrive at the revelation about man. It was impossible to remain at the stage of the patristic consciousness. Through humanism, man's activity is born in suffering, and it moves upward rather than downward. The truth of humanism is part of the religion of divine humanity, which predicates belief not only in God but in man as well.

§

Humanist anthropology reached its climax in F. Nietzsche, the most significant spiritual phenomenon of modern history. Nietzsche is the saving victim for the sins of modern times— a sacrifice of the humanist consciousness. After Nietzsche, his works and his fate, humanism is for ever overcome. *Zarathustra* is the most powerful human book without grace; whatever is superior to *Zarathustra* is so by grace from on high. *Zarathustra* is the work of man abandoned to himself. And never did a man left to himself and his own powers rise higher. In its final form the crisis of humanism had to lead to the idea of the superman, to the abolition of man and of the human. For Nietzsche the final value is not the human but the superhuman, since he has overcome humanism. For him man is a shame and a pain, man must be overcome, he must arrive at something which is higher than man, the superman. In Nietzsche humanism conquers not from above through grace, but from beneath through man's own powers —and this is the great achievement of Nietzsche. *Nietzsche is the forerunner of a new religious anthropology.* Through Nietzsche the new humanity moves out of godless humanism to divine humanism, to a Christian anthropology. Nietzsche is an instinctive prophet, as yet not possessing the Logos, a prophet of the religious renaissance of the west. Zarathustra's hatred for the lost man who has invented happiness is a holy hatred of the degrading lies of humanism. Zarathustra preached creativity, rather than happiness—he called man toward the mountain-top, rather than to bliss on the plain. Humanism is a level plain—it cannot stand the hills. As no one else ever has in the course of all history, Nietzsche senses the creative calling of man, a concept unknown alike to patristic and to humanistic consciousness. He cursed the good and the happy because they hate those who create. We should share Nietzsche's torment; it is religious through and through. And we ought to take upon ourselves the responsibility for his fate. Through Nietzsche there begins a new

90

anthropological revelation in the world, which in its final concept, in its Logos, must become the Christology of man. "What is great in man, is that he is a bridge, rather than an end."

Only one other person can be placed beside Nietzsche, one who is at once so like and so unlike Nietzsche—Dostoevski. In Dostoevski's anthropology something new was revealed to the world. In Dostoevski, the problem of man's consciousness of himself attains extraordinary acuteness. Dostoevski is interested only in man. After Nietzsche and Dostoevski there can be no return to the old; neither to the old Christian, nor to the old humanistic anthropology. A new era begins: boundaries and ends begin to be revealed. The end of everything passing and momentary begins. Nietzsche's ideas are false and must be rejected. Nietzsche did not know the way to the superman and finished in tragic helplessness. And what happened after his death is still more tragic, for he gave birth to Nietzscheism, a pitiful and powerless thing. But it is not Nietzsche's consciousness which is important, which is sometimes almost banal, but the man himself, his life-work, the torment of his seeking, his foresight. The true prophetic spirit was in him, not in the biblical but in the modern sense of that word. After Nietzsche, as after Dostoevski, man has to have a new consciousness of himself and must justify his calling, reveal his creative nature. "The last man" is something shameful which must be overcome. But this is impossible by the Christianity of the Fathers. And only the truth which has been revealed to certain mystics can help in overcoming the shame of "the last man".

In both Nietzsche and Dostoevski there occurred an extreme intensification of human self-consciousness, of anthropological consciousness. This is expressed in the fact that through them there was revealed to the Christian world the problem of the end of man, the problem of Antichrist. The impending and menacing image of the Antichrist compels the Christian world towards creative effort to discover a true

Christological anthropology. Man's highest self-consciousness, his anthropological consciousness, must be fully revealed because man is in danger of falling into the power of an Antichristology of man, a false anthropology which will destroy man. Man faces a dilemma: to have a Christological or an Antichristological consciousness of himself; to see in Christ the absolute man, or to see him in the Antichrist. In its godless and unspiritual development, humanism threatens to bring men to an Antichristological consciousness. The Antichrist is the final destruction of man as the image and likeness of divine being, as microcosm, as participant in the mystery of the Trinity through the Absolute Man, the Son of God. The Antichristological anthropology makes man a slave of the fallen angel who desired to have his own incarnation on earth, opposed to that of Christ. Making himself divine, and thus losing his sonship to God, man becomes the powerless slave of natural necessity, into which he was plunged by his fall. The man in the spirit of the Antichrist is separated from the sacrament of redemption which restores and lifts up man's fallen nature. The spirit of Antichrist promises man bliss in this world of necessity through renunciation of his god-like nature. But the spirit of Antichrist may be recognized not by superficial consciousness, not by dogmatic consciousness, not by sin, and not even by blasphemy against the Son of God, but by the secret condition of the depths of man's heart, which hates Christ and His Father with final and complete hatred. In face of the spirit of Antichrist man's self-consciousness must reach its highest and final effort. And our epoch stands under the sign of an exclusive anthropologism. We are on the eve of an anthropological revelation. Christianity's helplessness in the face of the modern tragedy of man is rooted in this very lack of discovery of a Christian anthropology. The new Christological anthropology must reveal the secret of man's creative calling and thus give to man's creative impulses a high religious meaning. The feebleness of man's Christological self-consciousness reinforces his Antichristological

92

self-consciousness. In this lies a grave danger for our epoch, the danger of the restoration of the Christianity of the Fathers, which has no true anthropology. Such a restoration might play into the hand of the spirit of Antichrist. When religious consciousness leaves an empty place, it is filled by the spirit of Antichrist. Religious demeaning and oppression of man lead to a false over-estimation of himself which finally destroys him. The anthropological religious turn in the world of to-day is a move in the cosmos from natural necessity toward human freedom. The anthropological revelation is bound up with a consciousness of relationship between the mystery of creativeness and the mystery of redemption.

# CHAPTER III

# CREATIVITY AND REDEMPTION

THE TRUTH OF THE New Testament, the Gospel, is absolute, the only truth assuring salvation. Not only those who are truly Christian by their consciousness but also those who have consciously left Christianity feel in the depth of their hearts the uniqueness, the extraordinary and incomparable truth of Christ. And the rationalist, Harnack, in his most profound feeling, bows before the absolute truth of the Gospel no less than do Orthodox or Catholics, although he does not really understand who Christ was. The truth-seekers of our time, having lost their old faith, are again and again turning to the Gospel and want to drink the living water from its absolute source. There are many attempts to justify and give meaning to life by means of the Gospel. In all these efforts, both within and outside the church, to justify and give meaning to everything in life, to give a basis for all life's values, and to do this by the New Testament, we feel a certain strain, a sort of violence done to the Gospel, the wilful intrusion into the Gospel of the values of another world. How can we religiously reconcile the creative values of life with the unique and absolute value of the Gospel story of salvation and redemption through Christ, the Saviour and Redeemer? Does the unique and absolute Gospel point the way towards the creation of life's values? Have we any religious right to turn the Gospel truth into an instrument for justifying our life-values and our creative impulses? These questions torment our time more sharply and hopelessly than they did in former Christian epochs. And we do violence to the Gospel with a wilfulness which earlier times never knew. Our distortion of the Gospel is born of religious thirst which amounts almost to religious despair, but the distortion itself is anti-religious and almost blasphemous. We seek at all costs to draw from the Gospel things which it does not contain. By means of a series of intervening links in a chain of discursive thinking, men try to derive from the Gospel that which they need but which is not therein revealed. Science and art, law and the state, social justice and freedom, sexual love, technics—everything by which modern man lives and which he cannot renounce must be justified by the Gospel for him who seeks the truth of Christ. All these fruitless, tragic efforts again and again lead to the old consciousness that the only justification of life which may be called New Testament and evangelical, truly expressing the religion of redemption, is that which was given in the Christianity of the Fathers, in asceticism. The religion of redemption is inseparable from asceticism and can accept life only as obedience to the results of sin, as a burden to be borne. The state, marriage, science, etc., justify the patristic consciousness as the bearing of burdens, as the sacred obedience of sinful man.

For the religious consciousness of the man of the new epoch there is only one way out: the religious realization of the truth that New Testament Christianity is a religion of redemption, the good news of salvation from sin, the revelation of the Son of God, the second hypostasis of the Holy Trinity in the aspect of God suffering for the sins of the world. This is one of the stages on the spiritual road. The second Gospel commandment of God and man has direct relationship only to the redemption from sin through divine love and grace. On the way of the spiritual life this is crucifixion on the cross of the rose of life. But does the mystery of salvation take in the whole of life? Is life's final purpose only salvation from sin? Redemption from sin, salvation from evil, are in themselves negative, and the final aims of being lie far beyond, in a positive creative purpose. Redemption from sin is only one epoch of the mystic life of the world, the core of the world-process. But the process of the world's life cannot be limited to redemption: it must contain other mystical periods. Like its Creator, man's life could not be created by God only for the purpose that, having sinned, he should atone for his sin, and should put into the work of his redemption all his powers, throughout the whole extent of the world-process. Such a conception of human nature would not correspond to the idea of the Creator and would demean the god-like dignity of man. The absolute Christian truth turns on the one hand towards redemption from sin and evil and on the other towards the positive creative calling of man: it reveals a Christology of man. The New Testament truth of the Gospels is only a part of Christological truth, oriented towards redemption and salvation; in it we cannot seek the direct justification of man's creative purposes. The Gospels reveal only one aspect of Christ, the Absolute Man redeeming and saving human nature.

§

There is not one word in the Gospel about creativeness: by no amount of sophism can we derive from the Gospel creative challenges and imperatives. The Good News of redemption from sin and of salvation from evil could not reveal the mystery of creativeness and show the way to creativity. The Gospel aspect of Christ, as God sacrificing Himself for the sins of the world, does not go so far as to reveal the creative mystery of man. That the ways of creativeness are hidden in New Testament Christianity is providential. We have precepts of the Holy Fathers on fasting and prayer. But we have not, and there could not be, precepts of the Fathers about creativity. The very idea of such precepts on creativity sounds strange to us and offends the ear. How pitiful are all the efforts to justify creativeness by the Gospel! Such justification usually amounts to saying: "The Gospel neither forbids nor excludes this or this—the Gospel permits creativity—the Gospel is liberal." Such an approach demeans both the absolute dignity of the Gospel and the great value of creativity. One is almost ashamed to refer to the Gospel's authority in justifying the creation of the values of life. This misuse of the Gospel has been too often made. The revelation about creativeness cannot be directly derived from the revelation about redemption. Man's creative activity has no holy scriptures: its ways are not revealed to man from above. In the holy scriptures which reveal to man the will of God, man always finds absolute truth, but it is another kind of truth and about something other. In creativeness, man is, as it were, left to himself, alone, and has no direct aid from on high. And in this fact the great wisdom of God is evident.

A justification of creativity through distortion of the Gospels is not revealed to us, but something else is, instead. We feel the *holy authority of the Gospel's silence about creativeness.* This absolute silence of Holy Scripture about man's creative activity is divinely wise. And to discern the all-wise meaning of this silence is to discern the mystery of man; it is an act of man's highest self-consciousness. Only the man who has not attained this higher self-consciousness seeks justification of creativity in the Holy Scriptures, and in holy indications about the ways of creativity, i.e. he would subject creativity to the law and the redemption. The man who still lives wholly in the religious epoch of the law and the redemption is not conscious of his creative nature; he wishes to create according to the law and for redemption, seeks creativity as obedience. *If the ways of creativeness were indicated and justified in the Holy Scriptures, then creativeness would be obedience, which is to say that there would be no creativeness.* To understand creativeness as obedience to the result of sin, as the fulfilment of the law or as redemption from sin, i.e. as either Old Testament or New Testament revelation, means denial of the mystery of creativeness, means not knowing the meaning of creativeness. The fact that the mystery and the ways of creativeness are not revealed in Holy Scripture is an evidence of the all-wise esoteric of Christianity. By its very nature the secret of creativeness is esoteric, it is not open for all to see but rather concealed. Only the law and the redemption can be revealed from on high. Creativeness is something mysterious and hidden. The revelation of creativeness does not come from above but rather from below—it is an anthropological, not a theological, revelation. God revealed His will to sinful man in the law and granted man the grace of redemption, sending into the world His Only Son. *And God awaits from man an anthropological revelation of creativity; in the name of man's god-like freedom, God has hidden from him the ways of creativeness and the justification of creativeness.* The law reveals the evil in man's sinful nature; it says "Nay, nay," and sets limits to man's evil will. The grace of the redemption restores human nature, gives it back its freedom. The power of redemption going out from Christ passes over into man. In the higher levels of religious consciousness, redemption itself is understood, immanently and inwardly, without that dualistic objectivization which we find in the legal doctrine of the redemption. Man is reborn a new creature through the cosmic mystery of the redemption. And man is reborn into the new Adam only if he has had an immanent experience of the crucifixion. But man's creative calling is not necessarily revealed in either the Old or the New Testament. Creativeness is a work of man's God-like freedom, the revelation of the image of the Creator within him. Creativeness is not in the Father, neither is it in the Son but in the Spirit, hence it goes beyond the borders of the Old and New Testaments. Where the Spirit is, there is freedom and there, too, is creativeness. Creativeness is not related to the priesthood and does not resemble it. Creativeness is in the spirit of prophecy. The Spirit cannot have its scriptures—it knows no directives: it is revealed in freedom. The Spirit breatheth where it will. Life in the Spirit is free and creative life. The anthropological revelation which has its origin in Christ is finally completed in the Spirit, in the free creative activity of man living in the Spirit. Creativeness is not yet revealed in either the law or the redemption; neither in the Old nor in the New Covenant of God with man. The secret of

98

creativeness is revealed in the Spirit; in the Spirit man's nature is known, without Scriptures, without commandments or directives from above. *In creativeness the divine in man is revealed by man's own free initiative, revealed from below rather than from above.* In creativeness man himself reveals the image and likeness of God in him, manifests the divine power within him. The breathing of the Spirit is not only divine, it is divine-human as well. The Church, too, is a divine-human organism. The mystery of the redemption was accomplished and is eternally being accomplished in the cosmos. After the redemption a new, creative being appears in the world and man is called to extraordinary activity, to creative upbuilding of profit for the Kingdom of God which is known as God-humanity.

§

The Creator's idea of man is sublime and beautiful. So sublime and so beautiful is the divine idea of man that creative freedom, the free power to reveal himself in creative action, is placed within man as a seal and sign of his likeness to God, as a mark of the Creator's image. *The compulsory revelation of creativeness as a law, as an indication of the way to go, would contradict God's idea of man, God's desire to see in man the creator, reflecting His own divine nature.* If there had been a revelation about creativeness from above, a revelation imprinted in the holy scriptures, then man's free creative deed would have been both unnecessary and impossible. There would have remained no room for an anthropological revelation. Such a passive concept of human nature makes man a being unworthy of the incarnation. Christ would not have been God-man if human nature is merely passive, unfree, and reveals nothing from within itself. For truly the God-man is a revelation not only of divine but of human greatness, and predicates faith not only in God but in man as well. The redemption itself was an inner growth of man. In the spirit of man, all the mystical events of the life of Christ are accomplished. Man's likeness to God in His Only

Son is already the everlasting basis for man's independent and free nature, capable of creative revelation. God did not reveal from above that He wills free courageous action in creativeness. If God had revealed and established this in Holy Scriptures, then free courageous action would be unnecessary and impossible. The truth about free daring in creativeness may be revealed by man himself, alone, only in a free act of his own daring. Herein lies hidden the great mystery of man. And there can be no divine revelation of this secret; it is inevitably hidden. The creative secret is both hidden from man and revealed by man. This is an esoteric mystery of divine revelation and of Holy Scripture. God the Creator, by an act of His almighty and omniscient will, created man—His own image and likeness, a being free and gifted with creative power, called to be lord of creation. This is an inner process in God. By an act of His almighty and omniscient power the Creator willed to limit His own foresight of what the creative freedom of man would reveal, since such foreknowledge would have done violence to and limited man's freedom in creation. The Creator does not wish to know what the anthropological revelation will be. Herein we see the great and sublime wisdom of God in the work of creation. God wisely concealed from man His will that man should be called to be a free and daring creator and concealed from Himself what man would create in his free courageous action. By a free act of His absolute will, God the Creator excluded from His creating all violence and compulsion, having desired only the freedom and the courageous activity of His creature. God waits for man's answering love: He waits for a free response to His call.

§

Creativeness is not only the struggle with sin and evil—it wills another world, it continues the work of creation. The law begins the struggle against sin and evil; the redemption finishes that struggle; but man is called to create a new and hitherto unknown world through free and daring creativeness, to continue God's creation. The fundamental duality of man's nature, his belonging to two worlds, corresponds to the duality of redemption and creativeness. As a fallen being, enslaved by the results of sin and caught by the force of necessity, man must pass through the mystery of redemption, in it must restore his god-like nature, regain his lost freedom. The creative secret of being is hidden by sin. Man's creative powers are weakened by his fall. Through Christ, man's nature is redeemed and restored; he is saved from the curse of sin. The old man is reborn into a new creature, the new Adam. But the mystery of redemption conceals the mystery of creativeness. As a god-like being, belonging to the realm of freedom, man is called to reveal his creative power. Here is the other side of man's dualistic nature, oriented towards creativeness instead of redemption. But true creativeness is possible only through redemption, Christ became immanent in human nature, and this makes man a creator like the Creator God.

§

Has the world ever seen creativeness in the religious sense of that word? The very question may appear strange. Who can doubt that there was a great effort of creativeness in Greece or in the period of the Renaissance? Throughout all history man has accomplished creative acts and in creative values the flowering of culture has appeared. And yet we must say that *the world has not yet seen a religious epoch of creativeness*. The world knows only the religious epochs of the Old Testament law and New Testament redemption. The world has lived in either religious obedience or sinful disobedience. And in the world one cannot create by obedience alone. Whatever has been called creativeness, no matter how great or valuable it was, was only a hint at true creativeness, only a sign, a preparatory stage. Man's whole history has been accompanied by creative impulses but his creative nature was rendered powerless by cosmic fall, by its being plunged into the lower spheres of being. When we speak of creativeness we usually have in mind the flowering of "science and art"—but seen from the religious point of view "science and art" may be revealed as forms of obedience, rather than creativeness. "Science and art", as well as the state, economy or the family, may be understood as obedience to the results of sin, as reactions to the necessity of the natural order. Even in the flowering-period of scientific and artistic genius the spirit of obedience drowned out the spirit of creativeness, fatefully and inevitably. In man, fallen and weak, there existed creative powers; but in the epochs of the law and the redemption, from the point of view of religion, those powers were swallowed up by submission to the results of sin, by the heavy burden of necessity. Man's creative activity was undermined and demeaned. And the impulses of great genius which have appeared in this chain formed by necessity have been like separate flashes of lightning. In the general and all-compelling march of world-culture even "science and art" have been a form of adaptation to necessity.

Economic materialism, very logically and very radically, interprets the whole of creative culture as obedience to necessity, as adaptation to man's condition, which has become more difficult through his being absorbed in the material spheres of being. Economic materialism is witness to the fact that, in the religious sense, the epoch of creativity has not yet dawned. Economic materialism is a most complete and extreme philosophy of sin, a philosophy of man unredeemed from sin and still knowing only the law. Marxism is not only not yet in creativeness but not yet even in redemption—it is in the Old Testament, in paganism. But there is a tiny bit of truth in Marxism, a reflected glimmer, a submissive consciousness of man's absorption in necessity. For Marxism, neither "science nor art" are creative—they are only adaptations. This radicalism and narrowness in Marxism is important for breaking down the naïve belief that "science and art" are true creativeness, the real revelation of man's creative nature. In this Marxism

102

approaches the very limit. And in its own way it stands higher than the middle-of-the-road, superficial *Kulturträger*, who have idolized the value of culture as genuine creativeness. We should stop to realize that much of "culture" comes from necessity rather than freedom, from adaptation rather than from creativeness. But in Marxism even this realization is an act of adaptation to necessity rather than an act of free creativeness. Economic materialism signifies the oppression of the human spirit. There is nothing free and nothing gifted. This sums up the whole oppression of the world.

We are standing on the threshold of a world-epoch of religious creativeness, on a cosmic divide. Up to now all the creativeness of "culture" has been only a preparatory hint, the sign of the real creativeness of another world. In the creativeness of "culture" there is expressed only the tragic dualism of human nature, struggling to escape from the fetters of necessity but not yet attaining another sphere of being. *Just as bloody pagan sacrifice was merely a foreshadowing of the world's true redemption through Christ's sacrifice on Golgotha, a foreshadowing which did not attain true redemption, so man's creative efforts, which have brought into being the values of culture, have been up to now only a foreshadowing of a true religious epoch of creativeness which will realize another sphere of being.* The religious epoch of creativeness will be a transition into another sphere of being, not merely to another "culture" or to another sphere of "science and art". The religious epoch of creativeness is a third revelation, an anthropological revelation following those of the Old and New Testaments. The ancient world moved towards redemption before the appearance of Christ. So the new world moves towards creativeness, but it has not yet known nor could it know creativeness until there is a cosmic anthropological turning-point, until there is great religious revolution in human self-consciousness. Then it will be seen that the creativeness of "culture" was a poor substitute for the creativeness of "being", in the epoch of the law and the redemption, when man's creative powers were still suppressed.

§

In the religious epoch of the law and the redemption, the moral side of human nature had to outweigh its æsthetic and perceptive side. The moral side of human nature is less creative; it has strong elements of obedience. And the fact that it prevailed was an expression of the subjection of human nature by sin. There was also the temptation to identify the religious with the moral, and a basis for this was found in both the Gospel and the works of the Church Fathers. The predominance of the moral element in the law is all too evident. There the moral is accepted in a restricted sense. In the work of redemption from sin the moral element is mystically transfigured and love and grace shine forth, but still the moral apparently predominates over the æsthetic and the perceptive. Salvation or perdition are connected with man's moral perfection, but not with his æsthetic or perceptive perfection. By his religious-moral perfection man redeems his sin, becomes a participant in salvation and wins eternal life. But can the same goal be reached by religious-æsthetic or religious-perceptive perfection? Can God refuse a man for his ugliness or want of knowledge if the man is morally perfect? Can man be refused because he does not create beauty or knowledge? Can man be saved and inherit eternal life by great accomplishments in beauty or knowledge? For man's eternal life, does God require only the moral man, or also the æsthete and the knower? Every kind of perfection, in everything like the perfection of God, ontological and not only moral perfection, all fullness of being, must be a participant in eternal life. But the religious consciousness says: "You may not be beautiful or wise but you must be moral." The work of redemption and salvation is accomplished by obedience and not by creativeness. Creative values are not necessary for salvation from perdition; they may even be harmful—in the terrible hour of death it would be better to forget them. This puts a tormenting problem to Christian consciousness.

If the religious life is complete with redemption from sin, then a higher creative fullness of being is both unattainable and unnecessary. Being is narrowed and simplified. In the religion of redemption creative values are not necessary to attain sanctity—neither beauty nor knowledge of any kind. Christian beauty and Christian knowledge are attained only through religious-moral perfection; they have no self-sufficient sources of equal value with the moral. The thirst for beauty or knowledge does not bring salvation. Creative desire is never of saving worth. In face of the principal and terrible task of redemption from sin, everything is vanity of vanities, everything is unnecessary and valueless. The one thing needful is perfection of obedience. In a time of the plague there can be no thought of knowledge or beauty and no thought of creative values. The sin which must be atoned for is the plague, and our sinful life is life in a time of plague, adapted to combating the disease. All life is occupied by one negative and imperative purpose. Under such a consciousness no one can believe in any kind of human activity or any kind of perfection here on earth.

From this tragic problem of Christianity there can be only one way out: the religious acceptance of the truth that the religious meaning of life and being is not wholly a matter of redemption from sin, that life and being have positive, creative purposes. *That higher creative, positive being, though unattainable at the time when redemption was begun, when God was still transcendent to man, is attainable in another period of religious life, after the redemption, when God in man is immanent.* Salvation from sin, from perdition, is not the final purpose of religious life: salvation is always *from* something and life should be *for* something. Many things unnecessary for salvation are needed for the very purpose for which salvation is necessary —for the creative upsurge of being. Man's chief end is not to be saved but to mount up, creatively. For this creative upsurge salvation from sin and evil is necessary. From the religious viewpoint the epoch of redemption is subordinated to the epoch of creativeness. A religion of thirst for salvation

105

and terror of perdition is only a temporary passage through a dualistic division. In various ways men of our modern time have felt that the sources of creativeness are to be sought neither in the New Testament religion of redemption nor in the Old Testament religion of law. Men have sought the sources of creativeness in antiquity. In the world of antiquity, in Greece, there were creative bases for an anthropological revelation: Greece is the homeland of human creativity, of beauty and knowledge. Every new impulse of human creativeness must of necessity turn back to the world of antiquity for its nourishment. This problem reached final acuteness in the life of Nietzsche. He burned with creative desire. Religiously, he knew only the law and the redemption in neither of which is the creative revelation of man. And so he hated God because he was possessed by the unfortunate idea that man's creativeness is impossible if God exists. Nietzsche stands on the world-divide of an epoch of creativeness but cannot recognize the indissoluble relationship of a religion of creativeness with the religion of redemption and the religion of the law; He does not know that religion is one and that in man's creativeness the same God is revealed One and Triune, as in the law and the redemption.

§

If redemption concerns only one aspect of Christ, the suffering and sacrificing Son of God, creativeness concerns another, that of Christ the glorified and mighty Son of God. The Christ who was crucified for the sins of the world under Pontius Pilate and the loving Christ, who will appear in glory, are one and the same Christ, Absolute Man, and in Him the mystery of man is revealed. The final mystery of man is revealed not only in the Christ who took the form of a servant but in His kingly aspect; not only in the image of Christ the Sacrifice but in the image of Christ the Victor. The creative mystery of human nature is related to the Coming Christ, to the power and glory of the Absolute Man. This creative mystery could not be revealed in the Gospel

106

image of Christ, since man still had to pass with Christ
through the mystery of redemption, through the sacrifice on
Golgotha. But can man, oriented as he is solely and completely towards the redemption, and seeing the Absolute
Man only under the aspect of the sacrificing Redeemer,
glimpse the Absolute Man in the creative image of the
mighty King of Glory? Is not this other aspect of Christ
hidden from him who is still in the redemption and has not
yet accomplished the daring act of revealing his own creative
nature? The Coming Christ will never appear to him who by
his own free effort has not revealed within himself the other,
the creative image of man. Only the courage of free creativeness will bring man to the Coming Christ, prepare man for
a vision of another image of the Absolute Man. And if great
obedience is needed for redemption, for creativeness there is
needed great courage. Only by great valour can we envisage
the Coming Christ. In the spirit of obedience we shall always
see only Christ Crucified, only His aspect as the Redeemer.
We need the sacrifice of valour, the heroic courage to cast
loose from all safe harbours. We must have the virtue of
living dangerously. *The third creative revelation in the Spirit will
have no holy scripture; it will be no voice from on high; it will be
accomplished in man and in humanity—it is an anthropological
revelation, an unveiling of the Christology of man.* God awaits the
anthropological revelation from man and man cannot
expect to have it from God. And one cannot merely wait for
the third revelation; man must accomplish it himself, living
in the Spirit; accomplish it by a free, creative act. In this act
everything transcendent will become immanent. The third
anthropological revelation, in which the creative mystery of
man will be revealed, is man's final freedom. Man is quite free
in the revelation of his creativeness. In this fearful freedom
lies all the god-like dignity of man, and his dread responsibility. The virtue of accepting a dangerous position, the virtue
of daring to do, is the basic virtue of the creative epoch.
Only he who possesses these virtues will vision the Coming
Christ: only to him will the mighty and glorified Christ

come. He who coward-like refuses the terrible burden of the final freedom cannot be oriented towards the Coming Christ—that man is not making ready Christ's second coming. Only a sacrificial resolve to take a risky and dangerous place, to sail away from safe shores towards an unknown and yet undiscovered continent from which no helping hands reach out—only this terrible liberty makes man worthy to see the Absolute Man, in whom is finally revealed the creative secret of man. The Coming Christ will reveal His creative mystery to him who himself does daring deeds of creativeness, who is preparing a new heaven and a new earth. Man's creativeness in the Spirit, in the higher spiritual life, is preparing for the second coming of Christ, just as the earth-mother of God prepared His first coming. The way to the second coming requires active, manly courage, not merely a passive femininity. Man is called not merely to wait and have a presentiment but to act and to create. Man must move out of a religious-passive and receptive condition into one of religious activity and creativeness.

God gave man the gracious aid of Christ's redemption which restored man's fallen nature. Through the redemption man's creative freedom is restored to him. And the time must come in the world for this creative freedom to be active. Man must create that for which he was redeemed, for which he was created. In man himself, in his terrible and final liberty, the change-over into the religious epoch of creativeness must take place. And it would be a new fall of man if he were to wait and demand that God should make this move for him, that the creative revelation should be accomplished not by man's inner freedom but only by the help of God from outside. The desire and expectation that God Himself should create what man ought to create is impious and displeasing to God. Such a passive religious consciousness is merely indulging human weakness and cowardice. And that old idea that man dare not create until the end of the world's redemption, until the end of the world, is false and atheistic. According to that old concept, man's lot in this world is only to redeem and shake off his sins, while creativeness will be possible only in the next world; and even this is not certain, since the other world is still represented statically rather than dynamically. This concept is contrary to the most profound essence of Christianity: Christianity makes God immanent in human nature and hence cannot admit a completely transcendent separation between this world and the next. This slavish feeling runs counter to the Creator's great idea of man: it is an expression of passive submission to necessity, a weak and cowardly refusal of freedom for the sake of quiet and safety. This is religious *bourgeoisie* within Christianity. Christ appeared before the law was completely fulfilled. And creativeness will begin before the redemption is completely accomplished. The law will not be completely fulfilled until the end of time, neither will the redemption, but the religious epoch of creativeness will exist along with the not-yet-excluded law and the not-yet-revoked redemption. The world's move over into the religious epoch of creativeness cannot be a betrayal of the law and the redemption. The revelation of the law and the redemption will find its final meaning and its final realization in the revelation of creativeness, since Christ, the world's Logos, is One and Eternal. In man's free creativeness his freedom is revealed, the freedom of the Absolute Man. The all-man fell very low, and the all-man will lift himself to dizzying heights.

§

The question of the religious meaning of creativeness has never before been put—such a question has never arisen in consciousness. This is the question of our time, one question, the final question to which the crisis of all culture leads us. Earlier epochs knew only the question of the justification of sciences and arts or of the organization of new forms of society but they did not know the religious question of creativeness, of the revelation of the creative mystery of man. The religious problem of creativeness is a problem of the ways of another kind of religious experience, of building up another kind of being. *Creativeness is neither permitted nor justified by religion—creativeness is itself religion.* Creative experience is a special kind of experience and a special kind of way: the creative ecstasy shatters the whole of man's being—it is an out-breaking into another world. Creative experience is just as religious as is prayer or asceticism. The creative experience is unique and self-sufficient—it is not something derivative; its roots go into the deepest depths. At its best, Christianity justified creativeness but it never rose to the consciousness that what matters is not to justify creativeness *but by creativeness to justify life.* In its religious-cosmic sense, creativeness is equal in power and value with redemption. Creativeness is the final revelation of the Holy Trinity—its anthropological revelation. This is a consciousness which has never existed in the world—it is being born in our epoch. But much that is in the world was preparing for the birth of this consciousness. It was prepared by the endless fatigue resulting from the forced Christian, evangelical justifications of creativeness. We now face the inevitable necessity of justifying ourselves by creativeness, rather than justifying our creativeness itself. The creative act should have its own inner justification—and any external justification is powerless and debasing. Man justifies himself before the Creator not only by the redemption but by creativeness as well. In the mystery of redemption the Creator's boundless love towards man, and His boundless grace, were poured out: in the mystery of creativeness man's boundless nature is revealed and his highest calling is realized. Love is not only grace but the activity of man himself as well. God himself, who gave His Only Son to be broken on the tree, atones for the sin of man and he expects that man, having partaken of the mystery of the redemption, will accomplish the great deed of creativeness, will realize his positive destiny.

Human nature is creative because it is the image and likeness of God the Creator. That the image and likeness of the Creator cannot fail to be himself a creator is an anthropological truth which was not recognized with sufficient intensity and fullness by former religious epochs. Religious consciousness was full of the mystery of redemption of human nature but the mystery of this to-be-redeemed human nature, itself, was unknown. What is the pre-destination of this redeemed human nature? Within the limits of the religion of redemption, there is no answer to this question. The usual Christian answer, that man's chief end is life in God, cannot satisfy us—it is too general and too formal. Those who give this answer are too much engrossed in the *way* to the final goal. Rest in God is usually thought of as victory over the evil and sin in human nature, as the extinguishing of this nature, as the absorption of the human by the divine. Man merely makes free within himself a place for God and returns to God's bosom without any profit. There is a fateful tendency toward monophysitism in historic Christianity. It is as though the man who is redeemed from his sins desired that his human nature should cease to exist—that only the divine nature alone should exist. But Christ is God-Man. He redeems and restores *human* nature to its likeness unto God. Human nature which knows itself, knows its independent and free being, must exist eternally only as a creative and creating nature. Human nature finally justifies itself before the Creator not by extinguishing itself but by its own creative expression. Man must absolutely *be*. Human nature, redeemed and saved from evil, has a positive human content and a positive human purpose. This content and purpose can be only creativeness. Man's creativeness is connected with the ecstatic element in him. This element exists in a fallen and sinful state. It is cleansed and enlightened by redemption, not quenched or destroyed. The cleansed and illuminated creative ecstasy realizes man's calling. Repentance or purification is only one of the moments of religious experience, one of the acts of the mystery of Christ. We must not stop at this moment: we must go on to positive spiritual living. The Christian mystery of redemption, at a certain level of the development of humanity, is objectivized; it is presented as something outside man, transcendent over man and his inner, spiritual way. In this manner Christ is acquired in an objective order, and man is relieved of the burden of the inner way of Christ, as the way of Man, as an anthropological process. This was the materialization of Christianity, its involution. Now, however, Christianity can stand only under the sign of evolution, of spiritual upsurge. The mystery of Christianity is transferred to the inner man: Christ becomes immanent in man and man takes upon himself the whole burden of measureless freedom. Christ ceases to be the only one in an objective series, among others. He, the All-Man, becomes man's Way, the mystery of man's spirit. Thus is revealed man's spontaneity and autonomy in creativeness, man's free activity on the way to the Coming Christ. God's will must be fulfilled to the uttermost; here there can be no difference of opinion among Christians. But we have to know what the will of God is. We dare not understand it in a purely formal way. And is not man's free creativity the fulfilment of the secret will of God?

# CHAPTER IV

# CREATIVITY AND GNOSSEOLOGY

THE CREATIVE ACT DOES not come under the jurisdiction of gnosseology, with its endless reflection. The creative act exists immediately in being: it is the self-revelation of the powers of being. The creative act justifies but is not itself justified; it is based upon itself and requires no foundation upon something outside itself. Man's consciousness of himself as a creative being is a primary, rather than a derived consciousness. And man should proceed from this consciousness of the creative act within himself: this is a revolutionary consciousness in man which cannot be arrived at by means of either logic or evolution. This, man's consciousness of himself as a creator, does not result from any doctrine about man: it precedes all science and all philosophy; it is before, rather than after, all gnosseology. Man's creative act is accomplished on a plane of being over which the competence of science does not extend and hence even gnosseological science has no bearing upon it. To justify or to deny man's consciousness of himself as a creator, by means of gnosseology, is neither possible nor desirable. Creativeness as a religious experience does not know any dualistic division into subject and object.

But critical gnosseology is a very serious phenomenon of modern culture—a serious symptom of the illness of creativity, of the tragedy of the creative consciousness now coming to birth. Critical gnosseology points up the crisis of culture and creativeness, lays bare the antagonism between culture and creativeness. Critical gnosseology provides a base and justification for various types of creativeness of a differentiated culture, but this instead of revealing, conceals the creative nature of man. The creative act is lifted out of the primitive sphere of being and transferred to a second sphere of consciousness, into being which is already rationalized and mediate, into a spirit already split into parts and prepared for a special purpose. Man's creative act does not create new being—in it being is not increased; it is critically separate from and contrary to being. Man is not a creator; and in his culture he is powerless to express creative nature. Here the nature of the critical philosophy of Kant is clearly revealed in its true light. This is nature under the law, Old Testament nature. In his Old Testament consciousness under the law, a state of mind so truly and conscientiously reflected by Kant, man does not dare to reveal his creative nature, he has courage only to create differentiated kinds of culture— for this differentiated creativeness is obedience to the law, a simple fulfilment of certain norms. The normativism of critical philosophy is one form of the Old Testament, under-the-law consciousness. A universally obligatory compliance with norms of logic, ethics or æsthetics, in the consciousness of differentiated culture, is obedience to the results of sin, adaptation to necessity, but not creativeness. This mark of sin and the resultant necessity is visible on the whole of culture; it does not express man's creative spirit. *Critical philosophy only reveals the law (norm) according to which sinful nature should live.* Gnosseological categories are categories of sin, of sinful being.

Critical gnosseology is just as much an obligatory form of existence of sinful nature as is the idea of the state with its courts and its police. Critical philosophy is a consciousness of the pre-creative epoch—it is not even in redemption but only under the law. It is a philosophy of law without grace. And its force lies in the fact that it corresponds to a certain condition of man, that it truly expresses something which is in man. Just as fallen man cannot live without the state police, so he cannot think without critical gnosseology. This is a measure taken by the law against sinful nature. Man's creative nature is rendered powerless by his fall and his sin; it has become a slave to necessity. Fallen, sinful man can

114

create only as he submits to law, only according to a certain norm. This subjection of man's creativity to law and norm is completely expressed in critical philosophy. Gnosseological consciousness lures man by Apollinism and classicism in creativity, by the completed coinage of the creative act, but in reality it only subjects sinful nature to the law. The man of the world's creative epoch, who is conscious of himself as a creator, is always a revolutionary as regards a creativity subject to law, normative, culturally-differentiated, since creativity can be neither obedience to the law nor obedience to redemption. Creativity is oriented towards, and is born of, another side of man's dual nature. This is why in the conscious, all-too-conscious, attitude of German culture to creativity there is a certain enslavement of the spirit which conceals man's creative nature. The extraordinary philosophical talent of the German race permitted its better expressing the consciousness that to sinful man only a culture opposed to the spirit of creativity is permitted, only a culture under law. Perhaps this is the positive mission of German thought, as expressing the final state of man's consciousness before he enters the religious creative epoch.

§

The attitude of Rickert and his school towards creativity is typical. This tendency is a *reductio ad absurdum* of the principles of critical gnosseology. Being is transformed into a form of existential judgement. In what sense does the philosophy of Rickert's school permit the creative act? In the immediate experience which precedes all rationalization or objectivization, there is nothing creative. Man as a primordial experience is a creature, but not a creator. Creativeness is already objectivization. In the creative act, as objectivization, life dies and being is sacrificed. This philosophy faces the dilemma: to be or to create. To be in the fullness of one's being does not mean to create: to create means to renounce being for the sake of values which transcend being. Creativity is not a revelation of man's being but rather its self-limitation, a sacrifice by means of being. We cannot expect that creativity will produce growth, the upsurge of being, the revelation of man. Creativity is not a disclosure, but rather a concealment, of man's nature. For such a critical consciousness the creative revelation of man is essentially impossible. There is a complete lack of equivalence. There is even opposition between man's being and every result of the creative act. When man remains in his own being, he does not create. When man creates he objectivizes values, produces something which is not to be measured by his own being, something not an expression of his own being. From this viewpoint one can create only culture, i.e. logical, ethic or æsthetic values, but not new being, another kind of life. Creativity is outside life—it is a conscious sacrifice to life, a conscious limitation of life. In objectivized culture, with all its values, you cannot find that life which was in the subjective spirit. Subject and object are hopelessly separated. Creative intuition, as transcending the contrast between subject and object, i.e. everything objectivized, is impossible. The culture of disciplined critical philosophy is thus seen as a consistent stifling of life, the quenching of being. To create normal science, normal art, normal society, means not to reveal but to limit life, to diminish being. The normative philosophy of values very cleverly reveals the contrast between a differentiated culture and being or life. Man's creative act fails to attain its purpose in the objectivized values of differentiated culture. We find no revelation of man in objectivized culture. The object does not in the least resemble the subject. This philosophy, remarkable in its way, faithfully reflects the sinful powerlessness of human creativity, the sinful break between subject and object, between man and the world. This philosophy, in spirit neither creative nor active, but rather compliant and adaptive, does not admit the idea that the sinful-limited condition of human nature, with its lack of power to create being, can be overcome—that the break between subject and object is not for ever. This is a philosophy of sin and hence it admits only life under the law. Life in grace is quite unknown to this philosophy. The philosophy of sin quite logically sees in the creative act an ascetic self-limitation of life and an ascetic abstention from being. A special form of asceticism characterizes critical philosophy, an asceticism without grace. And this critical asceticism clearly reveals that it remains wholly in the precreative epoch of world history, that it still belongs entirely to the law and the redemption. For critical philosophy man's self-consciousness is an act of obedience and humility towards the world's necessity, subjection to the shattered and compelling condition of the world. Man's creative consciousness of himself is the active overcoming of this shattered and compelling condition of the world: it passes out beyond the bounds of necessity. Despite its voluntaristic colouring, the philosophy of Rickert's school is will-less; it has no desire for another state of being, another degree of human power; it submits to the given condition as to fate, as to something unalterable. All it has left is to glorify the virtue of gnosseological submission, the perceptive humility of man's limitation and his scattered forces. In it there is no will to create another being; and hence no creative self-consciousness. Man is only a creature, not a creator. Man may not surpass the creation of God the Creator, may not surpass himself as a creation of God. There is no will to the identity of subject and object, and hence there is no true philosophy of identity. The philosophy of Rickert's immanentism in its own way asserts identity but this is an apparent, unreal and illusory identity, identity out of weakness rather than out of power. Modern immanentism affirms that being is immanent in knowing, rather than that knowing is immanent in being. But knowing is transcendent over being; it is outside and opposed to being. But a philosophy is possible which identifies subject and object, the creator and the created, a philosophy for which knowing is immanent in being and within it. A false immanentism asserts the immanent without the transcendent, but the final conquest of the transcendent finally overcomes the immanent

117

as well. Mysticism stands out beyond the very contrast be
tween the transcendent and the immanent; for mysticism,
God is both transcendent and immanent but at the same
time neither one nor the other. For true philosophy the
problem of the irrational is not a gnosseological problem, as
it is for the school of Rickert, but rather an ontological
problem. The light of knowing is completely immanent,
within being, but in being there is darkness as well as light,
i.e. in the depths of being there is the irrational, which has no
connection whatever with the doctrine of knowing and its
limits. The whole of critical culture is based upon transcendent feeling for and consciousness of God—on infinite
distance, on the dualistic separation between God and the
world. This immanent feeling for, and consciousness of,
God leads to the transformation of culture into being.

§

The critical-gnosseological theory of creativity explains
certain forms and phases of creativity. Not creativity as a
whole—in its profoundest manifestation creativity remains
unjustified. Only creativity subjected to generally valid
norms, realizing the ideal of classic perfection, can be
justified by critical gnoseology. Creativity in all spheres
of culture is normal and justified when it is classic, that is
when it is free from the spirit of life. The overflowing
Dionysiac creative forces are not justifiable by critical
gnosseology. These forces must be restrained; they must be
sacrificed for the sake of the ever-valid normal creative act.
For everything Dionysiac strives toward the elimination of
the contrast between subject and object; in the Dionysiac
element the subject passes into the object. Critical consciousness condemns the Dionysian creative act because it
does not achieve cultural values. Critical consciousness
refuses to recognize as valuable or significant any creativity
in so far as it is a revelation of man. Meaningful creativity,
producing value, is rather a concealment of man, it hides his
creative God-like nature. And here man's consciousness faces

118

the acute question; is a classic completeness of creativity, which creates values of differentiated culture, necessary or possible? Is freedom from the spirit of life possible in creativity? Was the creativity of the great creators in history classically perfect? Is not the creativity of the world's great creators a dawning revelation of man? Was not every great creativity free from all-compulsory norm, rather than free from life? The normal idea of a classic-complete creativity of culture is only a revelation of the tragedy, the sickness of creativity. *Classic creativity is a sickness which has been raised to the position of a norm.* Despite the well-known opinion of Goethe, there is more health in romantic creativity. The urge of romantic creativity is a thirst for release from this condition of illness, for overcoming the tragedy of creativity. It is healthy when romanticism desires to reveal man; classicism strives morbidly to conceal him. There is a healthy spirit of life in romanticism while in classicism there is an unhealthy spirit of the renunciation of life. In romanticism there is an urge to surpass being; in classicism, abnegation of all being. Classicism involves an immanent self-centredness; romanticism involves transcendent impulse. This romantic creative urge reveals the transcendent nature of creativity, which passes all bounds. The romantic creative urge is deeply related to the Christian feeling of life, to the Christian idea of another world.

In its essence, creativity is painful and tragic. The purpose of the creative impulse is the attainment of another life, another world, an ascent into being. But the result of a creative act is a book, a picture or a legal institution. Movement up or down is projected on a level. Herein lies the painful and tragic contrast between the aims of creativity and the results of creating. Instead of being, culture is created. The subject does not pass into the object; the subject disappears in objectivization. Classicism would recognize illness as a normal, healthy condition. For classicism the tragic contrast is significant and valuable, between the aim of creativity and its result. Romanticism feels the disease and suffers with it, and thus is more healthy than classicism. Romanticism does not desire an immanent reservedness, does not desire completeness; it thirsts for the transcendent impulse toward infinity. And romanticism responds better than does classicism, to the infinite nature of man, transcendent as regards the given world. It may be said that romanticism foretells the creative epoch, foresees its beginning. Classicism hinders the arrival of the creative epoch, fetters man in an immanent completeness, prevents his impulses towards another kind of being. Classicism would reconcile man to his illness, his limitations and his subjection to the law and create for him an immanent completeness which is fantastic and unreal. Romanticism will have none of this unreal completeness; it sees in the tragedy of creativeness a mark of man's higher nature. Critical gnosseology is only one of the forms of classicism. Classicism belongs entirely to the pre-creative epoch; it is under the law; it is a norm for sinful, not redeemed, nature. Romanticism has a foretaste of the creative epoch, but does not know the real religious-creative act. Here I am using classicism and romanticism not as æsthetic, literary categories but in a much wider sense as universal metaphysical categories which cover all phases of creativity, perception, moral life and everything. Classicism has a conservative, hindering inertia, while in romanticism there is revolutionary creative movement. Classicism is always something medial, while romanticism is final, not in its realization but in its intention. In essence, critical gnosseology legalizes classicism and denies romanticism. Creative romanticism will not recognize the power of gnosseology over creativity, the right of gnosseology to forbid, limit or justify it.

§

The dawn of the creative religious epoch also means a most profound crisis in man's creativity. The creative act will create new being rather than values of differentiated culture; in the creative act life will not be quenched.

Creativity will continue creation; it will reveal the resemblance of human nature to the Creator. In creativity the way will be found for subject to pass into object, the identity of subject with object will be restored. All the great creators have foreseen this turning-point. To-day, in the depths of culture itself and in all its separate spheres this crisis of creativity is ripening. At its highest, culture arrives at self-abnegation. Creativity in art, in philosophy, in morals, in social life, exceeds the limits of its own sphere, is not to be contained in any classic norm, reveals an impulse towards the transcendental. The creative man of to-day can no longer create science and art in the classic manner, just as he cannot play politics according to classic norms. In everything he strives to go to the limit, to the end, to pass all boundaries. Literature ceases to be only literature; it would be new being. Within the separate sphere of culture and its values the power to hold itself is lacking; the creative upsurge towards another type of being puts an end to the division of culture into a row of separate fields. At the heights of culture the question is put whether culture is the way to another kind of being or retention in the middle way, without any transcendental way out. Art is transformed into theurgy, philosophy into theosophy, society into theocracy. The norms of classicism are overthrown, according to which beautiful art, true philosophy and a just social order are supposed to be created. Symbolism in art passes beyond the boundaries and norms of classical art, reveals the final limits of the creative artistic act, and leads to theurgy. We find the same transition of the boundaries of art, the impulse to a final and other kind of being, in all the great Russian writers, Gogol, Dostoevski, Tolstoy. In the Russians the torment and pain of creativity reach their limits and the creativity of the Russian genius always overflows all boundaries. In socialism and anarchism we find the same surpassing of all boundaries of classic society with its legal, civic and economic norms, an impulse towards the transcendental, towards the final limits.

Nietzsche's creative work shatters all norms and all

barriers; the creative act overflows all the classic river-banks. The philosophy, the morals and the art of Nietzsche are final—they reach the limit. In Nietzsche higher culture surpasses all the limits of culture, goes to the very end. The renaissance of mysticism and occultism reveal a profound crisis of culture, the impossibility of remaining on the middle ground of classic values. The crisis of culture is directed against critical gnosseology, that advocate of classic, medium culture. In symbolism, in mysticism, in Nietzsche, in Dostoevski, in Tolstoy, in anarchism, in occultism—in all these expressions of the new spirit, the creative impulse rises against the classic and normal limitations of gnosseology. It is an integral, not a divided, spirit which lies behind the creative act; an upsurge towards another kind of being, towards the heights. This is not a sort of inner experience or some inexpressible communion with God. This is a fully expressible creative upsurge of man, revealing itself in the world-object. In the crisis of culture we feel the passage into a new creative epoch. The classicism of critical gnosseology, like all to-day's classicism, retards the passage into the creative epoch and hinders man's recognition of himself as creator. Critical gnosseology may be finally overthrown, not by some other gnosseology, not by philosophical thought, but by the creative act itself, by another form of being. Only an existential refutation of critical gnosseology can be radical and triumphant. The possibility of the creative act, denied by critical gnosseology, cannot be demonstrated by another gnosseology but by the creative act itself. And the existential crisis of creativity at the height of modern culture, proves the possibility of the creative act, outside the norms and boundaries established by critical gnosseology. Critical gnosseology merely reflected man's lack of creative power in the religious epochs of the law and redemption. Another gnosseology will be required to correspond to man's real and experienced transfer into another kind of being. Gnosseology depends upon the spiritual age of man and as yet we have no gnosseology which corresponds to the highest

122

spiritual being. Critical as well as rationalistic or empiric gnosseology is only a gnosseology which suits one of the conditions of man, one of the epochs of history. True immanentism must first of all recognize the immanence of perception in being and the possibility of creative development into higher states of spirituality, which are seen as transcending the given state of being. True Christian transcendentism means that this world transcends man and that God is immanent in man.

§

The question of the relation of gnosseology to creativity, which so troubles modern thought, depends upon a solution of the problem of the nature of knowing. Is knowledge a creative act, or is it obedience, adaptation to necessity? I spoke of this in Chapter I. Critical gnosseology demands of man's creative nature perceptive submission and humility. It even adds to its demand an ethical meaning, as though it desired man's ascetic self-limitation. Critical gnosseology gives a flavour of ascetic obedience to knowledge itself. And there is doubtless a strong admixture of moralism in this gnosseology. This type of gnosseology knows perception only as obedience, not as creativity. By its most profound nature perception cannot be only an obedient reflection of reality, an adaptation to the data at hand; it is also an active transfiguration, giving meaning to being, the triumph in being of the world-reason, the sunlight within being. But critical gnosseology orients itself exclusively by science, i.e. by knowing as an adaptation to the given world, as submission to necessity. But gnosseology itself reveals itself only as obedience to science—as obedience to obedience. And the partial truth of this gnosseology of science claims to be the whole truth. Competent only in the sphere of partial science, gnosseology dares to put the whole of life and being into chains. Gnosseology goes so far as to suspend being. Obedience becomes something obtrusive and audacious, it goes as far as disobedience to the higher Meaning of being. If

123

knowledge itself is not only obedience but creativity as well, how can the theory of perceptive creativeness limit or deny human creativity? The sphere of obedience to scientific knowing is very special and limited: the problem of creativity lies quite outside this sphere. The perceptive solution of the problem of creativity is possible only to the creative perceptive act. Creativity is known only by creativity, like knows like. Knowledge as obedience has nothing to say about creativity. Hence the nature of all creativity is unknown to science or the doctrine about science that is gnosseology. And this means that creativity neither demands nor permits a gnosseological justification or foundation. In no case can creativity be obedient to gnosseology. Man's creative nature is comprehensible only to creative knowledge, as one of the expressions of that same nature. Creative knowledge is an existential act, an act of ascension into being. Hence creative knowledge cannot be opposed to being and being cannot be killed in the creative act. Knowing is not outside being and cannot be considered as opposed to it: it is in the depths of being itself: it is activity within being. Knowledge is the sunlight which causes being to develop. Knowledge is creative development, the growth of being in the sun.

Creativity is existential and hence lies outside gnosseological judgement. Scientific gnosseology is always concerned with the secondary, while creativity deals always with the primary. And whatever scientific gnosseology has to say about the powerlessness of the creative act is only the powerlessness of gnosseology's secondary, rationalized nature. For critical gnosseology knowledge is not a form of creativity: it is the fettering of being, something which is in contrast to all creativity and resisting it. Knowledge (science) is a substitution for being. Gnosseology demands obedience to scientifically known being, but scientifically known being is a prison for man's creative nature, since scientific perception will never know that creative nature. In its latest conclusions critical gnosseology (e.g. Cohen) identifies science with being. Science is true being; mathematical

124

natural history is nature itself. But if science, mathematical natural history, is true being, real nature, in such being and nature the creative act is either impossible, or possible only in a limited and distorted sense. Being, however, is full of living creative forces, unknown to mathematical natural history. Science is not being, mathematical science is only a single form of adaptation to certain forms of being. That intellectualism which would identify being with science, nature with mathematical natural history, is truly demonic and destructive. And man's creative nature rises against this despotism of intellectualistic gnosseology. This rationalism is born of man's passivity. The understanding of nature as the same thing as mathematical natural history is Old Testament, and it is not strange that its clearest expression comes from Cohen, a Jew by blood and by conviction. The laws of nature are Old Testament: the revelation of law in nature.

§

Can man be externally dynamic, can he reveal his creativity objectively in the world, without the fatal division between subject and object and the fatal contrast between creativity and being, about which critical gnosseology has so much to say? This tormenting gnosseology faces modern consciousness. In what critical gnosseology has to say about creativity there is apparently much truth: culture is created in the break between subject and object, in this opposition between creativity and being. And it is easy to build a philosophy of culture which refuses to admit that in the creative act the subject enters into the object, that man reveals himself dynamically in the cosmos. Such a philosophy of culture, based on gnosseology, moves along the line of least resistance. This philosophy of created values has to deny the creative nature of man. This is a philosophy of the pre-creative epoch, but it is superior to the old scholastic and rationalistic philosophy: it reveals crisis and difficulty in both knowledge and culture. The philosophy of the creative

125

epoch cannot be so obedient: it is actual, it is itself the creative conquest of what had seemed fatal. For creative philosophy, truth is not a passive reflection of something: truth is rather activity in giving meaning to something. The attainment of truth presupposes creative activity of the spirit: the spirit must resist the separation of subject from object and the conflict between creativity and being. The creative epoch and creative philosophy are characterized by a new and different gnosseology which throws light on the relative and partial truth of the old gnosseology, under the law. This new and different gnosseology is based entirely upon the idea of man as a microcosm and the centre of the universe. The microcosm, in its creative and dynamic relationship to the macrocosm, knows no fatal separation, no opposition. Man is a relative and an image of the cosmos, not because he is a fraction of the cosmos but because he is himself a whole cosmos and of one structure with the cosmos. Man's cosmic nature was suppressed by sin and it will be fully and finally revealed only in the creative epoch. Then it will be clearly evident to philosophical consciousness, that the creative act has existential and cosmic significance. Man the microcosm is able to express himself dynamically in the macrocosm, he has the power to create being, to change culture into being.

§

True creativeness is theurgy, God-activity, activity together with God. But it is important that we understand that the problem of theurgy is not a problem of Christian creativity, of Christian culture. In the strict sense of the word, there can be no Christian creativity, and Christian culture is impossible. *We face the problem of Christian being rather than Christian culture, the problem of transforming culture into being, science and art into a new heaven and a new earth.* There never was a truly Christian culture. Culture was created outside Christianity; its only deep connection with Christianity was in the fact that in culture obedience to the results of sin were so strongly evident and sin was redeemed

126

by the tragic difference between the creative idea and its results. And in his culture, beginning with technics and economics and ending with the sciences and the arts, man, as it were, sought redemption from his sin, but his creativity was not theurgic. In the sweat of his brow man creates culture but cannot attain what is necessary for his creative nature. What man needs is a new heaven and a new earth, the transition of the creative act into another kind of being. This is the way of theurgic creativity. Critical gnosseology was an expression of the old spirit of culture. But what is creativity in the light of ontology? What is the relationship of creativity to being?

# CHAPTER V

## CREATIVITY AND BEING

THE BEING OF THE world is creature; being which has been and continues to be created. And the stamp of the creative act lies on all created being. A thing created, createdness, speaks of the Creator. Createdness is creativity. The creation of the world is creative development in God, His emergence from solitude; it is the call of divine love. Creativity presupposes movement and dynamic within divine life. The creative process is carried out in God from all eternity. Only the recognition of created being permits an original creative act in being, an act which produces something new and unprecedented. If everything in being was not created, but had always existed, the very idea of creativity could not have been born in the world. If we admit the concept of divine being in which there takes place only a rearrangement of data which have always existed, only an outflow, then the question of creativity could never in the world have arisen. If there had not been a divine creative act, in which something which had never been before was created, then the creative act in our world would be quite impossible. If divine nature is not capable of creativity, what sort of nature could be? The very idea of creativity is possible only because there is a Creator and because He carried out an original creative act in which that which never was came into being, something which did not proceed from anything which had been before and which neither weakened nor reduced the absolute power of the Creator. The creative act does not create out of the nature of the creator by reducing his powers through transforming them into some other state, but out of nothing. Creativity is not changing the creator's

128

powers into some other state, thus weakening the former: creativity is the production of new force from that which had not been, which until then had not existed. Every creative act, in essence, is creation out of nothing: the production of new forces rather than the changing or rearrangement of the old. *In every creative act there is absolute gain, something added.* The creative quality of being, the growth which takes place in being, the achievement of gain without any loss—all this speaks of a creator and of creativity.

The creative quality of being speaks of the creator and of creativity in two senses: there is a Creator who produced created being, and within this created being creativity is possible. The world was made not only created but creative. Createdness bears the image and likeness of the Creator, i.e. in createdness itself there are creators. Created nature would be something opposed to creative nature, if in the created there was not evident the image and likeness of the Creator. But human nature is the image and likeness of the Creator; it is creative nature. The soul is eternal, created by God the Creator before all worlds: the basic element of the soul is divine and independent of the world-process and its times. The pre-existence of souls is an absolute metaphysical truth. But the fate of the soul is bound up with cosmic development. The creative act is an absolute addition to being; the increase of power without any loss or diminution continues in created being itself, in man as in his Creator. Creativity in the world is possible only because the world is created. Being, as it is represented both in naturalistic materialism and naturalistic pantheism, knows nothing of creativity. This is a closed system of being in which there can be only a rearrangement of forces, but not gain or addition by growth. Whether we consider this being as material or as divine, the relation to creativity remains unaltered. For a purely pantheistic cosmology, also, there is little creativity, just as in the case of materialistic cosmology. The world may be Divinity, but neither in this Divinity nor in the world is there any creative act. Creative gain is born of the creator's freedom. Man is called to enrich divine life, for not only God and divinity should be absolute but man and humanity as well. The orthodox-biblical theology, cosmology and anthropology are too rationalistic: they presuppose a clear light, comprehensible to reason, as the basis of all being, rather than a mysterious abyss which for reason only creates an antinomy. This antinomy is revealed in the depth of German mysticism: it leads to the *Ungrund* of J. Boehme, the *Gottheit* of Eckhardt, to something greater than God Himself. The truth of pantheism may be extended only to this primitive and depthless divinity. But the creation of the world is something beyond, in God, in the Trinity as revealed in inner movement. Anthropogony has not been fully revealed in German mysticism—only theogony and cosmogony. But in God there is a passionate and anguished longing for man. In God there is a tragic deficiency which is satisfied by the great gain of man's birth in Him. The mystics taught the mystery of God's birth in man. But there is another mystery, that of man's birth in God. There is a summons, a call in man, for God to be born in him. But there is also God's call that man be born in Him. This is the mystery of Christianity, the mystery of Christ, which is unknown to the Hindu mystics, to Plotinus or to any of the abstract-monistic mystics. God and man together are greater than God alone. The substantial multinomial being revealed in One, is greater than a One undifferentiated. Only the myth of God's longing for man and for man's love can bring us near to the final mystery.

§

Penetration into the "createdness" of being brings us to recognize the contrast between creativity and emanation. If the world is created by God, this is a creative act, and creativity is justified. If the world only emanates from God, there is no creative act, and creativity is not justified. The mystic-pantheistic doctrine of emanation denies creativity

130

just as does the materialistic-naturalistic doctrine of evolution. If the world is only an emanation, an outflowing of Divinity, if in the world there is only an ebb and flow of divine power, diminishing according to its distance from its source, then in that same world there is possible only an outflow and transference of force, only a rearrangement of the power of being and not an increase of power by growth. The doctrine of emanation is a doctrine without increment. There is a mystical and ineradicable resemblance between consciousness of God and consciousness of the world. A consciousness of God which denies the creation of the world inevitably leads to a consciousness of the world which denies the creativity in it. The doctrine of emanation does not know the creative act in God, and hence it does not know the creative act at all—only outflow. For an emanational consciousness of God and of the world, power flows out and is variously dispensed but does not increase. God flows out in His emanation into the world. In Plotinus Divinity is not diminished in its power by the fact that its rays emanate into the world. But a consistent doctrine of emanation must lead to a doctrine of the diminution of Divine power. The world is divine, because God sacrifices Himself for the world, overflows into the world. Divinity is powerless to create a world, but it may become the world. And the divine power emanating into the world must necessarily be diminished and decrease. If the world emanates from Divinity, Divinity cannot retain all its power—divine force passes into the world. A purely pantheistic consciousness of God is for emanation and against creativity. A mysticism of the pantheistic-emanational type is forced to deny creativity— for this type of mysticisim life is an outflowing of Divinity into man and man into Divinity. For such a mysticism man is emptied completely into Divinity and Divinity completely into man, etc. There is no creative growth but only a re-arrangement of forces. Eckhardt, Plotinus and the Indian mystics all belong to this type. In fact, this type of mysticism does not know either God's creativity or the creativity of man. And the modern philosophic doctrine of loss, of the death of being in the creation of culture, is directly related to a pantheistic-emanational consciousness of God. In true creativity nothing is diminished: rather everything increases, just as Divine power is not diminished in God's creation of the world by the fact that this power passes into the world but rather new power is added which did not exist before. In its extreme form pantheistic-emanational consciousness of God leads logically to a denial of man. This is in no wise to deny the measure of truth in pantheism which enters into theistic god-consciousness. The idea of God surpasses those antinomies which are born of the idea of the world and its relationship to God. For both the antinomic theses are equally true: the world in God and the world outside God: God transcends the world and God is immanent in the world. The Bible story of the creation of the world is not the final truth: it gives only one of the antinomic theses: the other thesis of antinomy remains undisclosed—the creation of the world is an inner process of fragmentation and development in Divine being.

§

Materialistic evolutionism has a strange resemblance to the doctrine of emanation, despite the fact that in emanation everything deteriorates according to its distance from Divinity, while in evolution everything improves. Materialistic evolutionism accepts only a rearrangement of the elements of a closed universe, but refuses the idea of creativity. For this doctrine there exists only an outflowing, a pouring back and forth of given forces, but not creativity. Mechanical evolution and creativity are opposites. In the evolution taught by Darwin and Spencer the force of conservative inertia, rather than creating force, is active. In this evolution we may detect a positivistic similarity with mystic emanation. In both evolution and emanation nothing is created— everything is only flowing out and changing into some other form. And in the doctrines of both evolution and emanation there is submission to necessity. Materialism is profoundly opposed to theistic God-consciousness which admits the creative act but it may be compared with a pantheistic consciousness which denies the creative act. In the materialistic universe nothing is created—everything is merely rearranged and passes from one state to another. Materialism understands the law of the conservation of energy as a denial of creativity, as a conservatism of being. The doctrine of emanation also, in another way, has to recognize the conservative law of the conservation of energy. Creativity is an increase of energy not from some other energy but out of nothing and hence does not recognize the law of the conservation of energy as absolute and universal: it overcomes this law. Evolutionism may be simply deduced from the law of the conservation of energy, as Spencer tried to do. But the very starting-point, the hypothesis that the world's energy is a fixed quantity and cannot be increased, is not an absolute law: it is only a partial form of adaptation to necessity, to the sinful state of the world.

The denial of creativity in materialism and evolutionism is one of the accessory results of the mystical denial of creativity in abstract pantheism and emanationism. The theistic, or better the pantheistic, consciousness of God has to justify every creative act. Pure pantheistic God-consciousness does not admit the possibility of either God's or man's creativity: for this consciousness one divine state simply changes into another. Pantheism, with its emanation of the world out of God, does not admit of either God's independence and freedom or the independence and freedom of the world and of man. But the creative act always presupposes self-being, independence and freedom of personality, which is unknown to the pantheistic consciousness. Abstract metaphysical and mystical monism shuts out the possibility of a creative act, either in God or in the world. The creative act presupposes a mono-pluralism, that is the existence of a multitude of free and independent beings; in other words, a concrete all-oneness.

The question is not whether the world and man are outside divinity, but whether every person, every being, has free and independent existence. The transcendence of Divinity may be accepted only in the sense that the individuality of every personality cannot disappear and be dissolved in Divinity. The free and independent being of the personality unites with God but does not disappear in Him. Disappearance and dissolution presuppose a non-personal God: free union presupposes that God is personal. The personal God is the Triune God, the three persons of the Divine Trinity. Only with the Persons of the Divine Trinity is personal communion and union possible. A Unitarian God is non-personal. To the First-God, about whom Eckhardt taught, nothing personal applies. In the religious consciousness of India Divinity has not yet revealed the Trinity of His Persons to the world—that is a lower degree of revelation. In Christianity Divinity has already shown His Triune Face. The world is an inward drama of the Trinity. It may be said both that God is completely transcendent to man and that He is immanent in man. There must be revealed in me not only God and the Divine but man as well, my human nature—this means that man must be born in God. The plurality in the world has a positive religious meaning. Eternity is the heritage not only of God but of man, as profit from the world-process. This is the meaning of Christianity, as a religion of Divine-humanity. In the official theistic consciousness there is a dangerous tendency towards a fatal deism which finally separates God from the world. God surpasses the world, but the world is divine, divine energy overflows into the world. The theistic concept, which recognizes only a transcendent, distant and external God, is an immature, childish concept, which gives rise to religious fear. A mature courageous consciousness knows God as immanent, near us and within. The denial of process or movement in God is also a tendency towards deism. The doctrine of the Trinity of Divinity must recognize development in God and understand the rise and flow of the world-process as an inner dramatic movement in the Divine Trinity. The love within the *persona* of the Holy Trinity is divine dynamic. We must recognize creative evolution and development as a theogonic, cosmogonic and anthropogonic process.

§

The creative act is a free and independent force, immanently inherent only in a person, a personality. Only something arising in original substance and possessing the power to increase power in the world can be true creativity. Something arising from without, produced by a rearrangement of substance, is not creativity. Creativity is not a new relationship among the parts of the world—it is an original act of personalities in the world. If the world is not a hierarchy of personal substances which have free and original force in themselves, then creativity in the world is impossible. Only a personalist doctrine of the world, for which every being is personal and original, can give meaning to creativity. Such a personalist doctrine recognizes the originality of personality, derived from nothing outside or general, from no other means. God is a concrete personality and therefore a creator: man is a concrete personality and therefore a creator, the whole make-up of being is concrete and personal and hence possesses creative power. The world, through and through, is a hierarchy of living beings, original personalities, capable of creatively increasing being. The process which takes its rise in the substances of the world and their rearrangement is evolution. The process which arises from the internal force of substances, from their personal originality, is creativity. The materialization of the world, which admits only evolution and refuses to recognize creativity, is a result of the fall of personalities, their servitude.

This servitude has produced the false conception that God created being capable only of evolution, of rearrangement, of economics, but incapable of creativity. Created being is thought of as static rather than dynamic. Inertia and

the conservation of the elements are held to be the fundamental qualities of the created world. The Creator did not
communicate His creative energy to His creatures. In the
creative act the Creator closed and finished His creation and
demanded of it only absolute quiet and submission. The
dynamic in creation began only with man's fall: sin begot
movement. The conquest of sin should thus restore the
created world to its state of rest and stop all dynamic.
Creativity is evil. Such a concept was only a reflection of
man's inertia, passivity and static. In his fall man lost his
creative dynamic, became heavier, subject to necessity and
necessary evolution. The conquest of sin must restore man's
creative powers, give back to creation its dynamic. By its
nature created being cannot be something finished, something closed within God's act of creation. If created being
is dynamic, then the creative process is always active and
continuing. The Creator gives to man, to his own image and
likeness, free creative power. Man's creativity is like that of
God—not equal and not identical, but resembling it. Man
is not absolute and hence cannot have absolute power. In his
creativity man is related to other people and to the whole
world of beings: he is not almighty. But in human personality there is original creative force resembling that of God.
God is not the master, the lord, the commander. God's
management of the world is not an autocracy.

The Old Testament consciousness, suppressed and frightened, knows God as a terrible commander, an autocratic
master. Such a conception of God is incompatible with
Christianity as a religion of divine-humanity. There can be
no intimate relationship with a God who is a terrible commander, an autocratic master. Intimacy is possible only with
God as man, that is, with Christ. Through Christ God ceases
to be for us a master and commander and God's providence
ceases to be autocracy. There begins an inner, intimate life of
man together with God, man's conscious participation in the
Divine nature. Without Christ it is difficult to understand
God. At present man cannot accept God without Christ.

Without Christ, God is terrible and far-off and cannot be justified. Christ is the only theodicy. Non-Christian theism, without the Trinity and without Christ, is terrible, dead and useless. We cannot believe in God if there is no Christ. But if Christ is, then God is not master, not lord, not an autocratic commander—God is near us. He is human. He is in us and we in Him. God Himself is Man—this is the supreme religious revelation, the revelation of Christ. With Christ, God's autocracy ceases, for man as the son of God is called to immediate participation in divine life. The management of the world becomes divine-human.

§

In divine-human religion, God reveals His will. But man's will must be revealed by man himself. The divine-human religion predicates man's activity. If God created man in his own image and likeness, and if the Son of God is absolute Man, this means that man as a son of God is predestined to be a free creator, like his Father-Creator. Christ, the Son of God, Saviour and Redeemer, restores man's creative powers, which had been undermined and weakened. The way of Christ is the true birth of man. According to God's idea of man, a concept which cannot be revealed by God alone but must be revealed by man as well, man is called to continue God's work of creation. The creation of the world was not finished in those seven days. What was finished in seven days is the limited, Old Testament aspect of creation, for which the whole mystery of creation was not revealed. The stamp of sin's oppression lies on the Old Testament cosmogonic consciousness. But the New Testament religion of Christ reveals a new aspect of creation. *God's work of creation is continued in the incarnation of Christ the Logos.*

The appearance in the world of the God-man marks a new moment in the creativity of the world, a moment of cosmic significance. In the revelation of the God-man begins the revelation of the creative mystery of man. *The world is being created not only in God the Father but in God the Son.*

137

Christology is the doctrine of continuing creation. And creation may be completed only in the Spirit, only by man's creativity in the Spirit. The process of the world's creation passes through all the hypostases of the Trinity. The world-process is being completed in the Trinity. Hence everything earthly is completed in heaven. The mystery of creation cannot be revealed in the creative work of God the Father alone. In the consciousness of Christ's incarnation, as a continuation of the creation, there is already implicit man's creative role in the world. It is revealed in God the Son and God the Spirit that God continues His work of creation together with man and his free powers. God created such an astoundingly exalted image of Himself that in God's very act of creation there is justified the limitless audacity of man's creative act, man's creative freedom. Now the official doctrine of the creation, in both orthodoxy and catholicism, is Old Testament, it does not fully reveal the mystery of Christ that in Him the work of creation is continued by man. The cosmogony of Christianity has remained the biblical cosmogony of the creation of the world by God in seven days. The cosmic meaning of the appearance of the new Adam is not revealed by Christianity. Hence man's purpose in the world is understood as return to the bosom of God the Father, to the original state. Only an Old Testament conception could understand the life of the world as a return, as a victory over sin, i.e. as a process without gain or increment. Christian cosmology and cosmogony have truly remained Old Testament; they see the world and its creativity only in the aspect of God the Father. Up to now Christian consciousness has not known the creative revelation that man's task in the world is to create what has not yet existed, to supplement and enrich the creative work of God. The world-process cannot be only the experience of sin and redemption from it, only the victory over evil. *The world-process is the eighth day of creation, it is continuing creation.* All the mysteries of God are revealed in the cosmogonic world-process; the mysteries of creation and of creativity.

138

The world-process is a creative process of revelation, in which both the Creator and created being equally participate. In the creativity of created being the Son of God and the Spirit of God are revealed. The creating man partakes of Divine nature; in him the divine-human creation is continued.

§

The scientific-positive, evolutionary theory of development is conservative: it denies the creative nature of development, does not admit added growth or increment in the world. For materialism and evolutionism nothing new is created in the world—what takes place is merely rearrangement. The world is a closed set of data; it is inert. Evolutionism denies the creative subject. Creativity is freedom, while evolution is necessity. Creativity presupposes personality, while evolution is impersonal. Thus Darwinism, for instance, is a passive, compliant description of the factors of necessity in the natural world, without a glimpse of the freedom of the creator beyond that necessity. There is doubtless some truth in Darwinism, since in the present state of nature the struggle for existence and the natural selection of the fittest is dominant. But it has often been noted that for Darwinism the creative agent is hidden, that the subject of development is lacking in this doctrine. Hence the lack of completeness in Darwinism is now more or less recognized in philosophical circles. Darwinism remains merely an experiment of the economic and adapted description of the external factors of development—the "how". Darwinism does not penetrate to the inside of any development; it ignores the creative subject. Meanwhile we may consider the very subjection to the struggle for existence and to natural selection as one of the states of the creative subject, as his fallen state, his submergence in a lower plane of being and his adaptation to the results of the fall, i.e. an enfeeblement of his creative powers. Science can only describe the factors of the struggle for existence and natural selection, but philosophy puts the question of the origin of such an order of nature. In reality

139

Darwinism cannot explain the beginning of development, just as it does not know its ending: it describes only the middle part of the process of development and its external factors. And it is a false philosophy which tries to make of Darwinism a metaphysic of being. Darwinism only speaks eloquently of the non-creative state of our world, of the creative subject's oppression in material evolution.

Marxism speaks of the same thing, and not less eloquently. The marxist doctrine of social development is just as conservative, as non-creative, just as submissive to necessity, as the Darwinistic doctrine of biological evolution. Marxism denies the creative subject, just as does Darwinism. And, for Marxism, development is only a rearrangement of social material which knows no absolute increment. Marxism does not know the personality, it does not know freedom and hence does not know creativity. There is a bit of truth in Marxism, where it speaks of the state of oppression of man. But the falsehood in Marxism is in the fact that it presents itself as a metaphysic of being. Viewed from the religious standpoint, the non-creative, conservative doctrine of evolution, as it is best reflected in Marxism and Darwinism, is still completely in the epoch of the law and the redemption. Evolutionism teaches of the sinfulness of man. Science always has to do with sin and its results. Science, like the state, is Old-Testament and does not know creativity. This solidarity between the scientific and the religious consciousness in denying creativity is most surprising. The scientific denial of creativity is born of the religious denial of creativity. The mechanical and materialistic view of the nature of the world is the reverse of the Christian, ascetic sense of the world. Christianity drove out the spirits of nature and thus mechanized nature. In this sense science is a product of Christianity. Science is completely caught in the Christian consciousness of sin and the fall of man. And both science and religion are equally hypnotized by the redemption from sin and the necessity which is born of sin. And the orthodox consciousness of the eastern Church does not admit of creativity and

140

is afraid of it, just as is orthodox scientific consciousness.

Theosophical doctrine, too, attempting to synthesize science and religion, often takes the form of a doctrine of non-creative evolution. Theosophical evolutionism often is discovered to be related to naturalistic evolutionism. But both theosophical and orthodox consciousness understand that the natural order is a result of man's submergence in lower orders of being, involution into material—something which the naturalistic-evolutionary consciousness does not understand. The suppressed state of the creative subject is reflected in science, in religion and in theosophy as well. Science is penetrated through and through by the spirit of obedience and asceticism. For science the creative urge is just as demonic as it is for orthodoxy. In a certain sense Darwinism and Marxism are illegitimate children, bastards of the pre-creative epoch of Christianity.

§

The creative epoch must create a new creative doctrine of man, of the world and its development. *Creative development*, rather than evolution, must be revealed in the world. Knowledge in the creative epoch is active, not passive; it presupposes creative effort and hence reveals creativity. But the knowledge of evolution was only a passive adaptation. The doctrine of creative development predicates freedom as the basis of necessity and personality as the basis of every sort of being. The old spiritualism, Christian or simply philosophic, taught the freedom of the will and the substantiality of personality but did not teach creativity. This spiritualism was quite passive, and in it one felt the same suppression of the creative subject as in materialism. In the old spiritualism the idea of freedom of the person led only to a consciousness of responsibility and sinfulness, but not to a consciousness of creative force. In being itself, creative force existed only in a repressed and potential form, as was the case in spiritualistic consciousness. When creative force moves into a dynamic state in being, a new consciousness is produced:

141

for perception is being. The new knowledge of the creative force in man and in the world can only be new being. The creative impulses of the new man are symptoms of the dawn of new being and new knowledge. A state of passivity in face of necessity can know only evolution in the world; a state of activity and the urge towards freedom can know creative development in the world. Up to the present time both religious and scientific consciousness have expressed a state of being in which it is impossible to know either creative force or creative development. Only a philosophy of activity knows the creative dynamic of being. In the majority of cases mystical philosophy was passive and contemplative, hence the mystery of creativity was not revealed to it, either.

§

We face the task of overcoming a twofold consciousness: the scientific consciousness of the impossibility of creatively increasing the amount of energy in the world, and the religious consciousness of the impossibility of continuing creativity in the world. Creative philosophy recognizes the dynamic quality of created being. Created being is continuously created—it knows no limits to the creative process; it is not a closed set of data. Created being is through and through personal and plural, i.e. it consists of self-sufficient and creative individual beings. The cosmos is being created; it is not given, it is a task set. But is there a limit to the creativity of created beings? Are they completely like the Creator in His creative powers? There is an eternal and impassable limit which separates human creativity from divine creativity, from the creativity of the Creator. Created beings do not create beings—these are created only by God. Personality is created in God before all worlds. And every attempt on the part of created beings to create being leads only to the production of an automat, a dead mechanism. Such an attempt is always demonic—it is black magic. Only God has the power to create living being, personality. There is a divine basis for every being, every personality. The

142

creation of created beings can be directed only towards the increase of the creative energy of being, the growth of beings and their harmony in the world, to the production of hitherto non-existent values, new upsurge into truth, goodness and beauty—i.e. towards the production of the cosmos and of cosmic life—towards a "pleroma", towards a super-worldly completeness. But being in the image and likeness of God can be created by God alone. The very hierarchy of living beings in the world is made by the Creator to be the eternal composition of being. Substance cannot be created in the creative process. Every attempt to understand creativity as the reproduction of new living beings, rather than as an increase of energy, as growth and upswing created by God, is both godless and demonic. The mystery of the creation of persons is God's mystery. Every tendency in this direction leads to the production of an automatic and mechanical being, devoid of life. This is the creativity of the fallen angel.

§

In what sense are there two worlds: "this world" and "the other"? Ontologically, there is only one world, one divine being. But the fall of being shattered and divided it. The world came into a diseased state. "This world" is an illness of being, its captivity, its fallen state, a partial loss of its freedom and its subjection to external necessity. "The other world" is the health of being, its uplift, its liberation, its fullness. "This world" must be overcome and eliminated. But this does not mean hostility towards the world or the cosmos—it means hostility only toward its disease, its enslavement and its fall.

The question of the relation of creativity to being leads to another fundamental question—the relation of creativity to freedom.

# CHAPTER VI

# CREATIVITY AND FREEDOM: INDIVIDUALISM AND UNIVERSALISM

CREATIVITY IS INSEPARABLE from freedom. Only he who is free creates. Out of necessity can be born only evolution; creativity is born of liberty. When we speak in our imperfect human language about creativity out of nothing, we are really speaking of creativity out of freedom. Viewed from the standpoint of determinism, freedom is "nothing", it surpasses all fixed or determined orders, it is conditioned by nothing else; and what is born of freedom does not derive from previously existing causes, from "something". Human creativity out of "nothing" does not mean the absence of resistant material but only an absolute increment or gain which is not determined by anything else. Only evolution is determined: creativity derives from nothing which precedes it. Creativity is inexplicable: creativity is the mystery of freedom. The mystery of freedom is immeasurably deep and inexplicable. Just as deep and inexplicable is the mystery of creativity. Those who would deny the possibility of creation (creativity) out of nothing must inevitably place creativity in a certain determined order and by this very fact must deny the freedom of creativity. In creative freedom there is an inexplicable and mysterious power to create out of nothing, undetermined, adding energy to the existing circulation of energy in the world. As regards the data of the world and the closed circle of the world's energy, the act of creative freedom is transcendent. The act of creative freedom breaks out of the determined chain of the world's energy. From the viewpoint of an immanent world datum this act must always represent creation out of nothing. The timid denial of creation out of nothing is submission to determinism, obedience to necessity. Creativity is something which proceeds from within, out of immeasurable and inexplicable depths, not from without, not from the world's necessity. The very desire to make the creative act understandable, to find a basis for it, is failure to comprehend it. To comprehend the creative act means to recognize that it is inexplicable and without foundation. The desire to rationalize creativity is related to the desire to rationalize freedom. Those who recognize freedom and do not desire determinism have also tried to rationalize freedom. But a rationalization of freedom is itself determinism, since this denies the boundless mystery of freedom. Freedom is the ultimate: it cannot be derived from anything: it cannot be made the equivalent of anything. Freedom is the baseless foundation of being: it is deeper than all being. We cannot penetrate to a rationally-perceived base for freedom. Freedom is a well of immeasurable depth—its bottom is the final mystery.

But freedom is not a negative and ultimate concept, merely indicating the boundaries beyond which reason cannot pass. Freedom is positive and full of meaning. Freedom is not only a denial of necessity and determinism. Freedom is not a realm of chance and wilfulness, as distinguished from the realm of law-abiding and of necessity. Those, also, fail to understand the mystery of freedom who see in it only a special form of spiritual determinism—i.e. consider that everything is free which is born of causes within the human spirit. Although freedom is neither rational nor acceptable, this is the most rational and acceptable explanation of it. In so far as the human spirit is part of the order of nature, everything in the spirit is determined, just as are all natural phenomena. The spiritual is no less determined than the material. The Indian doctrine of Karma is a form of spiritual determinism. The Karma doctrine of reincarnation does not know freedom. Man's spirit is free only in so far as it is supernatural, transcending and going beyond the order of nature. Determinism is an inevitable form of natural being, i.e. including the being of man as a natural being, even though causality in man is spiritual rather than physical. Within the determined order of nature creativity is impossible: we can have only evolution. Freedom and creativity tell us that man is not only a natural, but a supernatural being. And this means that man is not only a physical being and not only a psychic being, in the natural meaning of the word. Man is a free, supernatural spirit, a microcosm. Spiritualism, like materialism, can see in man only a natural, although a spiritual, being and then subjects him to a spiritual determinism, just as materialism subjects to the material. Freedom is only the production of spiritual phenomena out of preceding spiritual phenomena in the same being. Freedom is a positive creative force, unconditioned by anything else and based upon nothing else, flowing up from a spring of boundless depth. Freedom is the power to create out of nothing, the power of the spirit to create out of itself and not out of the world of nature. Freedom is one's positive expression and assertion is creativity. Free energy, i.e. creative energy, is substantially inherent in man. But man's substantiality is not a closed circle of energy within which everything is spiritually determined. In man's very substantiality there are bottomless well-springs. Creative energy is increasing energy, not energy which merely rearranges itself. The mystery of freedom denies everything finite and all limitations. The old spiritualism understood spiritual substance statically and by this fact revealed its own non-creative character. For the old spiritualism, freedom was merely justification of moral responsibility, rather than a justification of creativity. Traditional spiritualism is a concept of the pre-creative epoch: it exists in the law and the redemption. The powers of evil, rather than of good, have resorted to freedom for their sustentation.

The lack of base, the infinite depth and the mysteriousness of freedom do not mean arbitrariness. Freedom cannot be rationalized—it is not subject to rational categories, but in

146

it the divine reason is alive. Freedom is positive creative power rather than negative arbitrariness. The negative consciousness of one's freedom as arbitrary free will is a falling into sin. Negative freedom, freedom as arbitrary free will, is freedom without content and void. To desire freedom for its own sake, freedom without purpose or content, is to desire emptiness, to turn away towards non-being. Freedom, conceived only formally, without purpose or content, is nothing, emptiness, non-being. Freedom in the Fall was this kind of negative, formal freedom and emptiness and non-being—it was freedom for freedom, i.e. freedom *from* rather than freedom *for*. Freedom in the Fall was not freedom for creativeness, not creative freedom. The falling away from God deprives freedom of its content and its purpose, impoverishes it, deprives it of power. Negative, formal, empty freedom is reborn in necessity: in it being is degraded. The positive, creative purpose and content of freedom could not yet be conceived at that stage of creation, the seven-day stage, since in creation there had not yet been revealed the Absolute Man, the Son of God, the revelation of the Eighth Day. In the seven-day creation there was possible only a trial of freedom. The position Adam occupied in paradise was not yet the position of man: the active-creative calling of man had not yet been revealed. The freedom of the all-man Adam had not yet been joined with the freedom of the Absolute Man, Christ, and in that earlier freedom were contained the seeds of the Fall and of sin. It might be said that Adam had the choice between absolute obedience and absolute wilfulness. Creative freedom is not revealed at this stage of creation. Adam's freedom was formal, rather than material. Material freedom is attained in another epoch of creation, the epoch of the revelation of the Absolute Man. This freedom is born of the union of the human nature of Jesus with the divine nature of Christ. The cosmic mystery of the redemption overcomes formal and empty freedom and the necessity which is born of it. Human nature, become son of God, rises to the consciousness of material freedom full of creative purpose. Freedom is penetrated by universal love. Freedom is henceforth inseparable from its universal content. Freedom *from* is in sin: freedom *for* is in creativeness. Adam's freedom in the seven-day creation is different from his freedom in the creation of the eighth day. The freedom of the new Adam, joined with the Absolute Man, is creative freedom, freedom which continues the work of God's creativity, freedom which does not revolt against God in negative arbitrary wilfulness.

There are two freedoms: divine and diabolic. The freedom of the first Adam could not be diabolic freedom, because divine freedom in its positive content could not be revealed in the seven-day creation. Adam's freedom was the first stamp of man's likeness to the Creator. And even in paralysing sin there was still a sign of man's power. The fall of the first man, Adam, had positive meaning and justification, as a moment in the revelation of creativity, preparing for the appearance of the Absolute Man. Theodicy, the justification of God, is also a justification of the meaning of evil. Evil, as absolute meaninglessness and loss, denies the absolute meaning of being and leads to dualism. The traditional Christian consciousness in the doctrine of evil approaches dualistic duotheism. This doctrine of evil, denying all immanent meaning in the experience of evil, was a pedagogic for the immature. There was no room for the truth of evil's antinomic nature. An exclusively transcendent view of evil gives rise to slavish fear. This slavish fear prevented man from comprehending his fall away from God as a tragic moment in the revelation and development of man's freedom from the old to the new form. But any antinomic solution to the problem of evil is impossible. It is equally true that a dark source of evil exists in the world and that in the final sense of the word there is no evil. The freedom of Adam the first man had to be destroyed in his experience of good and evil; it had to be swallowed up by necessity so that the true and higher freedom might be revealed through

148

the Absolute Man, Christ. The fall of the first Adam was a necessary cosmic moment in the revelation of the new Adam. This was the way to a higher completeness by means of a falling-apart. In Christianity the experience of sin is peripheral, exoteric. The deep experience of resisting God, of being deceived by God as an inward way of falling apart and division in divine life is esoteric. All the mystics have known this. Diabolic freedom was born after the appearance of the new Adam. Final evil is possible only after Christ. Diabolic freedom is a final and ultimate resistance against Christ: the destruction of man, the choice of the way of non-being. Diabolic freedom is revealed only in the eighth day of creation as a false likeness of creative freedom. The devil's creativity creates only non-being: it steals from God in order to create a caricature of being, a false image of being. Diabolic freedom is final necessity, final enslavement. Necessity is only a form of freedom. In Adam's fall freedom was reborn into necessity which was subject to the fallen angel. But this was still no final loss of freedom. Final loss of freedom and final enslavement are possible only in that epoch of creation where there is already the revelation of the Absolute Man, Christ, and when the Antichrist, a false image and caricature of the Absolute Man, tempts man by the blessed condition of non-being. Here we approach an eschatological problem. For the moment it has been important to state that two forms of freedom exist, corresponding to the two epochs of creation and revelation. The fall of Adam did not mean deciding the fate of the world. This was merely tempting a youth. The first Adam was not yet a part of the Divine mystery of the Trinity through the Absolute Man and hence did not yet know his creative freedom: he is only the first stage of creation. The final truth about evil is included in the genial works of J. Boehme. From the *Ungrund*, the abyss, light is born, God: the theogonic process takes place and out of it flows darkness, evil, a shadow over the light of divinity. Evil takes its source not in the God that is born but in the foundations of God, in the abyss, from which proceed both light and darkness. We can give reasoned meaning to evil only if we accept the principle of development in divine life.

§

Necessity is a creation of the freedom of the first Adam, a result of wrongly directed freedom, the freedom of the Fall. Freedom is not consciously accepted necessity, as the German idealists taught. Necessity is an evil, sub-conscious freedom, a freedom not illumined by the Logos. Obligatory necessity is only the reverse side of the world's fall away from, and estrangement from God. Those substances or beings of the world-hierarchy, which are estranged from each other and continue in strife and dissension, which are not united inwardly and freely, are inevitably bound and fettered outwardly. Man can be a slave only to that which is foreign and hostile. What is near and dear to man does not compel him. Those who love each other and are thus united are free: only those who are at enmity and not united are enslaved and know necessity. The materialization of the world, the compulsory and cumbersome relation of one of its parts to another—all this is born of alienation and enmity, i.e. of the fall of Adam the all-man. Necessity is fallen freedom, a freedom of enmity and dissolution, a freedom of chaos and anarchy. Obligatory necessity is always the reverse side of the medal of inner chaos and anarchy, a movement in the hierarchic system of the universe. True freedom is an expression of the cosmic (as opposed to the chaotic) condition of the universe, its hierarchic harmony, the inward unitedness of all its parts. The cosmic is always free; in it there is no obligatory necessity, no burden or pressure, no materialization of one of its parts for another. In the cosmos everything is alive, nothing is inert or overburdened, nothing compels by its material consistence. Every time that man's living spirit encounters the resistance of heavy and for him lifeless material bodies, he feels the fall of the all-man and the strife and alienation which were born of it. The lower

150

ranks of being were deadened, made burdensome, materialized by the fall of the all-man and by the strife and enmity
engendered by that fall. The obligatory "materiality" of
being is born of man himself. It is the result of man's loss of
his hierarchic position in the universe, his inward estrangement from the lower orders of the cosmic hierarchy, the
result of dualizing being. And the degree of obligatory
"materiality" is in direct proportion to the degree of inward
estrangement. The rocks are most obligatory for us and we
feel them to be the least living of all things because we are
the most estranged and separated from them. People who
are near to us in spirit are the least obligatory for us, and
we feel them to be the most alive of all things because they
are nearest to us, dear to us, joined with us. Love burns up
all necessity and gives freedom. *Love is the content of freedom—
love is the freedom of the new Adam, the freedom of the eighth day of
creation.* The world is bewitched by evil and can be released
from the spell only by love. The world's necessity is enchantment; the world's material "obligatoriness" is letting evil
take the lead; it is an illusory being, born of dissension.
The inert, heavy and oppressive material of the world can
be released from bewitchment, can be unfettered, made alive,
only by the power of the unifying love which the Absolute
Man, the new Adam, brings with him into the world. Love
is creativeness.

Man is responsible for the materialization of the world,
for the necessity and compulsion which reign in it; for man
is called to be king of the universe—and the world lives or
dies by him. The world is deadened by man's fall and it is
revived by man's uprising. But the all-vivifying and spiritual-
izing rise of fallen man is possible only through the advent
of the Absolute Man, bringing man's nature into communion
with divine nature. The Redeemer and Saviour of the world
exorcizes the spell and casts off the fetters of necessity. He is
the Liberator. *Without Christ the Liberator, the world would
have remained for all time shattered in necessity and determinism
would be for ever true.* Determinism is finally overcome only in

151

Christ the Liberator. Any philosophy which does not accept Christ the Liberator, which is not illumined by Christ the Logos, inevitably contains within itself to a greater or less degree an undissolved remnant of determinism. Without Christ the Liberator, freedom itself must appear to be the result of necessity. Freedom without Christ the Liberator is the freedom of the old Adam, freedom without love, freedom of the seven-day creation. Freedom with Christ is the freedom of the new Adam, freedom which by love removes the spell from the world—freedom of the eighth day of creation. After Christ, man is a new creature, knowing new freedom. For determinism only the old creature exists, under the spell of necessity. The naturalistic view of man and the world is the old view, born of the old consciousness, consonant with the epoch of unfinished seven-day creation. Determinism and naturalism will always persist until man's human nature is joined with divine nature through the Absolute Man. Individualism carries on a tragic but powerless struggle against the power of determinism and naturalism. Individualism is only an evidence of the crisis of naturalism and determinism—not a victory over them.

§

Individualism, which became so acute at the close of the nineteenth century, rose against the power of natural and social order over man's individuality. *Individualism is a convulsion of the freedom of the old Adam, of the old freedom.* Hence, in individualism, freedom is not creating the cosmos but rather resisting it. Freedom in individualism is a disunited freedom, estranged from the world. And all separation or estrangement from the world leads to slavery to the world, since everything foreign and distant from us is for us compelling necessity. For the individualist, the world is always violating him. Extreme individualism tries to identify man's individuality with the world and to cast off the whole world outside this inflated human individuality. But this identification of man with the world is realized only as an

152

illusion. This is demonic self-deception. In reality individualism denies that man is a microcosm and that he is in a cosmic situation. Individualism demeans man—does not wish to know his world-wide universal content. The individualist tries convulsively to free himself from the world, from the cosmos—and attains only slavery; for to separate oneself inwardly from the universe is inevitably to enslave oneself to it outwardly. Individualism is a devastation of individuality, its impoverishment, a diminution of its universal content, i.e. a tendency towards non-being. If individuality should attain absolute separation and alienation from the universe, from the hierarchy of living beings, it would turn into non-being—it would destroy itself completely. Individuality and individualism are opposites. Individualism is the enemy of individuality. Man is an organic member of the universal cosmic hierarchy, and the richness of his content is in direct proportion to his union with the cosmos. Man's individuality finds complete expression only in universal, cosmic life. In individualism, the individuality is empty, without content. In individualism, freedom is only an unhealthy convulsion. Did Ibsen's Peer Gynt affirm his individuality? Did he possess freedom? Convulsively asserting his individuality, he was deprived of it; he was not himself, a personality, but rather a slave of necessity. *Peer Gynt* is a work of genius presenting the tragedy of individualism. Individualism is the tragedy of empty freedom. Individualism does not say "I want this" (content): it says "I want what I want" (emptiness). But a free act of will must have content, an object, a purpose—it cannot be empty, purposeless, without an object. The free act of will desires something, and not just "what it desires". In this insistence upon the right to "want what I want" there is a slavish psychology, a psychology which has lost its freedom, a psychology of the age of childhood. The truly free affirm their will with definite content, not merely formally. They know what they want. Formal and empty freedom is the freedom of the old Adam, the freedom of the Fall, the freedom of the world's childhood. This formal and vacant freedom arises in individualism.

Individualism may be a symptom of world crisis, but it still remains in the pre-creative epoch of the world; it gives expression to its immature will, its lack of freedom. In individualism freedom takes a wrong direction and gets lost. Individualism and its freedom are confirmed only in universalism. A mature and free will directs its act of desire, its action on cosmic and divine life, towards a rich content for life, rather than towards vacuity. Mature and free will is creative will going out from itself into cosmic life. By its nature, individualism is not creative; it is negative and empty, since it deprives men of that universal content, towards which, alone, creativity may be directed. The whole concept of individualism is still confused and insufficiently explained. Sometimes individualism is understood as meaning the liberation of individuality from external pressure, natural or social, the pressure of an established moral or social order. If we understand individualism in this fashion, then we must recognize positive value in it. We cannot, for instance, deny the healthful elements in the individualism of the Renaissance. The human spirit is of greater value than the state, or customs and *mores*, or any external value—the human spirit is worth more than the whole external world. But in a strict sense, which is appearing only now in our time, individualism is opposed to universalism; it is the disunion of the human individuality from the universe; it is self-idolization. Such an individualism leads to the destruction of man, to his fall into non-being. Man is infinitely poor and empty if there is nothing higher than himself, if there is no God; and man is infinitely rich and meaningful if there is something higher, if God does exist. Movement is impossible for man if there is nothing higher, nothing divine—he has nowhere' to move. The liberation of man's individuality from God and from the world is murder; it is a diabolic enslavement. Man's freedom is bound up with the freedom of the world and is realized only in the world's

154

liberation. The world's necessity must be unfettered, released from the spell, in order that man should attain higher, free life. Individualism merely confirms that atomization, that estrangement among parts of the world, which is really enchantment and thralldom in compelling necessity.

§

The enslavement and bondage of the world's hierarchy of beings submit man to lower, moribund levels of being; they compel man by their material heaviness. This bondage, this heaviness of the lower hierarchy, conceal from us the creative secret of being. We see the world in an aspect of necessity, of moribund and petrified materialization. But is creativeness possible for necessity and out of necessity? We have already seen that in the realm of necessity only evolution is possible—the rearrangement of a given quantity of energy. Only freedom can create absolute increase in the world—only the free man creates. The determinism which is so compulsively forced upon us is false because freedom of personality does exist, creatively breaking the chains of necessity. We cannot understand the creative secret of being in a passive way, in an atmosphere of obedience to the world's heavy materialism. It can be understood only actively, in the atmosphere of the creative act itself. To know the creative activity of the person means being a creatively active person. Like knows like. The inner relationship between the subject of knowing and the object of knowing is a necessary condition of true knowing. Only the free man knows freedom; only the creating man knows creativity. Only the spirit knows the spiritual. Only the microcosm knows the macrocosm. To know anything in the world is to have this in oneself. Knowing is a creative act and we cannot expect to have knowledge of freedom from a slavish submission to necessity. We cannot expect to have knowledge of world freedom and of the world's creative mystery from an individualism which has separated and torn itself away from the world and set itself up against the world. The free creative power of individuality presupposes its universalism, its quality of the microcosm. Every creative act has universal, cosmic significance. The creative act of the personality enters the cosmic hierarchy, gives it deliverance from the power of lower materialized hierarchies, unfetters being. In its freedom and its creativeness the personality cannot be separated from the cosmos, cannot be divorced from universal being.

§

We find this anti-universalism which destroys individuality not only in individual schism but in the schism of sects. In the universe man is free: in a sect he is a slave. The error and untruth in all sectarianism lies in this breaking away from the cosmos, from cosmic breadth, in this refusal to accept the universal responsibility of every one for all men and all things. A sect wishes to be saved alone: it does not wish to be saved together with the world. In the sectarian psychology there is self-satisfaction, absorption with one's self, self-centredness. The sectarian psychology despises the world and is ever ready to condemn a great portion of it to destruction, as something of a lower order. In essence the sectarian psychology is not Christian: it has not got the Christian universalism or the Christian world-wide love. It does not want to recognize that Christ is not only saviour of me and my little ship, but the world's saviour as well. This schismatic psychology does not wish to bear the burden of responsibility for the fate of the lower hierarchic orders of being. Even in historic orthodoxy and Catholicism there is a tendency towards sectarianism, an insufficiency of the universal spirit. Individuality is smothered where there is no universal spiritual breath. The Christian conscience, the conscience of the universal Logos, cannot be reconciled either to individualism or to sectarianism: the apostasy and self-satisfaction of the single individual are equally repugnant to Christian conscience as are the apostasy and self-satisfaction of some small group. There may be an

156

individualism of a small group, its schism from the cosmos, its self-satisfaction with itself. Sectarianism is worse than individualism, for it produces an illusion of universalism, it appears to offer an escape from separatism, from the individual's diversion from the whole. And the individualism of a separate small group is more difficult to overcome than the individualism of one person. A sect is a false church, a pseudo-universalism: there is in sectarianism a super-personal magic from which it is difficult to be liberated. The wine of sectarianism intoxicates, gives an illusion of ecstatic uplift of being. In a sect, a false union takes place, a union outside the cosmic, universal hierarchy. In its mystic essence the Church is universality, a cosmic organism, a universal, cosmic hierarchy with Christ in the heart of being. In a sect, on the other hand, there is developed a false organism, a fiction. Everything which is not cosmic, not universal in spirit, is already a tendency towards sectarianism, although it may bear the stamp of official ecclesiastical authority. For the Christian conscience, the hermit is more acceptable than the sectarian. Individuality is, after all, a genuine reality and value: along its life's way, individuality may experience a condition of loneliness, of crisis; it may outgrow the old forms of union. But a sect is always a phantom, an illusion; it is unreal and does not possess value in and for itself. What the Church officially calls sectarianism may be a symptom and a sign of religious thirst for a higher spiritual life. But here I am using the sectarian spirit in its inward meaning and I can discover more of it in official ecclesiasticism than in the sects. Hence the sectarian spirit is worse than that of the lonely individual.

Solitude may be combined with genuine universality *sobornost* and true churchliness. And a man of œcumenical consciousness and churchly experience may be quite alone in his creative courage and initiative. Solitude is possible for the Christian in a transition-epoch, preceding the new world-epoch of creativeness. A sect, on the other hand, is a pseudo-church and hence it can scarcely have genuine œcumenicity and churchliness. Solitude is not necessarily individualism. Solitude, a man's being alone, is not alienation from the cosmos. It may be only a symptom of the fact that a personality has outgrown certain conditions under which others live, and its universal content is not yet recognized by the others. The supreme solitude is divine. God, Himself, knows great and anguished solitude. He has the experience of being deserted by the world and by men. Christ was solitary and not understood during His life. Men accepted and understood Christ only after His death on the Cross. Solitude is quite compatible with universality: there may be more of the universal spirit in solitude than in a herded society. Every act of courage, every creative initiative, gives a sense of solitude, of being unrecognized— transcends every given community. And there is always the temptation to overcome this solitude by some sectarian community rather than by the universal community. Solitude lies outside the contradistinction between individualism and universalism, hence there may be both universalism and individualism in solitude. The one may be more universal and œcumenical than a whole collective. In the single, lone Nietzsche there was more of the universal spirit than in many a sect, many a social collective. We must never forget that the religious way moves from the personality to society, from the inward to the outer, toward the cosmos by way of individuality.

§

God expects from man the highest freedom, the freedom of the eighth day of creation. This, God's expectation, lays on man a great responsibility. *The final, ultimate freedom, the daring of freedom and the burden of freedom, is the virtue of religious maturity.* To arrive at religious maturity means to know final freedom. The immaturity of Christian consciousness has hitherto made impossible a knowledge of man's ultimate freedom. Christianity has always been a training, a guardianship of the immature. And hence Christianity has not yet

158

revealed itself in fullness, as an experience of freedom. The religion of freedom is a religion of apocalyptic times. Only the final time will know the final freedom. Christianity, as a religion of training and guardianship of the immature, as a religion of the fear of temptation for the immature, is being deformed and is becoming torpid. But only a religion of freedom, a religion of daring and not of fear, can answer to man's present age, to the times and seasons of to-day. We can no longer refuse the time of freedom: Christian men are now too old, not only ripe but over-ripe for that. At the end of the Christian path there dawns the consciousness that God expects from man such a revelation of freedom as will contain even what God Himself has not foreseen. God justifies the mystery of freedom, having by His might and power set a limit to His own foreseeing. Those not free are not needed by God, they do not belong in the divine cosmos. Hence freedom is not a right: it is an obligation. Freedom is a religious virtue. He who is not free, the slave, cannot enter the kingdom of God: he is not a son of God; he is subject to lower spheres. There is a freedom which corresponds to the world's creative epoch. Before that there was only a freedom of the law and the redemption. What are the ways of freedom? Is asceticism which leads to sainthood the only way of liberation or is there another?

# CHAPTER VII

# CREATIVITY AND ASCETICISM:
# THE GENIUS AND THE SAINT

THERE IS A RESEMBLANCE among the techniques of religious experience of all religions, however they may differ in spirit: there is a resemblance in the methods of mystical experience of all the mystics, however much their types may differ. In the depths of every true religion and every genuine mystic there is the thirst for overcoming "the world" as a lower order of being, for victory over "the world", and hence we have asceticism as a way to this conquest and this victory. Without this ascetic moment, that is the conquest of lower nature for the sake of the higher, conquest of this world for the sake of another world, religious and mystical life is unthinkable. Asceticism, spiritual exercise, is an obligatory formal method for all religious and mystic experience, although the spiritual content of this formal method may be quite varied. Thus we cannot deny, for example, the formal, technical resemblance in the methods of practical mystics of the eastern yogis and those of eastern Christianity, although the two types of mysticism are very different, even oppose each other. The mystic practice of Yoga is a graceless way upward from below—a way of physical effort rather than of love. The mystic practice of eastern orthodoxy is based upon the acquisition of grace, on the presence of Christ at the very beginning of the way, and is permeated with the *pathos* of love towards God. But there is a formal, technical resemblance in method between the mysticism of St. Simeon the New Theologian, and Yoga. In one and the other there is *ascesis*, concentration, victory over passions, the overcoming of "this world" and the vision of another world. It is easy to

160

identify the practice of "mental effort" with the practice of the yogis. There is an eternal truth in Yoga, and it is well to remind ourselves of it now. The same technique may be found in the mystic practice of any religion. Asceticism is one of the eternal ways of religious experience. And we cannot doubt the religious value and effectiveness of this way. This way is considered pre-eminently a religious way. "The world" must be overcome and hence the struggle with passions which fetter man to "this world". Asceticism is only a technique of religious experience, only its formal methodology. No single mystic ever saw in asceticism a purpose and content of religious life, for content and purpose are already in another world, the acquisition of divine life. Viewed from outside, from a distance, we see only asceticism, only a technical and formal method, more denial than affirmation. But behind this there lies life in God, development into another life. The ascetic way is negative in its technique, but by its positive content it is return to the bosom of God.

But we are faced with the question: is there some other religious way, some other religious experience of creative ecstasy? By itself, the way of asceticism is not a creative way, and the ascetic ecstasy of saints and mystics is an ecstasy of return to God, the vision of divine light, rather than the creation of a new world, of life hitherto unseen. The experience of creative ecstasy as a religious way, is not revealed in the consciousness of the Church Fathers or in the consciousness of the old mystics. The creative experience, the creative ecstasy, is either denied completely by religious consciousness as "worldly" and of the passions, or else is merely admitted and permitted. Up to the present, religious consciousness has seen in creativeness not "spiritual", but rather "worldly" action. At the best, religious consciousness justified creativeness. But this very religious justification of creativeness presupposes that creativeness lies outside the way of religion. The very idea would have seemed forward and godless that creative experience does not need religious permission or justification but is itself a religious way, a religious experience of equal value with the way of asceticism. The old religious consciousness could only put the question of the justification of creative experience. The new religious consciousness puts the question of creative experience as in itself religious, as in itself justifying, rather than needing justification. Creative experience is not something secondary and hence requiring justification. Creative experience is something primary and hence justifying. Creative experience is spiritual, in the religious sense of that word. Creativeness is no less spiritual, no less religious, than asceticism. Such a statement of the problem could arise only in our time, in an epoch when the world is passing the divide into a new religious epoch of creativeness. In the religious epoch of the law and the redemption, the religious problem of creativeness was unknown. Only the "worldly", cultural problem of creativeness was posed and solved. In various ways man tried to combine the ascetic Christian way with the justification of worldly creativeness, i.e. culture. But in all these Christian justifications of the creation of culture, one always felt a strain, an eclectic compromise. The problem of creativeness was never considered religiously and could not be so considered, since the very putting of that question was already an entrance into the religious epoch of creativeness. Creative ecstasy is religious ecstasy: the way of the creative shaking of man's whole being is a religious way. This is a new, as yet unknown, religious consciousness—the consciousness of the creative epoch in the world.

Creativeness accepts and follows the Gospel commandment not to love the world or the things of the world. He who creates feels himself to be not of this world. Creativeness is the overcoming of the world in the gospel sense but a kind of overcoming other than that of asceticism although equal to it in value. In the creative act man passes out from this world and enters another world. The creative act is not an arrangement of "this world", but in it another world, a real cosmos, is set up. Creativeness is not an adaptation to this world, to the necessities of this world—creativeness is

162

transition beyond the limits of this world and the overcoming of its necessity. The gospel commandments "love not the world" and "overcome the world" remain valid for ever and can never be revoked. Not to love the world means to be free and to reveal our sonship to God: to cling to this world, however, means being a slave to necessity. Creativeness is not only faithful to this highest commandment of freedom from "the world", but it is also, by its very nature, a victory over that world in the name of another: it is a revelation of the meaning of the commandment "love not the world". The creative act is always an exit from this world, from this life. In its essence creativeness is an unshackling, a bursting of chains. In the creative ecstasy all the heaviness of the world is overcome, sin is burned away; another, a higher nature, shines through. The experience of overcoming the world in creativeness is qualitatively different from the ascetic experience of overcoming the world. It is not an experience of obedience but rather an experience of daring. And "the world" is burned away in the daring of creative activity, just as in the act of obedience.

The problem of religious justification of "the world" cannot even be put by the Christian conscience, true to the commandment of Christ. Any "deals" with "the world" are religiously impossible. This is all too clear in the revelation of the New Testament. Any justification of "the world" or "the things of the world" is a compromise with sin, for "the world" is not true being, it is fallen being and must not be confused with the divine cosmos. "This world" is only a shadow of the light. The world-cosmos is divine in all its multiplicity: "this world" has fallen away from Divine life. But creative values are not "worldly", not "of this world". The creative act is transcendental in relation to the world: it steps outside "the world". And the deficiency of the Christian New Testament revelation is not in the fact that Christianity does not justify "the world", but rather in that it does not justify creativeness or, better, that it is not yet a revelation of creativeness. The Christian consciousness ascetically denies "the world" and everything worldly—in this is the eternal truth of Christianity. And criticism of historic Christianity should be directed at its compromises and "deals" with "the world". In historic Christianity there is too much pagan adaptation to the world and the worldly; it is all adapted to the physical plane of being; it is lacking in consistent asceticism; in its expression it is not yet sufficiently spiritual. Christianity has not yet given a revelation of the creative mystery of the cosmos—there has been too much of the "world and the things of the world". In Christianity the attitude towards the world has been too pagan. In Christianity the attitude towards "the world" was one of obedience which was carried out into obedience to evil and could not yet be cosmic creativeness. But there is neither contradiction nor opposition between creativeness and asceticism. Creativeness does not assert what asceticism denies. That world which asceticism denies is denied by creativeness as well: what is affirmed by creativeness is quite another world. Hence the revelation of creativeness lies outside the gospel's denial of "the world". Creativeness presupposes an ascetic overcoming of the world—it is positive asceticism. Creativeness presupposes impoverishment, a diminution of "the world"—and this final poverty is the way to new creativity.

True creativeness can never be demonic: it is always a movement out of darkness. The demonic evil in human nature is burned up in the creative ecstasy, transforms itself into another kind of being. For every evil is shackled to "the world", to its passions and its burdens. The creative upsurge gives release from the heaviness of "this world" and transforms passion into another kind of being. The devil has no power to create and whatever is of him is not creative. He lies about his creation—he steals from God and makes a caricature. A creator may be demonic and his demonism may leave its imprint upon his creation. But great creation cannot be demonic, neither can creative value and the creative ecstasy which gives it birth. I think there was some demonic poison in the nature of Leonardo. But in Leonardo's

164

creative act the demonism was consumed and transformed into another kind of being, free from "this world". The demonism of Leonardo's nature is glimpsed in his *Gioconda*, in *John the Baptist*. But are the great creations of Leonardo's genius condemned to burn in the fires of hell? No, for in these creations the evil in Leonardo's nature has already been consumed and his demonism transformed into another kind of being, by passing through the creative ecstasy of the genius. In the *Gioconda* there is eternal beauty which will enter eternal life. Creative life is life eternal and not life corruptible. How powerless and pitiful is all moralizing about great creations! The beauty which is born in the creative act is already a transition from "this world" into the cosmos, into another form of being, and in it there can be no shadow of the evil which was in the sinful nature of the creator. A real picture or poem no longer belongs to the physical plane of being—they have no material weight— they enter the free cosmos. And the creative act is a self-revelation, of value for itself: it knows no judge outside itself.

§

The struggle with the darkness of sin begins with repentance. The spiritual life is unthinkable without the great mystery of repentance. Sin must be not only recognized but it must be consumed in the fire of repentance. Everyone who has passed through the religious way of repentance knows how complicated and how varied in quality is this way, not without its dangers. On the way of repentance the spiritual fruits of a higher life are ripened. But repentance is not always fruitful. Repentance sometimes may not bear fruit and may lead to feebleness, to spiritual suicide. Repentance may lead to a thickening of the darkness within oneself. When the way of repentance has reached the point of enfeeblement, then it is mystically necessary to take another way. One step further and the man dies, spiritually. The Fathers and the mystics say that repentance should be fruitful, that it should not lead to spiritual despair, for despair is the greatest sin. When repentance turns into despair it should stop there—it has not yet been justified by the birth of light. This point of despair and fainting of the spirit indicates the need for taking another way of spiritual action. The whole value of repentance is birth into new life. When deep despair sets in, when one is unable to arrive at new life through repentance, when the darkness within has attained its thickest concentration, then repentance loses its value and must itself be overcome. And there remains only one way of salvation from spiritual death, from self-expressed and self-incarnate darkness—the way of a creative shaking of the spirit. In a mysterious and wonderful way, repentance is reborn into creative impulse and renews the fainting and fading spirit, frees its constructive powers. Creativity cannot replace repentance. The way of repentance is inevitable, but the creative ecstasy and the creative impulse are a revolutionary birth into new life.

Repentance is necessary for creativity but creative shaking of the spirit differs in quality from that of repentance. In creativity, it is true, sin is overcome and shadow burned away, but this is another way of the spirit than repentance. By itself alone, repentance is not a rebirth. The rebirth is already in the creative impulse. In the creative rebirth, that cloud of darkness which could not be burned away in repentance is consumed and reduced to ashes. Those men are out of their minds who demand only repentance alone, who both forbid and fear the creative upsurge, who would bring man to spiritual despair and feebleness. These lovers of repentance alone, timorous opponents of creativity, are enemies of the spirit's rebirth, of birth into a new life, for creativity is just as much a religious act as is asceticism. In the religious creative experience there is a positive rather than a negative overcoming of "the world". The world must be conquered both ascetically and creatively. But by the ascetic way alone, solely by repentance, "the world" cannot be overcome, sin and darkness cannot be finally burned away. The asceticism of the Church fathers was once a new word, a new thing in the world, a heroic challenge to the old nature, to the old Adam. But to-day the asceticism of the Fathers has faded—it has become a mortal prison for the new man, for our new times. The revolutionary spirit of asceticism has changed into petrifaction and inertia. St. Isaac the Syrian was palpitatingly alive in his time and will remain so for ever. His work was revolutionary: it carried on a super-human struggle against the old nature: it had dynamic force for the greatest resistance to nature. To-day St. Isaac the Syrian, great and eternal, may become a source of death for us. The wrestlers of the spirit were mobile—now their work has lost its mobility. Now the world is moving towards new forms of ascetic discipline. The old experience of humility and obedience has turned into something evil. And it is necessary to enter the way of religious disobedience to the world and the evil of the world when the spirit of death is sensed in the fruits of obedience. Man is to face the world not with humble obedience but rather with creative activity. Even the experience of communion with God comes into the world as an act of creativity; for the once-revolutionary asceticism has turned into conservative guardianship of the past.

In Feofan the Hermit, who in the nineteenth century followed and restored Isaac the Syrian, the centre of gravity is no longer the mystic of resistance to the old nature, not transfer into another life, but first and foremost obedience to the results of sin and the justification of what is; the preservation of all the forms of that life. From this senseless ascetic mysticism was derived a system of living based on the maintenance of the things of this life, the life of "this world". The creative spirit is definitely recognized as sinful. Christianity itself, once young, new and revolutionary, has become lifeless and petrified. What once was life for others, has now become for us only a dead formula urged upon us from outside. The New Testament has become a religion of the scribes and Pharisees.

§

Our Christianity is no longer young—soon it will be 2,000 years old. The Christian Church is old. And we cannot measure Christianity by the individual age of a man, his personal merit, by the degree of his victory over sin. Each one of us is not thirty or forty or even fifty years old, if one counts by the time of the individual's conversion, but 2,000 years old. Each of us receives the world-religious experience of Christianity. Christianity is measured by times and seasons on a world-scale. It would be stupid to calculate Christian growth by our brief lives. The world-growth of Christianity, the times and seasons of its religious revelation in the world, do not depend upon my personal merits in the conflict with sin. I may have a larger revelation, not because I am a better man, more perfect in a religious way, less sinful, than one who lived a thousand years ago but rather because I live in another time and season, because Christianity has now ripened further on the universal scale. The adult is not better or less sinful than the child: but to him more has been revealed. Only an individualistic consciousness attempts to measure Christianity by individual growth.

To make the degree of revelation exclusively dependent on the degree of the individual's upward progress would be confessing religious individualism. But this individualism is in conflict with the very idea of the Church as a universal organism, which has its own super-personal life. There is a religious growth not only of man as an individual organism but of the Church as a universal organism. At the present time the universal organism of the Church is approaching its 2,000th birthday and is living through a crisis in connection with the times and seasons of the world. The perfection of the individual in his conflict with sin, and even individual saintliness, are powerless before this world-crisis of growth, before this entrance into another cosmic epoch, another stage of revelation. And this other stage of revelation, this other cosmic epoch, is not at all connected with man's great holiness or saintliness, as religious individualism thinks.

168

There used to be more saintliness than we have now. The saintliness in our world has diminished—it is as though man had been deprived of the gift of saintliness. And if we are to expect a new revelation, a religious renaissance out of personal saintliness, then man's situation is hopeless, tragically hopeless. Christianity, as a New Testament revelation of redemption, is becoming decrepit. The Christian blood is cooling off and all sorts of restoratory measures are being used to warm it up again. You cannot produce youth artificially. And Christian saintliness was related to Christianity's youth. In Christian saintliness there is an eternal and undying truth, but a truth which is incomplete, in which not everything has been revealed. Alone, this old and eternal Christian saintliness is unable to lead man over into a world-creative epoch. Each of us, poor Christian that he may be, having scarcely learned how properly to make the sign of the cross and having accumulated almost no spiritual gifts, is already living in a religious epoch other than that of the greatest of the saints and hence cannot simply start his Christian life from the beginning. Each of us receives a 2,000-year-old Christianity and this lays upon each of us a burden of world responsibility. The responsibility for the world-growth of Christianity, and not merely our personal growth, is laid upon us.

The root of the confusion and difficulty in our Christian life, its lack of health and its crisis, lies in this interweaving and mingling of two religious ages. The purely individualistic comprehension of the present stage of development of Christianity is a source of religious reaction and feebleness. The universal concept of this stage of growth calls us to creativeness and to re-birth. The individualist consciousness does not know the stages of the world's development and its epoch of revelation, hence it has no presentiment of the world's new epoch. This enfeebled individual Christian consciousness is now going through a stage of unhealthy depression and powerlessness. The old Christian consciousness which fearfully closed its eyes to man's religious growth, obliging him to undertake bold creativity, is doomed to disappear because we no longer have the sainthood and saintly living which there was in the youth of Christianity. Powerless envy of the religious life of the past gnaws at the Christians of to-day. This constant spiritual depression paralyses creativeness and gives birth only to religious cowardice. This eternal discouragement because one is powerless to become a saint is unworthy: this does not increase saintliness by one iota. And for the decadence of Christian life to-day it is not the worst who are responsible, but the best among the believers. We cannot depend entirely on the saints: we must take action ourselves. The old Christian individualistic consciousness does not wish to recognize the profound crisis of the anthropological element as it goes on throughout the whole of modern history. None of to-day's *startsi* (outstanding and specially revered monks) can give a reply to Nietzsche's torment: he answers him only with a condemnation of his sins. By the same token the *starets* has no answer for the heroes of Dostoevski. The new man is born in torment, he passes through abysses which the saints of old never knew. We are facing a new consciousness of the relationship between the saint and the genius, between redemption and creativeness.

§

At the beginning of the nineteenth century there lived the greatest Russian genius, Pushkin, and the greatest Russian saint, Seraphim of Sarov. Pushkin and St. Seraphim lived in different worlds; they did not know each other, and never had contact of any kind. Two equally noble majesties of holiness and of genius—they are incomparable, impossible of measurement by one standard—it is as though they bebelonged to two different sorts of being. The Russian soul may be equally proud of Pushkin's genius and of the saintliness of Seraphim. And it would be equally impoverished if either Pushkin or St. Seraphim should be taken away from it. And here I pose the question: For the destiny of Russia, for the destiny of the world, for the purposes of God's providence, would it have been better if in the Russia of the early nineteenth century there had lived not the great St. Seraphim and the great genius Pushkin, but two Seraphims—two saints—St. Seraphim in the Tambov Government and St. Alexander in Pskov? If Alexander Pushkin had been a saint like Seraphim he would not have been a genius, he would not have been a poet, he would not have been a creator. But a religious consciousness which recognizes saintliness like that of Seraphim as the only way of spiritual uprising will have to recognize genius like that of Pushkin as void of religious value, imperfect and sinful. It was only because of his religious frailty, his sinfulness and imperfection, that Pushkin was a poet-genius and not a saint like Seraphim. It would have been better for the divine purpose if two saints had existed, rather than one saint and one poet. Pushkin's work cannot be evaluated religiously, for genius is not recognized by means of spiritual upsurge and the creative work of a genius is not considered religious. The "worldly" work of Pushkin cannot be compared with the "spiritual" work of St. Seraphim. In the best case Pushkin's creative work is admitted and justified by religious consciousness but it is not considered a religious work. And it would have been better for Pushkin to imitate Seraphim, retire from the world in a monastery, enter the way of ascetic spiritual wrestling. In that case Russia would have been deprived of its greatest genius, would have suffered loss of its creativity. But the creativity of genius is only the reverse side of sin and religious poverty. Thus think the fathers and teachers of a religion of redemption. For redemption, creativeness is not necessary, only saintliness. The saint creates himself, another and more perfect being. The genius creates great works, accomplishes great deeds in the world. Only creation can save itself. The creation of great values may lead to ruin. St. Seraphim created nothing but himself and by this alone he transfigured the world. Pushkin created great, immeasurable values for Russia and the world but did not create himself. The creativeness of a genius is a sort of self-sacrifice. The work of a saint is first of all an ordering of himself. We may say that Pushkin destroyed his soul in the creative outflowing of his own genius. Seraphim saved his soul by spiritual effort within himself. The way of personal purification and upsurge (in yogism, in Christian asceticism, in Tolstoyism, in occultism) may be hostile towards creativity.

And now the question arises: In the creative ecstasy of the genius is there not perhaps another kind of sainthood before God, another type of religious action, equal in value to the canonical sainthood? I deeply believe that before God the genius of Pushkin, who in the eyes of men seemed to lose his own soul, is equal to the sainthood of Seraphim, who was busy saving his. The way of genius is another type of religious way, equal in value and equal in dignity with the way of the saint. The creativity of the genius is not "worldly" but truly "spiritual" activity. It is a blessing that in Russia there lived St. Seraphim and the genius Pushkin, rather than two saints. For God's purposes in the world, the genius of Pushkin is just as necessary as the sainthood of Seraphim. What a loss it would have been had the genius of Pushkin not been given us from above—a whole group of saints could not make up for such a loss. With the sainthood of Seraphim, alone, without the genius of Pushkin, the creative purposes of the world cannot be achieved. It is not that all cannot be saints, not all should be; not all of us are called by God to be saints. Sainthood is election and calling. And from the religious viewpoint he who is not called and predestined should not set out upon the way of sainthood. It would have been a religious crime before God and before men if Pushkin, in fruitless effort to become a saint, had ceased to write poetry. The idea of a calling is essentially a religious and not a "worldly" idea, and the fulfilment of a call is a religious duty. He who does not live out his calling buries his talent in the earth, commits a grave sin before God. Men are elected and called to the way of genius just as they are to the way of

172

sainthood. One may be fated to be a genius, just as one may be fated to be a saint. Pushkin was fated to be a genius-creator and he not only could not have been a saint, he should not, he dared not, be one. In Pushkin's creative genius there was gathered together the experience of a creative-world-epoch, a religious epoch. In every truly creative genius, there has been the sainthood of the creative epoch, another kind of sainthood, more sacrificial than ascetic and canonic sainthood. Genius is another kind of sainthood, but it can be recognized and canonized only in the revelation of creativeness. Genius is the sainthood of daring rather than of obedience. Life cannot be completely dissolved in sainthood without a residue, exaltedly harmonized and made logical. Perhaps a virtuous humility is not always pleasing to God. In the dark womb of life there ever remains some rebellious and God-resisting blood and the pulse of free, creative instinct.

The creative way of genius demands sacrifice—no less sacrifice than that demanded by the way of sainthood. On the way of the creative genius it is just as necessary to abjure "the world", to overcome "the world", as on the way of the saint. But the way of creative genius demands still another sacrifice: the sacrifice of an assured position, of assured salvation. He who has entered on the creative way, the way of genius, must give up the quiet havens of life, must renounce the building of his own house, the safe and assured ordering of his personality. Only he is capable of this sacrifice, who in it can transcend the bounds of "the world". The way of creative genius means casting off from all the safe coastlines. The way of sainthood is a difficult way of ceaseless effort and demands extraordinary spiritual power, renunciation of the lower spheres of being. But the way of sainthood includes the safe assurance of personal order. Genius is essentially tragic: it is not containable in "the world", and not accepted by "the world". The creative genius never responds to the demands of the world—he never fulfils the world's orders, he does not come under any of the world's categories. In genius there is always something of the unsuccessful from "the world's" point of view, almost uselessness for "the world". Genius is incomprehensible to "the world"; it does not classify under any of the world's differentiated categories of human activity. Genius cannot be objectivized in the creation of a differentiated culture: it is not related to any specific form of culture, does not produce any specific cultural values. In genius there is nothing specific—it is always a universal sense of things, a universal upsurge towards another kind of being. Genius is integral being, universal quality: genius is always the quality of a man, not only of an artist, a savant, a thinker or a social worker. Genius is religious in nature, for it involves resistance to "this world" by man's whole spirit; it is a universal assumption of another world and a universal impulse towards it. Genius is another ontology of human existence, its holy inadaptability to "this world". Genius is "another world" in man, man's nature "not of this world". Genius controls man like a demon. And genius is a revelation of man's creative nature, his calling to creativity.

The fate of genius in the pre-creative epochs of world history was always sacrificial and tragic. In genius there is revealed the sacrificial quality of all creativity, its incompatibility with the "safe and sound" worldly attitudes. Creativeness as revealed in genius is a sentence to perdition in this world. The genius is unable to defend himself in this world, he is incapable of adaptation to this world's demands. Hence the life of a genius is one of sacrificial heroism. The life of a genius holds moments of ecstatic happiness but it does not know peace and calm joy; it is always in tragic disharmony with the world around it. The sad fate of genius is all too well known. Even those men of genius whose lives were externally fortunate, as for instance Goethe or L. Tolstoy, internally were often near suicide and did not know real peace of mind. But the quality of genius is broader than the man of genius. In the strict sense of the word, few real geniuses are born. There is a bit of genius in

174

many men who cannot be called geniuses in themselves. Potential genius is inherent in man's creative nature and there is something of genius in every universal creative effort. There are persons who by their ontological nature or by their creative inadaptability to this world have a quality of genius, but they are not geniuses. The quality of genius is a special virtue, not given to every one, a special sense of the world, a special tension of the will, a special power of desire of something other, which may be confirmed and developed.

Genius is radically different from talent, has nothing in common with talent. Talent is a differentiated gift, specific, corresponding to the demands of various forms of culture. Talent is the quality of an artist, a savant, a social worker, but not the quality of a man. Genius is the union of a nature having the quality of genius with some specific talent. Thus an artist who is a genius combines in himself this "genial" nature with artistic talent. The nature of talent is not organic not ontological, but functional. The nature of talent is not universal. Talent does not know sacrifice or fatality. Talent may produce more perfect objective values than genius. It had adaptability to the demands of differentiated culture; it lies partly in success. From the viewpoint of culture, genius is not canonic while talent is. In genius man's whole spiritual nature palpitates with his desire for another type of being. In talent the differentiated function of the spirit is incarnate, adapted to the world's requirements. The nature with genius in it may burn out without having brought into the world anything of value. Talent usually produces values and is suitably esteemed. Talent is moderate and measured. Genius is always measureless. The nature of genius is always revolutionary. Talent acts in the midst of culture, with its "arts and sciences". Genius acts in ends and beginnings and knows no bounds whatever. Talent is obedience; genius is boldness and daring. Talent is of "this world"; genius, of another. In the fate of genius there is the holiness of sacrifice which is not found in the fate of talent.

§

The cult of saintliness should be complemented by the cult of genius, for the way of genius involves sacrificial heroism and the creative ecstasy of genius is no less religious than the ecstasy of sainthood. Transition into a creative religious epoch should first of all bring a recognition of the religious nature of genius. Not saintliness alone, but genius also, is a way. And if genius is not given to all, neither is sainthood. But the potentiality of genius, like the potentiality of holiness, lies in every image and likeness of God. The Creator fore-ordained man for genius. The creative experience of genius will be recognized as religiously equal in value with the ascetic experience of saintliness. Just as the will to saintliness has been recognized as a religious imperative, so the will to genius will also be recognized as a religious imperative. The ontological element of genius must be affirmed and developed as religious activity, as a way to overcoming "this world". *A will to genius is already possible because genius is will, first of all, a passionate will and desire for another kind of being.* And the will to incapacity is also possible, always connected with spiritual hesitancy and cowardice. Incapacity is a sin, the wrong definition of one's place and calling in the world. The will to incapacity is always a timorous adaptability to the world. The will to genius is a courageous overcoming of "the world". Genius is a positive revelation of the image and likeness of God in man, a revelation of man's creative nature, a nature which is "not of this world".

The old Christian consciousness tried to believe that in the higher degrees of saintliness, in the experience of the saints, there is revealed the creative secret of being, a secret surpassing that which is revealed in the creativity of genius. According to the old Christian consciousness, remaining entirely in the religion of redemption, saintliness is the only way to the secrets of being. On the higher stages of his spiritual ascent, everything is revealed to the saint: higher

176

knowledge, higher beauty and the secret of creativeness. According to this viewpoint, all the higher gifts are received as a reward for saintliness and outside this way of holiness they are unobtainable. Only holiness is the revelation of the creative secret of being. Only the saint is the true gnostic and the true poet. The saint in his contemplation learns the final secrets of being, and in developing his own saintliness he creates beauty. This consciousness leaves nothing to genius: everything is given over to saintliness. But can we admit that the gnostic gift or the poetic gift depend on saintliness or on religious-moral perfection? Is not the laborious sweat of all human effort opposed to every gift? And is not the gift of saintliness a special gift, different from the gnostic, the poetic, or others? I think the gnostic gift in Jakob Boehme was far stronger than in St. Francis, and the poetic gift in Pushkin was more powerful than in St. Seraphim of Sarov. To the genius of Boehme and Pushkin there were revealed things which were not revealed to the saintliness of Francis and Seraphim. Men who are imperfect and are not saints sometimes possess more knowledge and more beauty than the saints and the perfect ones. Saintliness is not the only gift of God, and is not the only way to Him.

The gifts of God are endlessly varied, the ways of God are varied, and in the house of the Father there are many mansions. There were saints who had a special gift of the mystic contemplation of divine mystery, but this gnostic gift was not present in all saints, by a long way. Other saints had the gift of beauty. Thus St. Francis was extraordinarily gifted with the sense of beauty; he was a poet. St. Seraphim possessed the gift of mystic contemplation. But there have been many saints who were very poor in the gifts of knowledge or beauty, who were not at all gnostics or poets. And not all the saints were mystics. At the same time there were great mystics who contemplated the higher secrets of being but who were not at all saintly. Poets have rarely been saints. That religious consciousness is deadened and reactionary which does not have the courage of creative

177

effort, of the daring act of creating knowledge or beauty, because it considers this heroic action only the portion of the saints; it takes from man the burden of free initiative, the burden of responsibility for revealing the secrets of creativeness. On this soil there grows up a powerless and unconscious envy of saintliness, a hesitant and cowardly inactivity in any kind of creative action. Those who are not foreordained to be saints should not dare to know how to create beauty and another kind of life. But then, religiously, we should condemn all the geniuses of the world, since they ventured to create without being saints. And in Christianity there is inherent not only a laborious sense of life, based on service in the sweat of man's brow, but a sense of life which is a gift. Every gift is something free, and only what is freely given is a gift. It is just Christianity which teaches of free grace, and in this it differs deeply from the religious consciousness of India which teaches of the law of Karma and will not hear of anything like free grace or free gifts of any kind. The new consciousness of the creative epoch must recognize in the psychological sphere the equal value of genius and saintliness.

§

On the way of creative genius it is possible that a special new type of monasticism should arise. This way demands no less renunciation of "the world" and its goods than the way of monasticism as now recognized. The life of genius is a monastic life in "the world". And the virtue of creative genius is the virtue of renunciation of peaceful order in personal living. The timorous refusal to take the creative road of genius gives quiet and security. The uncreative renunciation of the world's goods is rewarded with a firm and secure ordering of one's personal life and with personal salvation. But obedience to the results of sin makes man's life in "the world" secure. If you do not count the saints and the mystics in the monasteries, the "elders" and spiritual heroes, the monastic life is splendidly adapted to "the world" and

178

"the worldly", and there is no tragic sacrifice at all. The moderate asceticism which is practiced in monasteries is well equipped for adaptation to "the world", to everyday positivism and utilitarianism. There is a positivist type of asceticism which can be perfectly well carried on in "the world". But creative genius can never accept any kind of positivism. And the monasticism of the creative, the monasticism of the order of genius, demands more radical renunciation of the world and all its positive constructions than did the old monasticism. In fact, a positive-utilitarian economic approach and a "worldly" adaptability are characteristic for the "spiritual" world and the "spiritual" way of life. When you read the works of Feofan the Hermit, that classic spokesman of the orthodox of the nineteenth century, you are astounded at his combination of the mystic and ascetic with a positive-utilitarianism ordering of life and maintenance of quiet, his adaptation of the religion of salvation to the results of sin, i.e. to "the world". Bishop Feofan preaches an ideal of economic accountability and even a moderate accumulation of property. For a family it is even well to become rich. One does not have to strain too much to rise higher, spiritually; one does not need to be too spiritual. The worldly, bourgeois order of life is excellently justified by Feofan's asceticism. In his religious consciousness there is no place for tragic willingness to sacrifice. But only the religious way of creativeness carries mystic asceticism out to the real overcoming of this world, to the setting up of "another world". The old Christian consciousness inevitably passes over from the ascetic renunciation of "the world" to positive adaptation to it. In genius, the creative secrets of being are revealed, i.e. "the other world". But creativity and genius have a deep and mysterious connection with sex, and this connection must be comprehended religiously.

# CHAPTER VIII

# CREATIVITY AND SEX: MALE AND FEMALE: RACE AND PERSONALITY

THE STRONG FEELING of the central position of the problem of sex is characteristic of our epoch, as well as a deep desire to comprehend the elements of sex. It is as though sex had suddenly come into notice, something secret had become known. Man's concept and feeling for the world depends on sex. Sex is the source of being; the polarity of sex is the foundation of creation. The sense of being, its intensity and its colouring, has its roots in sex. With ever increasing acuity men begin to recognize, scientifically, philosophically and religiously, that sexuality is not a special, differentiated function of the human being, that is diffused throughout his whole being, penetrates all his cells and determines the whole of his life. To-day we cannot separate sex from the whole of life: we cannot assign to it only the importance of a special function of the organism. Sex is vastly broader and deeper than that which we are accustomed to call the sexual function in a specific sense. The specific sex function is itself the result of the differentiation of some sort of general, pre-sexual life. We cannot draw a sharp line scientifically between the normal and natural in sex and the abnormal and unnatural. This boundary line has been drawn not by the natural order of things but by general social morality, in which there is always very much of the conditional. From the philosophical viewpoint, we should do away with the category of "naturalness" as a criterion of good and evil. The "normal" and "natural" sexual function is the product of the differentiation of sex-life, outflowing through the whole physical and spiritual being of man. It is quite possible to say that man is a sexual being, but we cannot say that man is a food-digesting being. Man's sexual nature cannot be placed on the same level with other functions of his organism, even the most essential, such as the circulation of the blood. In man's sexuality we perceive the metaphysical roots of his being. Sex is the meeting-point of two worlds in the human organism. In this point of sex is hidden the secret of being. We cannot escape from sex. We may leave aside the differentiated function of sex, we may deny or conquer this "natural" function. But in this case man's sexual function is only transferred—and man still remains a sexual being.

Christian asceticism, having overcome the physical sexual life, was still powerfully conscious of the central problem of sex in man—felt it more strongly than many modern people who are living an ordered "natural" sex-life. Asceticism is one of the metaphysics of sex. St. Isaac the Syrian lives in the consciousness of the power and the central place of sex. This strong feeling lies behind his terrible words: "If you are compelled to speak with women, turn your face from the sight of them, and so converse with them. And from nuns, meeting or conversing with them, flee the sight of their faces, as you would flee from fire or the devil's net, so that in your heart your love towards God should not cool, and your heart should not be soiled by even the shade of passion. Even if they are your own sisters, guard yourself from them as from strangers. Beware of contact with your own kin, that your heart should not cool to the love of God. Better take deadly poison than to eat with women, even though they be your mother or your sister. Better for you to live with a serpent than to sleep under one blanket with a young man, even though it be your own brother." It would be a fatal error to identify sex with the sexual act, as is often done. A denial of the sexual act is not denial of sex. And a too-ardent refusal of the sexual-act is an ardent evidence of sex in man. Weakness or lack of interest in the sexual act is no proof of the weakness of sex in a man, for the sex-energy flowing out through man's whole being may have many expressions and take many directions. When it is said that a man has conquered sex in himself by the power of spiritual creativeness, this formula is only the surface of the phenomenon. In such a case sex has not been overcome, but sex energy has merely been given another direction—it is directed towards creativity.

In general the importance of the sexual act for sex-life as a whole must not be exaggerated. Sex-life is possible, even much more intense, without the sexual act. The sexual act, the sexual function, is conquerable, but sex is unconquerable. Asceticism can only transpose sexual energy, give it another direction, but it cannot conquer sex. Sex is related not to some part, but to the whole man. Sex is not merely one of many sides of man—it includes and determines the whole. Whatever way man turns, he is followed everywhere by sex-energy, and this leaves its stamp on all his activities. In everything we find the cross-section of sex. In knowledge itself there is an element of masculine activity and feminine passivity. Sex is related to the very secret of man's being and hence it has remained the element most shrouded in mystery. In all ages men have felt the uncanny relationship of sex with birth and death and hence it could never be considered by men as a special function (an important function but still less important than eating, for instance). It would be awkward and superficial to assert that a man who lives in sexual continence has no sex life. Even absolute chastity, of body as well as of spirit, predicates a sexual life. Chastity is through and through a sexual phenomenon—it is one of the directions taken by sexual energy. Man's integrity, his "whole-ness", is best maintained in chastity and hence sex-energy is not expressed in the fractional function of the sexual act—there is not even the thought of such fractionalization. The fractional function of the sexual act is a loss of integral sex-energy: it alienates this energy from the integral being of man. But chastity is not integral denial of sex— chastity means maintaining the integrity of sex, the concentration of sex-energy in man's integral nature as a whole.

182

The opposite of chastity, dissipation, is an extreme degree of the fractionalization of sex-energy, alienating it from man's integral nature; it is a loss of integrity. And in the sexual act there is necessarily an element of dissipation, for it is a fractionalization of sex-energy and its alienation from the integral life of body and spirit, making sex into a partial function. Virginity is not a denial, a minimizing or even the absence of sex; virginity is positive sex-energy; it is the maintenance of the integrity of sex, the refusal to let it be fractionalized. From this standpoint the very origin, out of the depths of sex, of a differentiated sex-function is in a way man's fall—the loss of integrity, the beginning of dissipation in the deepest sense of that word. For, in the true sex-life, one may give one's whole self but one cannot give a part—one cannot cut oneself in pieces. Sex is a cosmic force and may be comprehended only in the cosmic aspect.

§

From the fact that a person is identified either as a man or as a woman, it is clear that sex is an element diffused through all man's being and not a differentiated function. If sex is an infirmity, then it is an organic infirmity, not a functional infirmity of man's whole organism, physical and meta-physical. Sex is not only the point of contact of two worlds in man, but also the point of contact between man and the cosmos, microcosmos and macrocosmos. Man is joined with the cosmos first of all by sex. In sex we have the source of man's true connection with the cosmos and of his servile dependence. The categories of sex, male and female, are cosmic categories, not merely anthropological categories. The Christian symbolism of the Logos and the soul of the world, of Christ and His Church, speaks of the cosmic mysticism of male and female, of the cosmic conjugal mystery. Not in man alone, but in the cosmos as well, there is the sexual division into male and female and their sexual union. The spirit of the world, the earth, is feminine in its relation to the Logos—the light-bringing Man—and thirsts

183

for union with the Logos, longs to receive Him within herself. The earth, the bride, awaits her bridegroom, Christ. Nature awaits its ruler, man.

In the world order of things, the masculine is predominantly an anthropological human element: the feminine is a natural, cosmic element. The male, man, is related to the cosmos and to nature through woman; without the feminine element he would be cut off from the spirit of the world, from the mother earth. The woman, aside from connection with the man, would not be a complete person: the dark, natural element, impersonal and subconscious, is too strong in her. In the female element, separate from the masculine, there is no personality. The man recognizes the active purpose of the "anthropos" in regard to the cosmos and the necessity of overcoming all time and every hour. The woman is a part of the cosmos, but not a microcosm—she does not know the cosmos, for she thinks the cosmos is her own temporary condition, for instance her unrequited love.

But the world-differentiation into male and female can never finally wipe out the basic genuine bisexuality, the androgynous quality in man—the image and likeness of God in him. In truth neither man nor woman is the image and likeness of God but only the androgyne—the youth-maiden, the integral bisexual man. The differentiation into male and female is a result of the cosmic fall of Adam. Created in the image and likeness of God, the androgyne man falls apart, separates from himself the natural female element, is alienated from the cosmos and falls slave to the power of feminine nature. According to the remarkable teaching of Jakob Boehme, Sophia, the eternal virginity of man, flies away into heaven. But the feminine nature becomes person-less and powerless. Male and female are separated in man as the microcosm and in the world as macrocosm. And sex, differentiated and fallen—becomes the source, in the world, of tormenting, insatiable thirst for union. In truth the secret of every quarrel and the secret of every union is a sex secret. The disfigurement of the image

184

and likeness of God in man was the falling-apart of the androgyne, the male-female being. But this disfiguration and falling-apart could not be complete or final. The image and likeness of God was still preserved in man, in both man and woman; man remained in the roots of his being androgyne, a bisexual being. This is now beginning to be recognized anew by science, philosophy and religion. Man would be irrevocably lost if the androgynous image in him should disappear completely.

In all times, in various ways men have felt and recognized that all man's sexual life is only a tormenting and intense seeking for his lost androgynism, for the union of man and woman in one integral being. Plato, in his *Symposion*, has expressed this most profoundly. From earliest times it has also been felt and acknowledged that the root of man's fall was connected with sex, that man's sinful life, fettered in natural necessity, was preceded by the fall of the androgyne, the separation into male and female, the disfigurement of the image and likeness of God, and the slavish subjection of both male and female to natural-necessary attraction. The setting apart of the female element in the first mother Eve was the source of man's enslavement to natural necessity. Woman became the central, perhaps the only, weakness of man, the point of his enslavement to nature, which had become for him terribly foreign and strange. The natural became inwardly alien to man, who had remained the bearer of the anthropological element, and hence outwardly it became compulsory. Man attempts to restore his androgynous image through sexual attraction towards the lost feminine nature. But the whole of sexual life goes on in a strange natural-necessity. Man has become the slave of sexual attraction, the victim of his fallen "dividedness". The antique world produced the phallic cult, which became impossible in the Christian era; but the phallic cult is a bottomless deep and, even in a Christian era, men are powerless to free themselves from it. In the phallic cult there was expressed the intense, orgiastic thirst for the union of the two separated sexes, the urgent petition for cosmic sexual union. In it that phase of sex was deified in which alone the greatest contact and union of male and female was possible in our fallen world. Through this phase of sex man touches the veritable secret of being. In these forms of sex there is at once the greatest possible estrangement and conflict, and also the unifying contact by which a breaking-out through the boundaries of male and female is accomplished. The phallic cult is tragically powerless—it leaves man a slave but it is deeper than the modern secularized life of sex. And in every sexual love there is an enlightened and transfigured experience of the phallic cult.

§

Jakob Boehme's teaching of the androgyne and Sophia is very profound. "You are a youth or a maiden—but Adam was both in one person. Out of his lust Adam lost the virgin and in his lust he received the woman. But the virgin still awaits him, and if he only should desire to enter into a new birth, she would receive him again, with great honour." Boehme makes the distinction between the virgin and the woman. The virgin was the Sophia of the first Adam, whom he lost in the Fall. "Eve was created for this corruptible life, for she is the woman of this world." "But the wisdom of God is the eternal Virgin, rather than woman: she is immaculate purity and virtue and stands as an image of God and a like- ness to the Trinity." "This all-wisdom of God, who is the Virgin of beauty and an image of the Trinity, is in herself an image of man and the angels and has her origin in the centre of the cross, like a flower springing forth from the spirit of God." The "Sophia" quality of man is connected with his quality as androgyne. The fall of the androgyne meant the loss of the Virgin Sophia and the appearance of the woman, Eve. "The virgin is eternal, uncreated and unborn: she is the All-wisdom of God and a likeness of Divinity." Boehme's mystic doctrine of man as androgynous makes understandable why Jesus Christ, the absolute and

186

perfect Man, never knew a woman and in His own life did not realize the sacrament of marriage. The first Adam, also, did not know a woman, and was not married. "Adam was a man, and equally a woman, and yet neither, but rather a Virgin full of virtue, purity and incorruptibility, as an image of God. He had within himself the tincture of fire and the tincture of light in the gleams of which there rested his love for himself, as a sort of virginal centre, like a beautiful rose-garden, or garden of pleasure, in which he loved himself. And we shall resemble him after the resurrection of the dead, since according to Christ's words there they neither marry or are given in marriage, but live like the angels of God." "Christ on the Cross liberated our virginal image from both man and woman and in Divine love encrimsoned it with his heavenly blood." Christ restored the androgynous image of man and returned the Virgin-Sophia to him. "The image of God is man-virgin, neither woman nor man." "The Fire-soul must be tempered in the fire of God, and become brighter than pure gold, for it is the husband of the noble Sophia, out of the woman's seed. It is of the tincture of fire, just as Sophia is of the tincture of light. When the tincture of fire is completely purified, Sophia will be restored to it, Adam will again embrace his all-honourable bride, who was taken away from him at the time of his first sleep, and will become neither man nor woman, but only a branch on the jewelled tree of Christ which stands in God's paradise." "The woman, like Adam's virginity, was transformed or formed out of Adam's nature and being into a woman or a female, which, although lost to God, still maintained a holy virginity, as a tincture of love and light, but maintained it in a dead or faded form." Jesus again united in himself the male and female into one androgynous image and became "man-virgin". "Christ was then born of the Virgin in order to sanctify anew the feminine tincture and change it into masculine so that man and woman should become 'man-virgins', just as Christ was."

For Boehme the distinction between virgin and woman,

between Sophia and Eve, is important. His doctrine of Sophia is deeper and more complete than the cult of eternal virginity which we learn from Dante, Goethe or Vladimir Soloviev. Even the cult of the Mother of God as illuminated womanhood is not the final thing, for the Mother of God is still in the line of Eve, and is mystically like her. The cult of womanliness corresponds to man's passivity: in him the anthropological consciousness has not yet awakened. The cult of womanliness after all remains within the limits of the old man, from whom the womanly has been separated and set over against him, that is, until his new birth. Elements of a religion of feminine divinity slip into this cult. Into the pure cult of the Virgin Mary it is easy to mingle the idealization of the Woman, Eve. Christian mysticism still remains in a sexual polarization. But the consciousness of the anthropos must attain complete liberation from its immersion in the feminine sexual element, in this attractive and absorbing sexual polarity. The cult of the pure Virgin, carried out logically, leads to the cult of the androgyne and to Boehme's doctrine of Sophia as the divine virgin immanent in man. Boehme's doctrine of Sophia had as its objective the virginity of the soul, man's lost *Jungfraulichkeit*. We find the doctrine of the androgyne already in the Kabbala. And in their own ways certain of the Church Fathers had a foretaste of it, for example, St. Maxim the Confessor.

In the nineteenth century Franz von Baader revived Boehme's doctrine of the androgyne and of Sophia. Baader says that the idea of the androgyne should not have been foreign to the theologians, "least of all should the idea of a virginal androgynity have been strange to the theologian, since Mary gave birth without having known a man". "The nature of the soul is virginally androgynous, that is, each soul contains its nature (earth, bodiliness) within, and not outside itself." Baader sees the purpose of married love in the restoration of man's lost virginal nature, an androgynous nature. "Thus the secret and the sacrament of true love in the indissoluble bond of the two lovers, consists in each

188

helping the other, each in himself, towards the restoration of the androgyne, the pure and whole humanity, which is neither man nor woman, that is, nothing half and half." "The androgyne conditions the indwelling of God in man. Without this concept of the androgyne, the central concept of religion, that of the Image of God, remains uncomprehended." "The divine Sophia (idea) was the helper of the virginal human who was neither man nor woman: this human being, through his connection with her (Sophia), a connection which could not be sexual, should have confirmed the androgynity and thus eliminate the possibility of becoming man or woman. And even now, after the human being has become man and woman this same Sophia, as often as anyone turns to her inwardly, makes both man and woman participants, at least inwardly, of the androgynous, angelic nature." "God's will can be received only in a pure Virgin, that is, one free of all creative-will, and just as the earthly Virgin (Maria) was blessed by the awakening of the heavenly virgin in her, so every rebirth must receive a similar blessing. Virginity is purity from all creature-will." Man's rebirth as androgyne will mean his acceptance within himself of the whole of nature, the genuine revelation of man as microcosm. In the true birth of the integral man, both God and nature will be within and not outside him. External objectivity was bound up with sexual fractionization.

The teaching of the great mystics about the androgyne, about woman and about love, is reflected in a distorted form in Weininger. He gives a philosophical basis to the idea of the bisexuality of the human being. He considers woman to be the result of the fall of man. In the erotic, he sees a restoration of the integral androgynous nature of man. In Weininger the crisis of racial sex attains final acuteness. He feels the sinfulness of sexual life no less strongly than the Church Fathers did. And still there is lacking in him the something which would have made him the proclaimer of a great truth. Weininger has no contact with religious realities and hence he is speaking of the un-real woman. But woman is just as real as man or man is just as unreal as woman. In his teaching of the erotic, he strives towards the mystical, and the erotic then redeems him from the sin of sexuality.

§

Woman is the bearer of the sex-element in this world. In man sex is more differentiated and specialized: in woman it is diffused through the whole tissue of the organism, through the whole structure of the soul. In man sexual attraction demands more immediate satisfaction than in woman, but he is more independent of sex than is woman: he is a less sexual being. Man is greatly dependent, sexually, on woman; he has a weakness for the other sex, a radical weakness which may be the source of all his weaknesses. And for man his weakness for woman is something degrading. By himself man is less sexual than woman. In woman there is nothing which is not sexual: she is sexual in her strength and in her weakness, sexual even in the weakness of her sexual desire. Woman is the cosmic universal bearer of the sexual element, of the elemental in sex. The element of sex natural to the genus is a feminine element. The power of the race (genus) over man is realized through woman. This power entered the world of nature and took control of it through the first mother, Eve. Eve is the natural-racial womanliness. The creation of Eve brought the old Adam under the power of race-sexuality, fettered him to the natural world, to "this world". "The world" caught Adam and rules him through sex: Adam is fettered to natural necessity at the point of sexuality. Eve's power over Adam became the power of all nature over him. Man, bound to the birth-giving Eve, became the slave of nature, the slave of a womanliness separate and differentiated from his androgynous image and likeness of God. The attitude of the male man towards womanliness is the root of his attitude towards nature. He can escape neither womanliness nor nature—there is nowhere where he can get away. Deliverance is possible only through the new Adam, who comes into the world through a new womanliness.

190

The sinful power of female nature over the fallen man began with the woman, Eve: with the Virgin Mary began man's liberation from that natural power. In the Virgin Mary the earth takes into its bosom the Logos, the new Adam, the Absolute Man. *And if the fall and enslavement of the old Adam, the old man, confirmed in the world the rule of natural-racial birth through the sexual act, the new Adam, the new man, could be born only of a virgin, who conceived by the Spirit.*

This new birth from a virgin was a mystical conquest of the old birth in the natural order of "this world". Eternal womanliness, as the basis of a new world, liberated from sin, shall not give birth as the result of the sexual act of man. Eternal womanliness bears within itself release from natural necessity, since natural necessity rules over man only through the birthgiving sex. The religion of redemption denies both race and the sexual act, and sets up the cult of eternal womanliness, the cult of a Virgin giving birth only through the Spirit.

§

Sex life in this world is radically defective and spoiled. Sexual attraction torments man with an inescapable thirst for union. In truth this thirst is inescapable and union is unattainable in natural sex-life. The differentiated sexual act, which is the result of the cosmic fractionalization of the integral androgynic man, is inescapably tragic, painful and meaningless. The sexual act is the highest and most intense point of contact of two polarized sexes: in it each, as it were, goes out of himself into the other, steps out over the boundary of his own sex. Is union attained at this point? Of course not. The one fact alone speaks against the sexual act: that which is so easily profaned may become debauchery, which is diametrically opposed to any mystic of union. The union in the sexual act is illusory and this illusory union always has to be paid for. Sexual union is always momentary, passing and mortal. The ecstasy of the sexual act sets up goals which in the order of nature, where everything is temporary and passing, are unrealized. And this unrealized sexual unity is the permanent illness of the human race, the source of the race's mortality. The fleeting illusion of union in the sexual act is always followed by a reaction, a step backward, disunion. After the sexual act disunion is greater than before it. How often this painful sense of alienation astounds those who expected the ecstasy of union! In this mystic sense the sexual act should be of eternal meaning, union in it should reach the profoundest depths. Two bodies should be turned into one, each should permeate the other fully. Instead of this, there is performed an act of illusory union, all too temporary and all too superficial. The fleeting union is purchased at the cost of still greater disunion. One step forward is accompanied by several steps backward. The union of the two sexes, in its mystical sense, should be the permeation of every cell of our being into every cell of the other, the fusion of a whole body with a whole body, of a whole spirit with a whole spirit. Instead of this, what happens is a partial superficial contact; flesh remains separated from flesh. In the differentiated sexual act itself there is a sort of defectiveness and painfulness. The act of union of the two sexes ought to last for ever, never cease, be accompanied by no step backward into disunion: it should be integral, touching every cell of man's being, profound, endless. Instead, the sexual act in nature gives man over into the power of the evil endlessness of sex-attraction, knowing no end or satisfaction. The source of life in this world is spoiled in its roots; it is the source of man's slavery. The sexual act is inwardly contradictory and goes against the meaning of the world.

Natural sex life is always tragic and hostile to personality. Personality becomes the toy of the genius of race and the irony of the genius of race always accompanies the sexual act. This you can read in Shopenhauer and Darwin. The sexual act is totally impersonal—it is general, and always the same, not only in all men, but also in all animals. In this act there is nothing individual, nothing even specifically human.

192

In the sexual act personality is always caught in the power of the non-personal element of race, the element which makes the human world akin to the world of beasts. The mystical objective of personal union in one flesh is unattainable and unrealizable in a non-personal element. The inescapable tragedy of sex lies in this, that the thirst for personal union, in the natural race-element through the sexual act leads not to personal union but to child-birth, to the disintegration of personality in the begetting of children, to an evil endlessness instead of to a good eternity. In sexual life, which arises out of thirst for enjoyment and satisfaction, it is not the personal objective which triumphs but rather the interests of the race, the continuation of the race. The personal can never be realized through the impersonal. The sexual act is always a partial failure of the personality and its hopes.

Personality does not gain immortality and eternity in the sexual act, but subdivision into a number of new lives being born. The sexual act confirms the evil, endless relay of births and deaths. The birthgiver dies and gives birth to something mortal. Birth is always the sign of unattained completeness of the personality, of eternity unattained. Both the birthgiver and the child which is born are mortal and imperfect. The begetting of children is punishment for the sexual act and at the same time redemption of its sin. Birth and death are mystically bound together in sex. Sex is not only the source of life but of death as well. Through sex men are born and through sex they die. Corruption and death-bringing dis-integration came into the world through sex. Man's person-ality begins to decay and fall apart in sex; it begins to be pulled away from eternity. Sex shackles man to that decadent order of nature in which reigns the endless relay of birth and death. Only the mortal begets, and only the begetter dies. The law of Karma and the endless evolution of reincarnation taught by the religious consciousness of India is nothing other than the necessity of death and birth, connected with the sin of sexuality. Free grace in Christianity abrogates the inevitable results of the law of Karma. There is a profound antagonism between the eternal and perfect life of the personality and the birth of mortal lives in time, between the perspective of personality and the perspective of the race.

Race is the source of the death of personality—race is the source of birth-giving life. The Greeks knew that Hades and Dionysios were the same god—they felt the mystic connection between death and birth. This is why in the very depths of the sexual act, in sexual union, there lurks a deathly anguish. In the birthgiving life of sex there is a foreboding of death. That which gives birth to life carries with it death as well. The joy of sexual union is always a poisoned joy. This deadly poison of sex has always been felt to be sin. In the sexual act there is always the anguish of the shattered hopes of personality, the treasonable surrender of the eternal to the temporal. In the sexual union of this world not only is something born but something always dies. In the depths of the sexual act there is revealed the mystical nearness and relationship between birth and death. The sexual act is performed in the element of the race, outside personality. The sexual urge which holds man in its grasp is the submission of personality to the element of the mortal race. In the life of the race there is predestined the relay of birth and death, the disintegration of personality into an evil multiplicity. In the element of the race there is no way for the upsurge of personality, no road to perfect eternity.

The element of race is the result of man's fall, man who is decadent because of sex. The inward disunion of the fallen and sinful world has its reverse side in the external union in the element of race. The human race is false humanity—it indicates the decadence of humanity. In the human race, human nature is enslaved and oppressed. The racial element is the chief obstacle to the revelation of humanity, the revelation of man's creative nature. Race is an evil necessity —the source of man's slavery and mortal decadence. On the ways of race there is always hidden the fateful relay of birth and death. Man's true relationships by the spirit are basely

194

exchanged for the racial relationships by flesh and blood. People are bound together not by birth from a virgin, from the eternal womanliness in the Spirit, but by birth in the sexual act. The connection of the human race is a sexual connection; it presupposes that sexual act of which people are ashamed as of something unclean. People hypocritically conceal the source of their connection and their union in the human race. And the religion of the human race should be a religion of the sexual act—should lead to the deification of the very thing which people hide and of which they are ashamed. *Relationship by flesh and blood is relationship by the sexual act, an innate relationship.* The great importance of Rozanoff is in the fact that he demanded a religious recognition of this truth and of all the consequences proceeding from it.

Liberating the personality from the sexual act is liberation from the race, breaking the racial connection for the sake of another relationship by the spirit; it is escape out of the evil infinity of birth and death. The race and the personality are profoundly antagonistic—the two are mutually incompatible. Everything personal in man is hostile to racial sexuality. In personality a supreme concentration of sexual energy is possible. Without this energy a strong personality is impossible. But this energy cannot be directed towards race: it resists decline into an evil plurality. Personality recognizes itself and realizes itself outside the racial element. Personality cannot conquer death and win eternity on the basis of racial relationship. It must be born to life in a new humanity. After all, the relation of parents to children is still biologic and zoologic. In this man is very like the chicken or the dog. The relationship of children to parents may be mystical. Here it is possible to resist the order of nature; here resurrection is possible, the transformation of race into spirit. I am speaking here of an active attitude towards deceased ancestors, not of a passive following in their footsteps which is racial slavery. Man is responsible for the death of his parents and ancestors; he must achieve their resurrection.

But this resurrection is possible only outside race, in relationship by the spirit. A mystically-active attitude towards one's ancestors transforms the racial relationship into a spiritual one, the mortal into the immortal.

At the heart of Feodoroff's religious consciousness is the idea of the awakening of deceased ancestors. He saw the essence of Christianity in awakening (awakening, not resurrection). But in Feodoroff's consciousness there was dualism which he could not overcome. On one hand, he firmly and boldly turns his gaze forward, calls man to creative activity, and believes in man's capacity to awaken the dead by his own activity. On the other hand Feodoroff is a conservative. His most creative activity is not directed forward to the creation of something new, but rather backward, toward the re-establishment of the old life. Within the racial element Feodoroff is revolutionary: he desires a reverse movement within it. But he does not get out of the racial element. His religion is essentially a religion of the race. He confirms a connection by race, by flesh and blood, not by spirit. For him the dead must be resurrected in the race rather than in the spirit. His idea of relationship has an aftertaste of the race. It is a mark of his genius that he sees in the Holy Trinity an image of all relationships, but it is as if he implied to the Divine Trinity a racial relationship, rather than seeing it as an image of spiritual relationship. In the life of the race death is inescapable. Only in the spirit is the victory over death possible, the resurrection of the dead. The first birth in the race is not man's real birth. Only the *second birth* in the spirit, of which all the mystics have taught, is man's final birth. But humanity has to pass through the mortal way of the race, and on this way religion must sanctify sex-life and fill it with the spiritual.

§

Christianity, as a religion of redemption, refuses and overcomes the racial element and racial necessity. The man of the racial element is the old Adam, and he who would

196

participate in the revelation of the new Adam, the revelation of personality, must divest himself of this old nature. The Gospel revelation refuses the racial connection among men by flesh and blood, by the sexual act, in the name of a higher connection by the spirit. The New Testament reveals to him who recognizes himself as a personality a way out of race, out of racial necessity. But this way out predicates a heroic struggle to overcome the fallen and slavish attitude towards sexual inclination. The Christian family, the Christian ordering of racial sex life is merely an inevitable compromise with the world, only obedience to the consequences of sin. In this Christian ordering of sex, this adaptation to race, there has not yet appeared the revelation of the mystery of sex. In Christianity only the ascetic denial of the sex life of the old Adam is truly profound and truly religious. Man's enemies are of his own household. The great spiritual wrestlers, who burned away the old sex in the fire of their devotion, turned sexual energy in another direction quite opposite to any perspective of race. In the most extreme of these, St. Isaac the Syrian, there was a transfigured sex-energy. But the new sex, in a positive form, was not revealed in the religion of redemption. The old race, the old sex, remain in the Old Testament and in paganism. The whole of natural sex life with its limited laws carries on, on the Old Testament, pre-Christian level. Whatever is *personal* in sex is already on the level of the New Testament, for the New Testament is above all a revelation about personality. The confirmation of the non-racial in sex life is the beginning of the revelation of the new sex. This will be positively revealed only when the nature of love is revealed, the essence of the erotic.

In Christian consciousness up to the present time all positive confirmation of sex has been superficial and compromising. The only really profound thing was the denial of sex. Christian sex-asceticism was genuinely mystical. The Christian virtuous order established for sex was utilitarian and bourgeois. In the New Testament period in the world's history there was lighted a consciousness of relation by the spirit, union in freedom and not in necessity. But how this was to be applied to the relation between the sexes, to sex life, to the mystical union of male and female, remained unclear and unexplained. There is a symbolism of sex in the depths of Christianity: Christianity reveals the mystic of sex in the relationship between Christ and His Church, between the Logos and the soul of the world. Nevertheless the Christian world remains outside a positive revelation of the new sex. Christianity cannot simply kill sex, destroy it completely. And beside the ascetic denial of sex in Christianity there still exists the affirmation of the old sex, the racial relationship between man and woman. In Christianity sex is either completely denied or else it is justified as giving birth to an evil continuity, but not eternity. There remain the visions of Christian mystics and Christian poets. It must be openly admitted that in the epoch of redemption, the New Testament epoch, the new, creative sex is not revealed. The revelation of the new sex is the revelation of the new creative world-epoch. In sex, Christianity affirms only obedience: either ascetic obedience, or obedience to the old sex, under the limitations of the law. There has not yet occurred in Christianity a positive revelation of sex-life outside the racial element and the necessity of nature. There has not yet been set the task, fully, religiously conceived, of the transfiguration of sex—transfiguration, rather than killing sex or submitting to it. In the pre-creative world-epoch it could not be completely realized that the very orgiastic in sex must be transfigured, taken out of the circuit of race and nature and directed towards the creation of new life, a new world, rather than being destroyed. In truth, all creative energy is related to sex-orgiasm, which is always stepping out beyond its borders. Sex-orgiasm is positive, creative energy which may just as well lift man as demean or enslave him. But up to now in Christianity we have had only an ardent denial of sex orgiasm.

198

§

The religious self-consciousness of personality is a crisis of
the racial element, the beginning of an exodus from race.
We live in an epoch of world-shattering of the racial sex.
Only now are the final results beginning to be evident of
that breach in the racial basis for sex which Christianity
brought into the world. The naturalism of sex, its "natural"
norms, are now shaken. The crisis of race is the most painful
in the life of the new humanity; in this crisis man strives
towards freedom from the element of race, strives towards
the new sex. Never before have there been such widespread
deviations from the "natural", birthgiving sex; never before
has there been such a feeling and recognition of man's
bi-sexuality. The "natural" boundaries between female and
male are blurred and confused. It becomes possible to put
the question whether, in the higher sense of the word, the
birth-giving, racial sex with the sexual act is natural,
whether it is normal. Is not the sexual act itself an anomaly?
Only in our present transition-epoch can we seriously
doubt this. Everything organic-racial finds its end in the
mechanical-artificial and automatic. It has never been
finally recognized that the religion of Christ obliges us to
recognize the "natural" sex life as abnormal, the "natural"
sexual act as perversion. Christianity gave its blessing to the
begetting of children only as redemption of sin, only as the
sole justification of the mystical unnaturalness and abnormality of birth-producing sex-life. Christianity mystically and
radically refuses the "natural" criterion of racial sex.
Christianity recognizes as natural, normal and proper, only
birth by the Spirit and in union with the Spirit. But the
religion of redemption, which gives liberation from the sin
of racial sex has not yet revealed the new transfigured sex.
Christianity admitted only asceticism, or else the old family
as an adaptation to the results of sin. But this profound
Christian denial of sex, this condemnation of the old sex,
could not remain without effect in the course of centuries

and thousands of years. Racial sex was undermined and shaken. The "natural" norms and boundaries of sex were brought into question. Personality rose up to demand another birth and another relationship. The inescapable longing of sex took hold of man. The tragedy of sex poses the problem of the relationship between creativity and birth.

§

The sex-urge is creative energy in man. In it there is a superfluity of energy which demands outlet into the world, into an object. The profound connection between creativeness and birth-giving, their relationships and their contradictions, is indubitable. The creative energy of sex finds its outlet in begetting new lives. In the element of race, in the order of natural necessity, sex-energy is discharged in the begetting of children, creativeness is exchanged for begetting, immortal creativity for the mortal. There is a profound antagonism between creativity of the eternal and the begetting of the temporal. Individual perfection and the begetting of children are in inverse proportion to each other. Biology teaches this, and so does mysticism. The creative power of individuality is reduced and deteriorated in begetting children. The personality disintegrates in the evil endlessness of race. He who begets the most creates the least. Begetting takes away energy from creativity. Creative genius is hostile to the elements of race, and can only with difficulty be combined with begetting. In the creative sexual act there is always an enslavement of personality, an insult to the creative impulses of the individual. Man becomes the slave of his creative sexual energy—he is incapable of directing it towards a creative act. In sex life the feminity of Eve, rather than eternal virginity, conquers; the race lords it over the personality.

The results of sex-life fail to correspond to its creative task. In natural sex-life the union of man and woman is not attained—neither is the creation of eternal being. And each one who is born must start all over again this circle of evil

200

plurality. Creative energy is fettered by the chain of birth-giving. And sex-life with its begetting is the chief obstacle to the dawn of the creative world-epoch. The human race, remaining in the element of the old Adam and the old Eve, is powerless to create, since it spends its creative energy on the continuation and ordering of the race, on obedience to the results of sin. The resurrection of departed ancestors, to which N. Feodoroff calls us, presupposes the transfer of energy from begetting children to the resurrection of the fathers. The fatal impossibility of overcoming natural necessity, the inevitability of adaptation to the given order of the world, are concentrated in the point of the sexual act of begetting. Only from this point can there begin a world-movement, a world-liberation. The change of direction of creative energy must take place in sex. Begetting sex must be transformed into creative sex. The dawn of the creative world-epoch will be marked by a change in the order of nature, but this change will begin first of all in the point of sex—the point where man is bound to natural necessity. In the depths of sex, creativeness must conquer begetting, personality must conquer race, union in the Spirit must conquer the natural union by flesh and blood. This can only come as the expression of a new creative sex, the revelation of the creative mystery of man as a sexual being. By the same token, this can only be the revelation of the androgynous, God-like nature of man. The sexual act of begetting, which turns man into a slave of the elemental-feminine order of nature, will be transfigured into a free creative act. Sexual activity will be directed towards the production of a new world, the continuation of original creation. This was foreseen by the genius of Plato.

Sex-energy contains the source of creative ecstasy and the prophetic vision of genius. All true genius is erotic. But this creative genius is oppressed and held down by the element of race, by the sexual act of begetting. In essence the sexual act is profoundly opposed to all genius, to all universal conception and universal creativity. Genius is through and through erotic but not sexual, in the specific, differentiated sense of that word. The genius can live a specific sexual life, he may devote himself to the most extreme forms of vice, but his genius will remain despite such use of sexual energy; and in the racial element, in his begetting sex, a tragic breakdown is always inevitable. Genius is incompatible with a bourgeois-ordered sex-life, and it is not unusual to encounter in genius some sexual anomaly. The life of genius is not a "natural" life. Profound vacillations in sex-life indicate the dawn of a new world-epoch. The new man is above all a man of transfigured sex who has restored in himself the androgynous image and likeness of God, which was distorted by the decadence into male and female in the human race. The mystery of man is closely related to the mystery of the androgyne.

§

But the holy, mystical idea of androgynism has its dangerous caricature-like counterpart in hermaphroditism. The "this worldly" travesty of androgynism takes the form of hermaphroditism. But all hermaphroditism is a caricature, a distortion, pseudo-being. Hence the revelation of heavenly androgynism had to remain esoteric, since there was danger of just this vulgarization in hermaphroditism. Franz von Baader understood this profoundly. Androgynism is man's likeness to God, his supernatural upsurge. Hermaphroditism is an animal, natural mixture of two sexes, not transformed into higher being. Up to now the idea of woman's emancipation has been based upon the profound enmity between the sexes, upon envy and imitation. The feminine movement is the last place in which to seek the "ultimate men", the androgynic mystery of union. Out of envy and enmity, by mechanical imitation, woman assumes for herself male qualities and becomes a spiritual and physical hermaphrodite, a caricature, a pseudo-being. The enmity between the sexes, envy and competition and imitation, are opposed to the mystery of union. The emancipation of woman is, of course, a symptom of the crisis of the race, the breakdown of sex now evident, and it is better than the hypocritical compulsion in the old family, but its bases are old: in it we find neither the new man nor the new life. In the crisis of sex I know no more profound phenomenon than that of the gifted youth Weininger with his fatal longing for sex, his inescapable sex anguish, which attained the highest tragedy, his horror of evil femininity. Feeling his way in the darkness, in his own fashion, Weininger helplessly approaches the mystery of androgynism as salvation from the horrors of sex, but he is powerless to partake of this mystery. Philosophically he understood and accepted the bisexuality of the human being, but religiously he was held away from the mystery of androgynism as the image and likeness of God. Weininger stood completely in the unfulfilled, longed-for redemption, but since he was not a Christian he did not know of eternal femininity receiving the Logos in itself: he did not understand the womanliness of the Virgin Mary. It is touching to see how this unhappy youth exerts almost superhuman efforts to rise to a divine erotic, to love which redeems the sin of sex. In his own way he had an intimation of the religious truth that the female element fell away in the fall of man and became the object of an evil and false tendency, the source of enslavement. But he did not wish to know that in the female element there is just as much of the eternal God-likeness as in the male.

The man-androgyne is not a man, not a fractional, disintegrated being, but a youth-maiden. The mystics felt the androgynism of the new Adam-Christ. Only androgynism can explain in the Absolute Man, in whom there should have been the fullness of being, the absence of sex-life similar to that of the human race. In the absolute Man, the new Adam, there cannot be the differentiated and decadent life of sex. And the new, eternal sex is not yet revealed to us in that aspect of the absolute Man in which he appears to us as the Redeemer, in the aspect of the sacrifice on Golgotha. The positive revelation of the new sex is possible only in the

203

revelation of the absolute Man in creative power and glory, and it is being prepared in the new life of sex, gradually evident in man, in every one of us—the creative sex. The cult of eternal womanliness is inwardly present in the epoch of redemption, it is connected with the New Eve, with the Virgin Mary and the Redeemer's entrance into the world through her illuminated womanliness. The cult of eternal womanliness was a way of liberation from the evil and enslaving womanliness. But in eternal womanliness the new man, the creative mystery of man is not yet revealed. The Christian cult of eternal womanliness is still completely in the old fractionization of the sexes. The cult of eternal womanliness will not be the characteristic of the new creative world-epoch, but rather the cult of the androgyne, the youth-maiden, of man as the image and likeness of God. In this will be revealed the mystery of man. And the way to this all-uniting revelation leads through love. For the coming world-epoch and the new world-life, womanliness will be confirmed in the aspect of virginity rather than motherhood. The whole world crisis is culminating in the crisis of motherhood, and by this very fact the crisis of material itself. We witness the beginning of the futuristic, technical end of the religion of race, the religion of the material, and no power can protect from destruction the racial, maternal and material organic life. There will be left of the material only a transfigured sensibility and an eternal form of illuminated corporeality, freed of all weight and of the organic necessity of race.

# CHAPTER IX

# CREATIVITY AND LOVE:
# MARRIAGE AND THE FAMILY

THE EVERYDAY "CHRISTIAN" consciousness agrees fully with the everyday "worldly" consciousness in recognizing only three conditions of sex: the normal family under the law, asceticism, and debauch and unchastity. This average everyday consciousness admits nothing else in the realm of sex, and this quite regardless of whether the consciousness is religious or positivist. We must admit that during its long history, Christianity has often been the most genuine positivism. It is very important to emphasize the fact that all three recognized conditions of sex are determined by the sexual act and in relation to it: in all cases sex is identified with the sexual act. This evidences the hypnotic power of the element of race. One speaks only of the sexual act, which is morally and socially ordered and accepted in the family in the interest of reproduction, is completely denied in asceticism, and rules uncontrolled in the disorder and disorganization of debauchery. This prevailing consciousness in various forms speaks, shamefacedly it is true, of the sexual act, but maintains complete silence about sexual love. Men speak of sex but strangely forget about love. For in truth sexual love cannot be placed in the category of the family or in the category of asceticism or in that of debauchery. Love is not an ordering of the sexual act for the purpose of begetting children and the social organization of the race; neither is it an ascetic denial of all flesh in sexual life; nor is it unbridled and unlimited indulgence in the sexual act.

Love is in no sense whatever the sexual act: it has neither the positive nor negative relation with the sexual act which is vaguely felt by people with racial consciousness. And love, in a very profound sense, is the opposite of the differentiated sexual act, but opposite in quite another way than is asceticism. In the realm of sex, people with racial consciousness, both religious men and positivists, are concentrated on the sexual act itself and on its consequences, and fail completely to see the universal significance of sex, as well for the whole man as for the whole cosmos. The secret of sex is not at all the sexual act, performed either for virtuous child-begetting or for perverted enjoyment. First of all, we cannot believe that the sexual act was ever indulged in, anywhere or by anyone in the world, solely for the virtuous purpose of begetting children: it is always done elementally, in passion, for a fleeting self-satisfaction. The race triumphs in the sexual act not because a man is moved by racial virtue as his purpose but because it unconsciously dominates man and makes fun of his individual purposes.

The mystery of sex is revealed only in love. But there is no sphere of life where there reigns such inert conservatism and such conditional hypocrisy as in that of sexual love. The most extreme revolutionaries are very often conservative when the question of love arises. The revolutionary consciousness is encountered most rarely in the sphere of sex and love, although here it should be the most radical, I would even say the most religious. The socially minded and learned radicals and revolutionaries think only of the social and physiological ordering of sex—they never go any deeper. Love is wiped off the worldly account-books and turned over to the poets and the mystics. When these "Christians" or positivists speak of sex, do they recall the love of Tristan and Isolde, of Romeo and Juliet, the love which was sung by the Provençal troubadours or by Dante? Neither their theology nor their science, neither their morals nor their sociology, see in love a world-problem. We can say how Christian theology and ethics, scientific biology and sociology react to the sexual act, but how they consider love is unknown. The old racially-conceived theology and science cannot even know love.

206

In love there is something aristocratic and creative, something profoundly individual, unracial, something neither canonical nor normative—it surpasses the average-racial consciousness. Love lies in another plane of being than that in which the human race lives and orders its existence. Love lies outside the human race and passes beyond the consciousness of the human race. Love is not necessary to the race, to the perspective of its continuation and ordering. It remains, as it were, at one side. Sexual dissipation is nearer and more comprehensible to the human than love—in a certain sense it is even less dangerous. Man can adjust himself in "the world" with sexual dissipation—he can even limit and put it into order. Love will submit to no setting in order. In love there is no perspective of adjusting life in "this world". In love there is the fatal seed of perdition in "this world": the tragic loss of youth. Romeo and Juliet, Tristan and Isolde, perished from love, and it was not accident that their love brought death with it. The love of Dante and Beatrice did not permit well-being in "this world": innate in it was the inescapable tragedy within the boundaries of "this world". We cannot theorize about love, nor moralize, nor sociologize, nor even biologize—it is a foreign flower, perishing in the midst of this world. The growth of love is a tragic impossibility. To this all the great poets and writers of all ages bear witness. Is it not therefore natural that love has been left out of all "worldly" calculations, that the solution of the problem of sex has always been attempted outside of the problem of love?

§

By its very nature the family has always been, is now and always will be, a positivistic, secular institution of good order, a biological and sociological ordering of the life of the race. The forms of the family which have so greatly varied in the course of human history have always been forms of social adaptation to the conditions of existence, to the economic conditions of the world. No other phenomenon in human life can be so successfully explained by economic materialism as the family. In this sphere sociological materialism won its greatest victory. The family is first of all an economic unit and its connection with sex is always indirect rather than direct. And the connection of the family with love is much more tenuous. Man's sexual life was never held within the limits of any form of the family, it always flooded over all boundaries. But in the process of racial self-protection and the ordering of humanity it was necessary to work out forms of adaptation and limitation. The continuation of the human race and its orderly existence on the earth had to be placed in a certain independence of the natural orgiasm and chaos of sex. A legalized, normal form of sex had to be developed as an inevitable adaptation to the given condition of being. The religious consecration of the family is just as necessary as the religious consecration of the state. The mystery of love, as an absolute mystery of two persons, is something the comprehension of society cannot attain; but society has been accustomed to regulate everything which relates to the continuation of the human race. *The family was born of necessity and not of freedom.*

Religiously the family is completely Old Testament, in the law which convicts of sin. The family is obedience to the results of sin, adaptation to the necessity of the race. The family is always an acceptance of the inevitableness of the procreative sexual act, an adaptation to the necessities which result from it, the moral redemption of the sexual act by acceptance of the yoke of sex. The basis of the family is fallen sex, the unconquered differentiated act of sexual life, the lost integrity of sex, loss of chastity. The family is a moral and social justification of sinful fallen sex by the fact of procreation, and it arose for procreation. By this very fact, every ideology of the family recognizes that only that union of man and woman is good and justified in which the sexual act is accomplished. The whole *pathos* of the family is born of the sexual act and any other union of man and woman is not recognized as family, is not considered justified.

208

Without the sexual act there is no begetting of children, i.e. the justification of the family, that for which it exists. Any union of man and woman in which the sin of the sexual act is overcome and in which the integrity of sex is re-established is not a family union and has no justification in a family. The family appears as a lower form of the intercourse of the sexes, an adaptation to the inevitable sexual sin. Any rise in sex, any upsurge into new forms of intercourse of man and woman, eliminates the family and makes it unnecessary. And the ideology of the family, which has become a conservative force in the world, fears any upsurge or upflight in sexual life, fears it worse than sin and degradation. The family consents to being a setting-in-order of the sexual sin and of vice, in the interests of the ordering of the race, and it fears more than anything else a revolution in sex which would threaten the racial order.

The moralists of the family are ready to justify the sin of sex as the bearing of a burden and as obedience. They cannot reconcile themselves to the heroic and titanic efforts to overcome the old sex for the sake of revealing the new sex and new sexual union, not in the elements of the race but in spirit. The moralists of the family do not know what to do with the fact of the union of men and women outside the sexual act; they do not know how to evaluate such union. To them one of three cases is necessary: the procreative sex-life of the family, debauched sex-life, or the ascetic absence of any sexual life at all. And it is most surprising that in the usual ideology of the family, be it religious or positivist, the attitude towards that very sexual act on which the whole ideology is based remains unexplained. Orthodox and Catholics alike do not believe that men can completely overcome the sexual act, just as they do not believe that men can completely abstain from eating meat. Is the sexual act something good and justified in itself, or is it good and justified only as a means, as an instrument of procreation? At this central point of the problem of sex and of the family there has been heaped up a mountain of hypocrisy. The moral *pathos* of the begetting of children which prudishly scorns the sexual act is essentially hypocritical: from both the religious and the moral viewpoint, the *pathetic* attitude towards procreation should be transferred to the sexual act itself. If the begetting of children is divine, then so is the act on which it depends. Here Rozanoff, the brilliant challenger and interrogator of the Christian family, is completely right. If the sexual act is sinful, if it is a fall of sex, then there cannot be an innocent moral *pathos* of procreation. There is always something hypocritical lurking in the ideology of the family. The religious bases of the family remain unelucidated, just as the attitude towards the central mystery of sex remains unclear. The family continues to be justified on the bourgeois surface of the world. The family is above all the *bourgeoisie* of "this world", and the depths of sex in it have never been sounded. The fact of the existence of families "outside the law" reveals the socially-adaptable nature of the family. And yet the family, like every other law, has a religious meaning and justification, just as does the state.

§

In the profound mystic of its substance, the New Testament denies the family, just as it denies the sexual act as a fall and a sin of sex; it denies the race, it denies "this world" and all its bourgeois institutions. A genuinely "Christian family" is no more possible than a "Christian state". The family is a racial institute; it is putting the race in order. The New Testament revelation overcomes the element of race, and a law of the good-order of the race, a law of the family, can no more proceed from the New Testament than can a law of the state. But the New Testament, which does not know the law, which overcomes the law, does not abolish the law for a world plunged in unredeemed sin, a world enslaved by the elements of nature. Like the law of the state, the law of the family is essentially Old Testament, pre-Christian, but the New Testament justifies it as obedience to the Old Testament subjection to the law, obedience to the results of sin. The Christian family is merely a disinfection of the sexual sin, which renders it harmless. Christianity knows full well that men are born in sin, that the union of the sexes in the natural family order of things is sinful, and tries to weaken this sin and render it harmless by means of adaptation and obedience. The family under the law does not mean the creation of new human relationships or new life: it is obedience to "the world"; it is "the world's" burden. Truly surprising is the tolerant attitude of Christianity toward the sin of the sexual act and the sin of the economic well-being of the family, i.e. towards just that in the family which is of "the world", that which is an adaptation to "the world". Beget children in a decently moral sexual act, and then install them in economic well-being! That is the *pathos* of the Christian family. Read that pillar of orthodoxy, Theophanes the Hermit. For him only two aspects of the family are important: the physiological, the procreative sexual act, and the economic well-being of wife and children. Bishop Theophanes, who has absorbed the mysticism of the early Church Fathers, speaks of this physiological and economic aspect of the family with moral *pathos*. The ascetic bishop turns out to be a good husbandman in "the world", a good bourgeois. For Bishop Theophanes the spiritual aspect of the family is exhausted by obedience, by the obedient bearing of burdens. In Bishop Theophanes you cannot find one word about the new love in the Spirit, about the new union of men and women in a higher order of being, about the marital mystery.

It is astounding, almost frightening, this silence of orthodoxy and of the whole of Christianity on the subject of love—the denial of marital love! For in marital love there is no place for the physiology and economics with which the builders of the Christian family are exclusively concerned. There is no marital mystery in the family. The family is not set up and put in order for marital love but for the good order and the well-being of the race. The family may even be polygamous, if polygamy turns out to be the best form of social adaptation—a polygamous family would be less hypocritical than a monogamous one. The mystical marriage is something outside this whole contrast. Not only the positive-social ideology of the family but the Christian-moral ideology of the family as well are penetrated through and through by economic utilitarianism. Like the state, the family is not a spiritual phenomenon: it is not in the Spirit. The mystery of marriage is not revealed in Christianity. Blessing the family union, the Church merely renders harmless the sin of sexual life. The Church blesses the Old Testament idea of the state as well. In the New Testament, in a religion of redemption, there can be only the ascetic conquest of sex. The mystery of love, of marriage, is in spirit, in the epoch of creativeness, in the religion of creativity. The sacrament of marriage is not the family, not the natural sacrament of birth and the continuation of the race. The sacrament of marriage is a sacrament of union in love. Only love is the holy sacrament. The sacrament of love is above the law and outside the law: it means going outside the race and racial necessity; in it is the beginning of the transfiguration of nature. Love is not obedience, not the bearing of the world's burdens, but rather creative intrepidity. This mystery, the mystery of marriage, has not been disclosed either in the revelation of the law or in the revelation of redemption. The mystery of love is the creative revelation of man himself. It was conceived in mystic love which always breaks through the boundaries of the utilitarian and racial physiology and economy of the family. The family was a school of love, but not of true marital love.

Love in this world is tragic and admits no careful ordering: it is subject to no norms. Love means failure in this world rather than the well-ordered life. The supreme thing in love, what maintains its mystical sacredness, is its renunciation of all perspective in life, its sacrifice of life. All creativeness demands this sacrifice, and so does creative love. Well-being in life, the good ordering of the family—these are the grave of love. Love is more closely and intimately and deeply

212

bound up with death, rather than with birth, and this relationship, which the poets have dimly felt, is the pledge of its eternity. The contrast between love and procreation is profound. In the act of procreation love disintegrates, all the personal in love dies, and another sort of love triumphs. The seed of this disintegration of love is sown in the sexual act. "I never yet have found a woman by whom I would wish to have children, because I love you, eternity." Thus spake Zarathustra. The genuine other-worldly love, the love which creates eternity, excludes the possibility of the sexual act, overcomes it for the sake of another kind of vision. It is well known that to one deeply in love there is sometimes no specific sexual attraction—this is not necessary. And a strong impulse to the sexual act has all too often no connection with real love, sometimes even predicates revulsion. Those truly in love desire absolute union and absolute fusion, spiritual and physical. The sexual act separates: revulsion and murder are at the bottom of it. But love is a creative act, creating a new life, overcoming "the world", and conquering the race and natural necessity. Personality, unique and unrepeatable, is confirmed in love. Everything impersonal and racial, everything which subjects the individual to natural and social order, is hostile to love, to its unique and unspeakable mystery.

There is not, nor can there be, a law for love: love knows no law. The creativeness of love is not obedience, as in the family, but rather free and daring upflight. Love is not to be contained in the category of the family or in any other category: it is not to be contained in "the world". The sacrificial quality of love, its renunciation of worldly prosperity and well-being, make it free. Only the sacrifice of security gives freedom. Whatever is connected with adaptation to "the world", with obedient bearing of its burdens, is never free from fear, from the burdens of daily care. In love the burdens of the world are conquered. In the family there is always the difficulty of good management and of security, the fear of the future, daily burden-bearing, just as in other forms of adaptation, in the state, in economics, in positive science. Love is a free act. In love there is no trace of economics, no hint of care. And this freedom is purchased only at the price of a willingness to sacrifice. The freedom of love is a divine truth. But men also make the freedom of love truly vulgar. That freedom of love is vulgar which seeks above all the satisfaction of the old sex, which is most of all interested in the sexual act. This is not freedom of love, but enslavement of love, this is in opposition to any upsurge of sex towards something higher, every upflight of love, every victory over the burden of natural sex. There is in love an ecstatic and orgiastic, but not a natural-racial, element. The orgiastic ecstasy of love is supernatural—it opens a way out into another world.

In the creative act of love the creative secret of the loved one is revealed. The lover sees the loved one right through the shell of the natural world, through the rind which covers every person. Love is the way to revealing the secret of the person, to a comprehension of the person in the depth of his being. The lover knows things about the person of the loved one which the whole world does not know, and the lover is always more right than the rest of the world. Only the lover truly comprehends personality, solves the riddle of its genius. The rest of us, who do not love, know only the surface of the person, do not know the final mystery. The deadly vacuity of the sexual act lies in the fact that in its impersonality the mystery of the person is smothered and torn apart. The sexual act leads into the mælstrom of impersonal nature; it stands between the person of the lover and the loved, and hides the mystery of the person. Not in the sexual act and not in the race is accomplished the true union of love which creates another, a new life, the eternal life of the person. In God the lover meets the beloved; in God he sees the beloved person. In the natural world lovers are separated. The nature of love is cosmic, super-individual. The mystery of love is not to be known in the light of individual psychology. Love gives communion with the cosmic hierarchy of the world; in the androgynous image it brings together in cosmic union those who in the natural order were torn apart. Love is the way whereby every man reveals in himself the man-androgyne. There can be no accident in true love: in love there is predestination and vocation. But the world cannot pass judgement on the mystery of two, the marital mystery: in it there is absolutely nothing of the social. Only a few achieve the true mystery of marriage, for only a few is it known: it is something aristocratic and predicates election.

§

What is debauchery (licentiousness) in the deeper sense of the word? Debauchery is the direct opposite of all union. The mystery of debauchery is the mystery of disunion, of falling apart, of strife and hostility in sex. The mystery of union cannot be debauched. Where true union is attained there is no debauch. There is an inevitable element of debauch in the sexual act, because it does not unify but rather separates; because it means reaction; because it gives birth to enmity. The family gives no protection from this debauchery of the sexual act, from this superficiality, from this superficiality of the contact of one being with another, from the impossibility for one being truly to penetrate to the interior of the other, this impossibility of fusing all the cells of man and woman. Debauchery is disunion: it always transforms the object of sexual attraction into a means rather than an end. All the physiology and psychology of debauchery is built upon this transformation of means into ends, upon the substitution of attraction for the sexual act itself or substituting the act of love for attraction to the object of love. Love of love, instead of love of a person—this is the psychology of debauch. This psychology offers union with no one. In it there is no thirst for union: there is a divisive, almost alienating psychology. In it the marital mystery is never realized. Love for the sexual act instead of love for a fusion into one flesh—this is the physiology of debauch. In this physiology there is no thirst for union with anyone, there is even no desire for union: this is a physiology of natural enmity and alienation. In the element of debauch sexual life is the furthest separated from the integral life of the personality. In debauchery the personality does not connect any of its fond hopes with sex. Sex somehow is separated from man and from the cosmos, it becomes isolated, lost in itself.

Any attempt to include sex in the cosmos is directly opposed to debauch. The isolation or separation of sex, its differentiation from the integral essence of life which we see in the world of nature, is always debauchery. This can be conquered only by restoring to sex its universal significance, reuniting it to the meaning of life. The ordinary everyday, "worldly" "bourgeois" ideas of debauchery are often directly opposite to the truth; they are superficial, conditional, utilitarian; they do not know the metaphysics of debauchery. Conditioned moralism and social traditionalism with their bourgeois spirit are powerless to decipher the mystery of debauch, the mystery of non-being. In so-called marriage debauch finds asylum, just as in other places where it cannot be justified. It finds its place everywhere where there is another aim than the union of the lovers, a penetration through love into the mystery of the person. The problem of debauchery is not moral but metaphysical. All the biological and sociological criteria of debauch are conditional—in them speaks the voice of this bourgeois world. In the ordinary use of the word, debauch is any forbidden form of sexual union, when in reality it is the lack of all union which is vicious. The sexual act is vicious just because it does not give sufficiently profound union. Equally superficial are the current ideas of the viciousness of some anomalies of sexual life. Our sexual life is all one anomaly, and sometimes the most "normal" may prove to be more vicious than the "abnormal". Debauch cannot be prohibited: it must be ontologically overcome by another type of being. Love is one antidote for debauchery. Another antidote is a higher spiritual life. Passionate lust is not vicious in itself. Only that lust is vicious which divides, which does not penetrate its object, which is lost in itself. And holy is the ecstasy of love which melts the lovers into one.

The laws of love are absolute and unconditional. There is no sacrifice in life which could not be justified for the sake of true love. First of all the sacrifice of security and well being for the sake of the absolute laws of love is justified. In love there is no wilfulness of the personality, no personal will, no personal drive which knows no limit. Love is supreme fate and predestination and a will that is higher than the will of man. In the family there is sacrifice for the sake of human welfare: in love, courageous sacrifice for the sake of a higher will. Truly, the divine will joins two lovers, predestines them one for another. Love is a creative act, but not an act of wilfulness, or of personal profit. The law of love is duty, it is the highest commandment of obedience to love. Obedience to love is higher, more spiritual, than obedience to the family. The duty of love overcomes the suffering caused to people by love. Love is always cosmic, necessary for the world's harmony, for divine predestination. Hence love should not fear the suffering to which it gives birth. From the cosmic nature of love we must inevitably conclude that unshared, one-sided love is impossible, and so it should be, for love is above people. Unshared love is a fault, a sin against the cosmos, against the harmony of the world, against the androgynous image which is sketched out for us in the divine world-order. And all the strange tragedy of love lies in this tormenting search of the androgynous image, the cosmic harmony. Through sexual love the fullness of man is realized in each of the two participants.

The union of the sexes is four-membered rather than two-membered: it always means the complex union of the male element of the one with the female element of the other, and of the female element of the first with the male element of the second. The mystical life of the androgyne is realized not in one bisexual being but rather in the quadripartite union

of two beings. For many, the way towards a single androgynous image leads through a multiplicity of unions. The
cosmic nature of love makes jealousy a fault, a sin. Jealousy
denies the cosmic nature of love, its relationship to world-
harmony, for the sake of individualistic bourgeois property.
Jealousy is the feeling of a bourgeois proprietor who does not
know the higher world-meaning of love. A jealous man
thinks that the object of his love belongs to him, when
actually it belongs to God and the world. In the mystery of
love there is no such thing as a proprietor, and no such thing
as private ownership. Love demands the sacrifice of all
private ownership, of all bourgeois pretensions to possess the
loved one only for oneself. In love the personality is revealed
only by the sacrifice of personal interest or profit. Since it is
cosmic in its meaning, love cannot take man away from the
cosmos. It is just this mystical and cosmic meaning of love,
just this faith in divine predestination and election in love,
which predicates free conflict in love and the free, living
expression of those strong in love, for a mystical predestination needs no defence.

§

There is a profound and tragic difference between female
and male love, a strange lack of comprehension and a shock-
ing alienation. Woman is a being of quite another order than
man. She is much less human, much more nature. She is
primarily the bearer of the sex element. In man, sex is of
lesser significance than woman. Woman is all sex: her sex-
life is her whole life, which occupies her completely, in so
far as she is woman rather than human. In man sex is much
more differentiated. By her nature woman always lives by
one: she does not take many unto herself. And woman does
not well understand this capacity of man to comprehend in
himself the fullness of being. Woman in greater measure
gives herself to one person, the one who possesses her at the
moment, gives herself to one experience which crowds out
all the rest of life, all the rest of the world. With woman the

one becomes the all, she sees everything in the one, she puts everything into the one. Woman identifies the whole of being with the mood which possesses her at a given moment. To the question "What is being?" the woman who suffers from unrequited love always answers: "Being is unrequited love." Her comparatively feeble sense of personality and her dependence on times and seasons, on sensations which change with the times, is directly connected with this peculiarity of woman's nature. In man's nature there is a stronger sense of personality and great independence of conditions which change with the times, a greater capacity to accept within himself the fullness of spiritual being at all times. Man's nature has the capacity to experience within himself at all times, independently of the times, all the fullness of the spiritual life of his personality, the capacity to feel himself at the height of his powers at all times. Man is not inclined to give himself up completely and exclusively to the joy of love or the suffering caused by some misfortune: there is always with him his creativity, his business, all the fullness of his powers. In the field of male consciousness one thing may occupy the foreground and another move back, but nothing disappears or loses its importance completely. Woman, on the other hand, gives herself up exclusively and wholly to the joy of love or the suffering from misfortune: she dissolves completely in this one, puts herself wholly into it. Woman's personality is constantly subject to the danger of falling apart into separate sensations and the sacrificial offering of herself for the sake of these sensations. This is why woman's nature is so inclined towards hypnosis or possession. Female hysteria is related to this peculiarity of woman's nature, and its roots are metaphysical. All that is high and noble in woman, as well as all that is low, is bound up with this, her uncanny strangeness towards masculine nature. Woman experiences eternity otherwise than does man. Man considers the fullness of the spiritual powers of his nature as independent of the change of time, independent of the power of temporary experience over the fullness of personality.

Woman is powerless to resist the power of temporary conditions, but in these temporary conditions she invests all the fullness of her nature, her eternity.

Profoundly different are the masculine and feminine attitudes toward love. Woman is often a genius at love: her attitude toward love is universal. She puts into love all the fullness of her nature and stakes on love all her fondest hopes. Man is more often talented in love, rather than a genius at it: his attitude towards love is not universal but rather differentiated; he does not put the whole of himself into love and will not be completely dependent upon it. For man there is something uncannily frightening in the elements of woman's love, something which, like the ocean, is terrifying and can quite engulf him. And the demands of woman's love are so limitless that they can never be satisfied by man. Out of this ground grows the inevitable tragedy of love. The separateness of male and female, this sign of man's fall, makes the tragedy of love inescapable. The man seeks beauty in the woman, loves the beauty in her, thirsts to worship this beauty, since he has lost his virgin. But for man this beauty remains something exterior, outside him: he does not take it into himself, does not make it a part of his nature. This is why it is so difficult to love a woman with eternal love, that in love, man wishes to adore a beauty which is outside himself. In the cult of masculine love there is a nucleus of idolatry. But the woman is rarely that image of beauty before which one may kneel, which can be idolized. This is why love brings man such searing disillusionment, why he is so wounded by the dissimilarity between the image of the woman and the beauty of eternal femininity. But the higher, mystic meaning of love is not in worship or idolization of woman, as exterior beauty, but in communion with femininity, in the fusion of male and female natures into the image and likeness of God, into the androgyne. In the creative act of this higher love male and female natures cease to be so terribly foreign and hostile to each other. This must come to pass as a final liberation and cleansing from the erotic idolization of sex and femininity, which must be transferred to divine life itself.

Sexual love is connected with the very essence of personality, with man's loss of the image and likeness of God, with the fall of the androgyne in which femininity was not an element foreign to him, attracting him from without, but rather an inner element in man, the virgin indwelling in him. And the religious meaning of sexual love, of the erotic, lies in the fact that it is the source of an upward movement of personality, the creative upsurge. The meaning of love is not to be sought in the static of life's arrangement but in the dynamic of life's movement, in the creation of another kind of life. Every victory of the static over the dynamic in love deadens and petrifies love; it transforms it from creativeness into obedience, into adaptation to the conditions of existence. In true love there is a creative upsurge into another world, a conquest of necessity. And they know not what they do who would transform love into obedience. This means changing freedom into necessity, creativeness into adaptation, changing the mountain into a plain. Love is of the heights, not of the plain: they have nothing in common with love who would adapt it to the plain of life. Love cannot be held to the plain: here it withers and becomes something different. Love is no dweller on the plain of life. In love there is nothing of the static, nothing of arrangement. Love is flight which destroys every trace of "arranging matters".

§

In friendship based on love (*Liebesfreundschaft*) there is not that uncanny alienation and uncanny attraction of the object which characterizes sexual love. In friendship there is not that polarity, attracting opposite elements, neither is there that uncanny combination of love and hostility. Friendship is not bound up with the very roots of personality, with the very integral image and likeness of God in man. Friendship fills the life of personality with positive content, but does not touch the very bases of personality.

Sex permeates the whole man; friendship touches only a part of him, only his spiritual function. But in genuine, profound friendship there is an erotic element, a relationship with sex, if not direct, then indirect. The sex energy, the energy of thirst for union, may be directed towards friendship, just as towards any other creative act. And only that friendship is filled with high significance in which sexual energy, the energy of every union, is active. The mystery of sex is a mystery of creative insufficiency, of poverty which gives birth to riches. Friendship is not whole but partial love: it does not contain the ultimate secret of two, although it may approach this. In friendship there is no union of two into one flesh (not only in the sense of the sexual act, but in another far higher sense); there is only contact. Hence friendship is a high degree in the hierarchy of feelings which unite, but not the highest and not the ultimate. But in true friendship there must be a penetration into the unique secret of the beloved person or, better, the reflection of one in the other and a profound mutual understanding.

§

Sexual love, erotic love, is considered as profoundly and absolutely different from general human love, brotherly love, "Christian" love. Oh, of course it is different! Sexual love knows the secret of two and it is rooted in the polarity of disintegrating elements. "Christian" love, like humanist love, has become transformed into complete abstraction, bodiless and bloodless, into "glass love" as Rozanoff has it. Even the holy fathers call us more often to "harden your hearts", than to love. We have said before that Christian love has not yet been revealed by humanity in the religion of redemption. The revelation of Christian love demands a creative act. It calls us to another union, "not of this world", a union of all in a Christian all-humanity, to the union of all in the free Spirit, rather than in the necessity of nature. Hitherto Christian humanity has known natural union, union out of adaptation to necessity. This adaptation to necessity has been not only in the state but in the church which has come to resemble the state. The physical history of the church has been anything but religious. The church's incarnation in history has been cultural and has shared all the peculiarities of culture. In universal, all-human Christian love there should be creative upsurge towards another world, that vision of the human face of every brother by the Spirit in God, which is found in a high degree in erotic love. In true Christian love, not "glassy" and not abstract, there is a reflected flash of heavenly erotic; it means directing the energy of sex towards all humanity and the whole world. Sexual love overcomes the sinful falling-apart of male and female, in a union of the two which is not of this world. Christian love overcomes the sinful falling apart of all the beings of the world, all parts of the world, in a union of all, that is not of the here and now. The fall and decadence of man was related to sex. And so is the ultimate reunion. Only in the heavenly erotic there is not the *ennui* of adaptation to necessity. In the long course of history men have tried to transform Christian love into the *ennui* of adaptation to the here and now. And they justified this crime by the mysticism of obedience to the results of sin. True Christian love was considered by the Christian world to be a dangerous risk—the pride of too dizzying upflight. And even love was denied to sinful man, as to one unworthy of it.

§

Is the mystical connection between love and androgynity now sufficiently clear? In this connection the ultimate meaning of love is revealed. Androgynity is the ultimate union of male and female in a higher God-like being, the ultimate conquest of decadence and strife, the restoration in man of the image and likeness of God. Love is the restoration to man of the lost virgin-Sophia. Through love, the alienated feminine nature is reunited with masculine nature and the integral image of man is restored. In love this reunion is always connected with the person of man, with the unique

223

and unrepeatable person. Hence love is the way of fallen man's ascent towards likeness to God. In erotic there is the redemption of man's sexual sin, redemption realized and passing over into creativity. The sin of fallen sex is overcome negatively by asceticism and positively and creatively by love. In androgynity the natural although distorted bisexuality of every human being receives its supernatural, mystic meaning. In androgynity there is the mutual interpenetration of all cells of male and female nature: a final and ultimate fusion. Every cell of man's being is androgynous, bears in itself the reflection of divine nature. And the union of male and female must be profound rather than superficial. The ultimate mystery of androgynous being will never be unravelled completely in the limits of our present world. But the experience of erotic love gives us communion with that mystery. The connection of erotic love with androgynity is just its connection with personality. For in truth every personality is androgynous. Androgynity is the restoration of the integrity of sex in the Godlike being of personality. In love there must be revealed neither the mystery of femininity nor that of masculinity, but rather the *mystery of mon*. But on the way to the revelation of this mystery the revolutionary overthrow of the family is just as much a falsehood as the revolutionary overthrow of the state. The law must be fulfilled, but there is a world which stands above the law.

The erotic is connected in the same inseparable way with creativity. Erotic energy is the eternal source of creativity. Erotic union is accomplished for creative upsurge; and just as inseparably the erotic is connected with beauty. The erotic shock is the way of revealing beauty in the world.

CHAPTER X

# CREATIVITY AND BEAUTY: ART AND THEURGY

ARTISTIC CREATIVENESS best reveals the meaning of the creative act. Art is primarily a creative sphere. It is even an accepted expression to call the creative element in all spheres of spiritual activity "artistic". A clearly creative attitude towards science, social life, philosophy or morals, we consider artistic. And even the Creator of the world is considered in the aspect of the great artist. The expectation of the creative epoch is the expectation of an artistic epoch, in which art will have the leading place in life. The artist is always a creator. Art is always a victory over the heaviness of "the world"—never adaptation to "the world". The act of art is directly opposed to every sort of added burden—in art there is liberation. The essential in artistic creativity is victory over the burden of necessity. In art man lives outside himself, outside his burdens, the burdens of life. Every creative artistic act is a partial transfiguration of life. In the artistic concept man breaks out through the heaviness of the world. In the creative-artistic attitude towards this world we catch a glimpse of another world. To receive the world unto oneself in beauty is to break through the deformity of "this world" into another. The world which is forced upon us, "this world" is deformed, it is not cosmic, beauty is not in it. Accepting the beauty in the world unto oneself is always creativity. In freedom, not in compulsion, we attain to the beauty in the world. In every artistic activity a new world is created, the cosmos, a world enlightened and free. The scurf falls from the face of the world. Artistic creativity is ontological rather than psychological in its nature.

But in artistic creativity we see the tragedy of all creativity —the gap between aim and realization. The aim of every creative act is boundlessly greater than its realization. This has often been noted. The aim of every creative act is to create another type of being, another kind of life, to break out through "this world" to another world, out of the chaotic, heavy and deformed world into the free and beautiful cosmos. The aim and purpose of the artistic-creative act is theurgical. The realization of the creative artistic act is the production of a differentiated art, of cultural æsthetic values. Creativeness goes out not into another world, but into the culture of this world. Artistic creativeness does not attain ontological results: it creates the ideal rather than the real, symbolic values rather than being. In artistic creativeness there is clearly revealed the symbolic nature of all cultural creativeness. *The tragedy of creativity and the crisis of creativity form the basic problem passed on by the nineteenth century to the twentieth.* In Nietzsche and Ibsen, in Dostoevski and Tolstoy, with the symbolists, the world crisis of creativity reached its final intensity. What a surprising epilogue to the whole creative life of Ibsen: "When we Dead shall awake"! Here the problem of the tragic contrast between creativeness and being, between art and life, is put with extraordinary power: should one create life itself or create works of art? And the whole life of Leo Tolstoy was a tormenting transition from the creation of perfect works of art to the creation of a perfect life. This tragedy of the artist-creator has now become so acute that perfect, classically beautiful art has become almost impossible. The classic ideal of the beautiful, canonic, normalized art stands between creativeness and being, separates the artist from life. Creativity is re-cast into perfect art rather than into perfect life. For the artist-creator, another, higher type of being is unattainable.

Canonic art does not permit creative energy to pass over into another world; it retains it in this world; it admits only symbolic signs of another kind of being, but does not admit the reality of such being itself. Canonic art with its differentiated norms still remains obedience to the results of sin, just like canonic science, the family or the state. Canonic art is the adaptation of the creative artist's energy to the conditions of this world. Canonic art may be beautiful, but its beauty has not the essential of being, in the final sense of that word, just as the truth of canonic science or the justice of the canonic state fails to have it. The canon in art always hinders creative energy, as a necessary adaptation to this world, as obedience to the result of man's sin. This hindrance prevents the creation of another world. Canonic art is immanent in this world, rather than transcendent. It seeks only cultural values, does not strive towards new being. Canonic art does to the creator of beauty, what the canonic family does to creative love. Canonic art never was creativity in the religious sense of the word: it belongs in the pre-creative epoch: it is still in the law and the redemption. The great artists always had great creative energy but it could never be adequately realized in their art. In the creative ecstasy, there was a break-through into another world. But the classically-beautiful canonic art leaves one in this world, giving only hints of another. The canon of differentiated art is the law of obedience. The way of canonic art is opposite to the way of creative daring. The world crisis of creativity is the crisis of canonic art.

§

There is a profound contrast between pagan art and Christian art or, better, the art of the Christian epoch. Pagan art is classic and immanent. Christian art is romantic (I use the word here not in the narrow, but in the wider sense of the word) and transcendent. In classic pagan art there is an immanent completeness, an immanent perfection. Classically beautiful pagan art strives for finality and perfection of form here on earth, in this world. The heavens are closed above pagan art and the ideals of perfection are of the here and now, rather than of the beyond. Only in pagan art

227

do we find that classic perfection of form, that immanent attainment of beauty in this world, by the means of this world. The ideal and finished perfection of the Pantheon is possible only in pagan art. The finished perfection of pagan art does not call man away: it leaves him here in this world. In this classically beautiful perfection of form of the pagan world there is no upsurge towards another world: this attained perfection closes man in in this world. Antique sculpture and architecture rest on this belief in the possibility of enclosing beauty in this world by means of perfection of form. In the classically beautiful art of antiquity there is no transcendent longing, no transcendent upsurge: no abyss opens above or below. In the pagan world heaven itself was a complete and closed dome, beyond which there was nothing. Perfection in beauty is attainable not out there, beyond our limitations, but here, within these boundaries. The art of the pagan world speaks not of longing for a beautiful other world but rather of the attainment of beauty in this, under the closed dome of heaven. And the pagan, pre-Christian aspiration towards classic and immanent perfection of form produces one of the eternal traditions in art which has come over into the Christian world.

Christian art is of another spirit. Heaven opened above the Christian world and revealed the beyond. In the art of the Christian world, there is not, nor can there be, a classic finality of form, immanent perfection. In Christian art there is always a transcendental intention towards another world, towards an upsurge beyond the limits of the immanent world; there is romantic longing. A romantic incompleteness and imperfection of form characterizes Christian art. Christian art no longer believes in final attainment of beauty here in this world. Christian art believes that final, perfect, eternal beauty is possible only in another world. In this world only a striving towards the beauty of another world is possible, only the longing for that beauty. The Christian world permits of no closing-in, no finality in this world. For the Christian world, beauty is always that which speaks of

228

another world—that other world's symbol. Christian transcendent feeling of being produces a romantic tradition in art which struggles against the classic tradition. Romantic Christian art sees unearthly beauty in imperfection, in the lack of finality itself, in this groping toward an upsurge beyond the limits of this world. Christian art does not leave us in this world, in beauty already finally attained, but leads us out into another world, with beauty beyond and outside the limits of this.

In pagan art there was classic health. Christian art is romantically ailing. The thirst for the redemption of the sins of this world, the thirst for communion with another world, are imprinted on the ideals of Christian art. A comparison of medieval Gothic with the classic architecture of antiquity will make clear one contrast of the two types of art. In pagan art there was a structure of this world, a structure in beauty, like the structure of the pagan state or of pagan science. In classic pagan art the artist's creative act is adapted to the conditions of this world, to life and beauty here. In a world of classic finality, the creating act does not lead out into another world but rather holds us in this. This classic finality of the pagan world forms the tradition of classic art, sets up the canon for the attainment of perfect, final form. Romantic art is not canonic. But in the Christian world the classically beautiful art of the antique world is changed. It contains much that is eternal and deathless but also much that is all too temporal, confining, reactionary in the deepest sense of the word. The art of antiquity is the eternal source of creativeness and beauty. But the canon of classicism may easily become a confining conservative force, hostile to the spirit of prophecy. Antique classicism can be deformed into dead academism. And it is not at all a question of form in contrast to content, since in art the form is itself the content. But form-content may be finished and closed-off or else it may be unfinished and breaking through. The final crisis of canonic art is becoming evident only now in our time, and men are beginning to reason out the relationships of pagan and Christian tradition. One can best understand the nature of art with its classic finality and its romantic tendency in Italy, the holy land of creativeness and beauty, by an intuitive penetration into the early and the late Renaissance.

§

The great Italian Renaissance is vastly more complex than is usually thought. In the Renaissance there was an extraordinary uprising of human creativeness: the problem of creativity stands out with an acuteness never felt before. In the Renaissance man attempted to return to the antique sources of creativeness, to that source of creative nourishment, which never failed in either Greece or Rome. But it would be an error to think that the Italian Renaissance was pagan, that it stood under the sign of the renaissance of paganism. This simplified viewpoint has been abandoned by the historians of art. In the creative upsurge of the Renaissance there occurred such a powerful clash between pagan and Christian elements in human nature as had never occurred before. In this lies the significance of the Renaissance for the world and for eternity. It revealed the activity of the pagan nature of man in creativeness, and at the same time the activity of his Christian nature. Antiquity, with its ideals of immanent finality, could never be restored, because in general the restoration of any previous historical epoch is impossible. The historians of culture are more and more discovering the Christian elements in the Renaissance. We cannot find the antique pagan integrity in the Renaissance: this is a period when man was profoundly divided, a period of extraordinary complexity born of the clash of different elements. The restorers of paganism must admit that the blood of the people of the Renaissance period was poisoned by the Christian consciousness of the sinfulness of this world, and the Christian longing for redemption. The Christian transcendental sense of being had so profoundly possessed men's nature that the integral and final confession of the immanent ideals of life became impossible. The men of the

230

Renaissance were split Christians: in them two conflicting streams of blood gushed against each other. The Christian-pagans were divided between two worlds. You cannot find the pagan-integral, immanent feeling for life in the Renaissance; that is something men have invented. After Christ and the cosmic changes of human nature bound up with him, there can be no complete return to antiquity, to the immanence of paganism. The coming of Christ magically inoculated human nature with the feeling that it belonged to two worlds, with the longing for a world other than this. Even in the life of Benvenuto Cellini, so masterfully recounted by himself, in the life of this amazing man of the most pagan period of the Renaissance, the sixteenth century, there is still all too much of Christianity. Benvenuto Cellini was just as much Christian as pagan: he was not an integral man, possessed exclusively of the immanent sense of life. The description of his religious awakening in prison, the submission to the will of God by this adventurer and maker of scandals who had murdered people right and left, is deeply moving. On all the creativeness of the Renaissance there lies the seal of the stormy conflict of opposing elements, the eternal struggle of Christian transcendence with pagan immanence, of romantic incompleteness with classic finality.

The few centuries of the Renaissance (fourteenth, fifteenth, sixteenth centuries) are marked by an intensity of man's creative powers never before witnessed. But there are several renaissances, and it is important to distinguish among them. There is the early Renaissance, the trecento—all tinged with Christian colour. It was preceded by the sainthood of Francis of Assisi and the genius of Dante. Mystic Italy, the source of the early Renaissance, was the highest point of all western history. It was in mystic Italy, in Joachim de Floris, that the prophetic hope of a new world-epoch of Christianity was born, an epoch of love, an epoch of the spirit. These hopes nourished the creativeness of the early Renaissance, which was through and through Christian in its tendencies. Giotto and all the early religious painting of Italy, Arnolfi and others, followed St. Francis and Dante. But the hopes of mystic Italy were ahead of their times. Man was as yet unable to realize that towards which St. Francis and Dante travelled, although by different ways; that which Joachim de Floris had prophesied. A churchly-Christian creativeness, a culture, an art, in the final meaning of the word, had not yet come into being and could not have arrived. A true anthropology had not yet been revealed. The great rise of man in humanism was yet to come. The Renaissance of the fifteenth century, the quattrocento, did not realize the ideals of Dante and St. Francis, did not continue the religious art of Giotto—the fifteenth century revealed the struggle between the Christian and the pagan elements in man. The split man appeared, man who had not yet reconciled his pagan sources with his Christian sources: here man's creativeness struggles through to freedom. But in the quattrocento certain unhealthy artists appear, men divided against themselves, with a secret infirmity which hindered them from realizing to the full their great purposes, men of strange and tragic destiny. This unsound break is felt in Donatello, we find it in Pollajuolo and Verrocchio: it attains great intensity in Botticelli, and culminates in Leonardo. The art of the quattrocento is beautiful but painfully divided: in it Christianity encountered paganism, and this encounter deeply wounded the spirit of man.

The Florentine art of the quattrocento strove towards classic perfection of form and made great gains in this direction. But we may trace in it also marks of Christian romanticism—a transcendent longing which did not permit of classic perfection. The fountain springs of the Renaissance, St. Francis and Dante, were not forgotten in the fifteenth century. Fra Angelico continued the spirit of the trecento. And we can unravel the explanation of the tragic fate of some chosen artists of the quattrocento only if we peer and penetrate deeper into the divided, non-integral soul of the quattrocento, this soul torn by the struggle between Christian and pagan elements. The tragic fate of Botticelli,

232

that greatest artist of the Renaissance, who has only become intelligible and near to us in recent times, gives us a key to unlock the secret of the Renaissance, even to-day not completely understood. Botticelli is the most beautiful, the most deeply moved, the most poetic artist of the Renaissance, and the most divided and unsound, one who never attained classic completeness. In the trembling soul of Botticelli the quattrocento passed over from Lorenzo the Magnificent to Savonarola. In the fate of Botticelli the quattrocento recognized its betrayal of the great hopes of the early Christian Renaissance. The pagan Renaissance of the quattrocento began to degenerate at the end of the period: its aims were discovered to be unattainable and the appearance of Savonarola was inwardly thoroughly logical and inevitable. Savonarola was not at all the fanatical enemy and destroyer of art and beauty which he is sometimes painted. He called to mind the great aims of art, struggled with its deformations; but he was the expression of only one extreme element which like the pagan Renaissance was also unable to dominate in life. When Botticelli was the great artist of the pagan Renaissance and painted his Venuses for Lorenzo the Magnificent, he was not giving expression to the classic pagan element. His Venuses always resembled his Madonnas, just as his Madonnas resembled his Venuses. As Berenson has well said, Botticelli's Venuses have left the earth and his Madonnas have left heaven. In the work of Botticelli there is a longing which does not permit classic finality. The artistic genius of Botticelli created only a rhythm of lines more beautiful than anything known before. In the whole life-work of Botticelli there is a sort of fatal failure: he did not realize either the aims of the Christian Renaissance or those of the pagan Renaissance. Botticelli is not a perfect artist: he is less perfect than Giotto on one side and less perfect than Raphael on the other. And still Botticelli is the most beautiful, the nearest to us and the most moving artist of the Renaissance. One cannot approach his pictures without a strange inner trepidation. In Botticelli, in his art and

233

in his fate, the secret of the Renaissance was incarnated. In Botticelli there is revealed the most fatal failure of the Renaissance, how the dream of the Renaissance was unrealizable, incapable of fulfilment. *The secret of the Renaissance is that it did not succeed.* Never before had there been sent into the world such creative powers, and never before had there been so clearly revealed the tragedy of creativeness, the great gulf between aim and realization. In this failure of the Renaissance there was a real revelation of the destinies of human creativeness: in this there is an extraordinary beauty. The Renaissance did not take place, although it was marked by the greatest intensity of creative energy. A pagan Renaissance is impossible in the Christian world, for ever impossible. Classic immanent perfection can no longer be the portion of the Christian soul which has been touched by transcendent longing. The great experiment of a purely pagan Renaissance in a Christian world had to end in the preaching of Savonarola, the renunciation of Botticelli. Decline and distortion, a dead academism, are inevitable as the end of a pagan Renaissance in a Christian world.

The quattrocento is the heart of the Renaissance; in this central point is the secret of the Renaissance. Botticelli and Leonardo faced the riddle of man, which the trecento did not know. But the final great effort of the pagan Renaissance to realize here the ideal of classic and finished perfection, was made in the sixteenth century in the Roman High Renaissance. It may be argued that Michelangelo, Raphael, Giulio Romano, Bramante—the whole architecture of the High Renaissance, refute the statement that the Renaissance failed. It may be said that Raphael was a success; that he succeeded in perfection; that not Botticelli was the great figure in the Renaissance, but Raphael. But the art of the cinquecento with Raphael at its head is the beginning of a decline, of the failure of the spirit. When you wander through the Vatican, that kingdom of the High Renaissance of the sixteenth century, you are overpowered by a deadly *ennui*, you long for the Florence of the quattrocento,

234

less perfect, less finished, but uniquely beautiful, near and dear and intimately moving. What is Raphael? He is the abstract limit of the classically perfect tradition in art, the ultimate in the finished and the final. The art of Raphael is abstract perfection of composition—it is the law of perfected artistic form. Raphael is the least individual, the most impersonal artist in the world. In his perfect art there is no vibration of the living soul. It is not surprising that he has become the totem and example of all the academicians, who are still learning from him to-day. You can have no romance with Raphael—you cannot love him intimately. Raphael had great artistic gifts and an extraordinary adaptability, but we may doubt that he was a genius. He is not a genius because he never knew the universal conception of things, never felt the longing which passes out beyond the limits of this world. Raphael is not an individualist of genius—he is abstract form, perfect composition. Raphael's classicism in the Christian world produces an impression of deadly rigidity, almost as though it were superfluous, a failure more complete and fatal than the imperfection and division of the men of the quattrocento. All the high, perfect art of the sixteenth century is essentially unoriginal; in the sense of world development it is imitative and reactionary. We find in it no new beauty, hitherto unknown to the world.

The art of antiquity was original and beautiful: it was exclusively and uniquely alive. But beneath the perfect forms of the sixteenth century we may sense the beginning of moribund decline. The beauty of the cinquecento bears the stamp of unoriginality, of the passing and temporary, of unreality. Raphael's very approachability, the ease with which he is understood, his general recognition, are fateful qualities for him. Michelangelo had greater genius, was more original and more tragic than Raphael. But the very perfection of Michelangelo with its lack of charm was his failure: he too failed to realize the aims of the pagan Renaissance. The health in the art of Raphael and Michelangelo

235

is only apparent, external. The unhealthy art of the men of the quattrocento is much more original, more valuable, more significant. Despite their great differences, we find in both Botticelli and Leonardo the magic of charm. And neither Michelangelo nor Raphael possess this magic—one senses in them a sort of sexlessness. Michelangelo and Raphael are the beginning of the decline of art. After these comes the school of Bologna, dead academism. The final result of the Renaissance with all its failures, was baroque, which attempted to unite the Catholic reaction with the attainments of the pagan Renaissance, to utilize the pagan Renaissance in the service of the Jesuit church. Baroque is more original than the High Renaissance, and it succeeded in decorating Rome with fountains and stairs. Baroque conquered the whole of Europe, but in the false grimace of baroque there is imprinted the fatal lifelessness of a union of Christianity with paganism. The whole of paganism entered once more into the Catholic Church, but this failed completely to produce a renaissance. And a Christian ecclesiastical renaissance is just as impossible as is a pagan renaissance. Culture is not adequate to either pagan or Christian religious creativity. The tragedy of creativeness, its failure, is the final teaching of the great epoch of the Renaissance. In the great failure of the Renaissance lies its greatness. For the Christian world absolute finality and perfection lie in the transcendent distance.

§

Art, also, may be the redemption from sin. There is redemption in classic, canonic art whose attainments are in contrast to the aims of the creative act; and there is redemption, also, in romantic art, breaking all the canons and surpassing all limits. In art, as everywhere else in the world, the sacrifice of Golgotha is repeated. But the creative artistic act, by its purpose, by its intention, passes beyond the epoch of redemption. *The creative act is hindered in the world by the redemption, and therefore it becomes tragic.* By its very essence

236

creativeness passes out beyond the religious epochs of the law and the redemption, beyond both Old and New Testaments. But in these world-epochs it is forced to adapt itself both to the law and to the redemption. The adaptation of creativeness to the law produces classic art: its adaptation to the redemption produces romantic art. The creative act which gives birth to art cannot be specifically Christian: it is always beyond Christianity. But the realizations of that creative act may be carried out in a Christian milieu. In the strict sense of the word, creativity is neither Christian nor pagan: it rises above and beyond them. In the creative artistic act darkness is overcome and transfigured into beauty. We have already said that the demonic darkness of Leonardo burned up in his creative act and was turned into beauty. Art is pagan-classic or Christian-romantic not because of the nature of the creative act itself, which always surpasses the boundaries of both paganism and Christianity, but because of the world atmosphere in which the realization of art is operated.

The ancient and everlasting contrast of classic and romantic art takes on new forms in the nineteenth century. On the one hand realism is born, and on the other symbolism. Realism in art is an extreme form of adaptation to "this world". Realism does not, like classicism, strive to attain values of beauty here, immanently; it is not, like classicism, obedient to a canon of law, but rather to reality, to the data of the world. Realism is the furthest removed from the essence of every creative act: it is the least creative form of art. Realism, as a tendency, depresses and quenches the artist's impulses. And if the realists of the sixteenth century were sometimes great artists, this was only because tendencies in art in general are of small importance, and because the beauty of eternal art and the eternal creative act shone through their temporary realist shells. Balzac and Tolstoy can be called realists only conditionally. In no less measure they were mystics, and above all they were artists of genius. The programme of realist art always means the

237

decline of art, the demeaning of creativeness, submission to creative powerlessness. The creative act of an artist is essentially the non-submission to this world and its distortions. The creative act is a daring upsurge past the limitations of this world into the world of beauty. The artist believes that beauty is more real than the distortion of the world. The realistic tendency believes that distortion is more real than beauty and summons us to submit to this distortion in the world. Realist art is bourgeois. The degeneration of realism into naturalism was the last word in this adaptation and submission. Increasing heaviness in distortion is creative decline. There can be no art without an impulse to beauty. But we must distinguish between the submission of classicism, which produced the immanent value of beauty, and the submission of realism, which passively reflects the world. Artistic creativeness, like knowledge, is not merely a reflection of actuality: it always adds to the world's reality something which has never been before. And in the great art of the nineteenth century, which is conditionally termed realistic, we may discover both eternal classicism and eternal romanticism. Even more: in to-day's realistic art there are traces of a symbolism which reflects the eternal nature of all art. But realism has now been finished. The art of the end of the nineteenth century and the beginning of the twentieth, stands under the sign of symbolism. Only in symbolism is there revealed the true nature of all artistic creativity. And in symbolism the tragedy of creativity reaches its climax.

The difficulty of the problem of symbolism lies in the fact that, on the one hand all art is symbolic, and on the other there is a new symbolic art which marks the birth of a new spirit and a form of creativeness hitherto unknown. Of course Dante and Goethe were symbolists. And of course we may discover symbolism in the very essence of every genuinely great art, in the very nature of the creative act, which gives birth to the value of beauty. In art, new being is not created but only signs of new being, its symbols. Art always teaches us that everything passing and temporal is a symbol of

238

another form of being, permanent and eternal. The final reality of being is created in art only symbolically. For the creative act, truly final and secret being is attainable only symbolically. Hence symbolism is not only the strength of art but its weakness as well. Symbolism points up the eternal tragedy of human creativeness, the great distance which separates artistic creativeness from the final reality of being. The symbol is a bridge thrown across the gulf from the creative act to hidden, final reality. Art cannot be realistic, either in the empirical sense, or in the mystical. We can speak of realism in art, only conditionally. Mystic realism already exceeds the bounds of art as a differentiated cultural value. A final, mystic realism would mean the conquest of the tragedy of creativeness. At its peaks, symbolism in art merely makes the tragedy of creativeness more acute and throws out a bridge to a new and unheard-of creation of being. In the great art of antiquity, for instance in Dante, the mystic rose was only a symbol of the final reality of being. But even the art of Dante was powerless to create new being.

Not only all art, but all culture as well, is symbolic. In culture and its values there are created only signs, symbols of final being, rather than being itself or reality itself. Even economic culture is only a sign, a symbol of man's final power over nature, rather than the being of that power itself, its final reality. The final and most real power of man over nature will be theurgic rather than economic. There is symbolism in all human creativity. Symbolism is creativeness unfinished, creativeness which has not attained its final goal, is not finally realized. Art should be symbolic—the highest art is the most symbolic. But symbolism cannot be the final slogan of artistic creativity. Beyond symbolism is mystic realism: a way rather than a final purpose. Symbolism is a bridge over to the creation of new being, but it is not new being itself. Symbolism is the eternal in art, because all true art is a way to new being, a bridge into another world. This eternal symbolism of the artistic creative act is found in both classic

239

and romantic art. Even the realism of the nineteenth century was unable finally to suppress the symbolic nature of art.

But there is also a "symbolism" as direction or tendency of a new art. This new symbolism is characteristic of the new spirit and a new epoch of man's creativeness. The symbolism of Mallarmé, Maeterlinck, Ibsen and in Russia of V. Ivanov, A. Byelii and others, is bringing new values into the world, new beauty. This is not the symbolism of Goethe, nor is it the symbolism of the earlier great creators. In the new symbolism both the great creative intensity of the human spirit and the creative tragedy and illness of the spirit attain their final limits, reach the highest degree. The new man, in creative impulse, strives upward beyond the boundaries of art which have been set by this world. The symbolists refuse all adaptation to this world, all submission to this world's canons: they sacrifice all the values of well-being in this world, which this world hands out as rewards for adaptation and submission. It is the destiny of the symbolists to lead the way of new life in creativeness, new life which is sacrificial and tragic. Goethe's symbolism was after all canonic, adapted, obedient to the laws of the world. Even the symbolism of Dante was obedient to the word of the middle ages. The new symbolism pushes right away from all firm coasts: it seeks what has hitherto never been known. The new symbolism seeks the final, the ultimate: it passes the bounds of the average, ordered, canonic way. In the new symbolism creativeness outgrows itself. Creativeness presses forward, not towards cultural values but towards new being. Symbolism is a thirst for liberation from symbolism through a recognition of the symbolic nature of art. Symbolism is a crisis of cultural art, a crisis of every medium culture. In this lies its world-significance. But "condemned to die are the all-too-early messengers of an all-too-early spring". The first symbolists had to perish, to fall as sacrifices, just as Nietzsche was sacrificed and perished. Prophecy of new being breaks mightily forth in symbolism but we must not seek in symbolism either final perfection or

240

complete attainment. The tragedy of all Christian creativeness with its transcendental longing reaches a climax in symbolism. The paganism of so many of the decadents is a superficial phenomenon. Symbolism is the final word of the world-epoch of redemption and the entrance court into the world-epoch of creativity. The symbolists are the sacrificial forerunners and heralds of the coming world-epoch of creativeness. But the symbolists still have their roots in the epoch of redemption.

§

I do not know a phenomenon more noble, inwardly more tragic, and in its own way more heroic, than the Catholic writers of the nineteenth century, and a very special kind of Catholic, not official, not adapting themselves to the Catholic "world". I speak of Barbey d'Aurévilly, E. Hello, Villiers de l'Isle Adam, Verlaine, Huysmans, Léon Bloy. These "reactionaries", in most cases æsthetic royalists, clericals and aristocrats, hated the bourgeois world of the nineteenth century with a holy hatred. They were men of the new spirit, who lived palpitatingly beneath the garments of the restoration. They were reactionary—revolutionaries, adapted to nothing: their whole lives were spent in poverty, failure and lack of recognition. These men would not enter into any sort of compromise with the bourgeois spirit; they loved only their dream, and sacrificially devoted their whole lives to it. The biographies of these men move us with their tragedy, their own type of heroism. The beauty in which they lived was always for them the other world, in every way contrasting with the distortions of "this world" which they hated. Their very reactionism was revolt rather than adaptation. These men had no hopes whatever of earthly well-being. Their spirit projected them out beyond the limits of this world. This world called forth in them only scornful aversion. As André Gide says "Baudelaire, Barbey d'Aurévilly, Hello, Bloy, Huysmans—all had this in common: lack of knowledge of life, even hatred of life, scorn, shame, pure disdain. There are all the nuances—a sort of religious rancour against life." What a contrast in this noble, truly aristocratic spirit, to the bourgeois modernism which self-satisfiedly plays at being pagan! The art of these new French Catholics, unrecognized and scorned by everyone, is the last late flower of the world-epoch of redemption. Their beauty is still the beauty of the redemption. These weary spirits are the redemptive sacrifice for the sins of the bourgeois world, this world which has betrayed nobility. Here the Catholic spirit is refined to the point of losing all the contours of this world, all the heaviness of a catholicism become worldly. But neither in the wonderful stories of Villiers de l'Isle Adam nor in the vows of Verlaine, nor in the evil anger of Léon Bloy against the bourgeois world do we find the creative daring of the new world-epoch. These spirits stand at the boundary between two worlds: in them, as yet unconsciously, there trembles the future in which they do not believe; but theirs is a way of sacrifice and they are powerless to create new life. The new symbolism in France has a profound connection with Catholicism. And higher than these recent Catholics who have taken unto themselves the whole beauty of the redemption, this sacrificial nobility and this powerless heroism—higher than these stand only three: Nietzsche, Ibsen and Dostoevski.

The profound crisis of art is also felt in the painting of recent times, in cubism, in futurism. No matter how the art of to-day is destroyed by advertising and charlatanry, beneath this scum lies something more profound. The cubism of Picasso is something very significant and deeply moving. In Picasso's pictures we feel the real pain of the world's coming apart, layer by layer, the world's dematerialization and decrystallization, the atomization of the world's flesh, the rending of all the veils. After Picasso, who in his painting felt the movement of the cosmic wind, there can be no return to the old expression-forms of art. Futurism is the final break with the antique, the crisis of humanism, a shattering of the very image of man.

§

The new art, the new symbolism, are valuable and important first of all as a world-crisis of art, as indications of the crisis of all culture: what its enemies called decadence is connected with this great crisis of human creativeness. The artistic achievements of the new art are not as great as are its searching and its suffering. The new art is in essence a transition—a bridge to another type of creativeness. Art has arrived at such a profound crisis as the history of culture has never yet known. The profoundest revolution in human creativity is reflected in the tormented searchings of art. Even the epoch when Christianity appeared in the world did not know such a revolution of creativeness. Christianity was not a creative revolution in the world: Christianity was a revolution of redemption. The art of the catacombs was antique art; with the Christians creativeness remained pagan. Later Christianity introduced into art the longing for the transcendental, but even then art remained within the bounds of earthly achievements of artistic values, although these were not perfect. To-day the deep, revolutionary question is put concerning the impossibility of art as cultural value. The creative artistic act is transfused from culture into being. Symbolism is culture's dissatisfaction, an unwillingness to remain in culture: it is a way to being. We are living at the beginning of the end of medium, human art, cultural art. This phenomenon is deeper than the crisis of canonic art: it is the crisis of all art as a differentiated value of culture, the switchover of creative energy to a new way. We no longer have classically beautiful art: it has already become impossible. The art of Dostoevski, Leo Tolstoy, Ibsen, Baudelaire, Verlaine is not classically beautiful art, is not canonic art. Modern academism in art is always lifeless and no longer beautiful. And there can be no return to the pre-revolutionary period in art.

The art of Goethe, like Goethe's feeling of life, are lost to us forever—a lost paradise. Any attempt to return to Goethe is lifeless and reactionary. The catastrophic feeling for life has imprinted itself upon our art and permits no return to the ideal of Goethe. Goethe was a genius and a symbolist, but his art was still human-average-cultural, was a halt within boundaries. Goethe did not know that catastrophic sense which does not permit us to rest on medium values, does not permit adaptation to long perspectives of life-construction and welfare. To-day the ideal of Goethe holds us in the middle way: hinders the development of the end. Goetheism is a conservative slogan. To-day creativeness is revealing ends, limits. The prophecy of new being seeks an outlet for itself in the creative act of the new spirit. Everything canonic, classic, culturally differentiated, everything mediocre, adapted to "this world", everything Goethean, Kantian—all these set up conservative, hindering barriers to the prophetic creative spirit. And a return to the canonic, classic ideals of culture can be only a temporary reaction of weariness and weakness. The future belongs to the creative catastrophism of Dostoevski, Nietzsche and the genuine symbolists. Art has, after all, been an adaptation to "this world" and creative catastrophism must come to a sacrificial denial of art, but through art and within art itself. The sacrifice of culture for the sake of higher being will be super-cultural, and not pre-cultural or extra-cultural. It will justify the highest meaning of culture and art, as its great expression.

§

The new æstheticism was not an academic classical art for art's sake. Æstheticism strove to become a new religion, an exit from the disfigured world into the world of beauty. Æstheticism tried to be everything; to be another life; it flowed out over the limits of art, it thirsted for the transformation of being into art, for a renunciation of being, for the sacrifice of the world's life for the sake of beauty. In the religion of æstheticism there was its own kind of asceticism, its own wrestlers of the spirit. Such was the æstheticism of

Huysmans. Huysmans is a hermit and a spiritual wrestler of æstheticism, renouncing the life of this world, as did the best French symbolists. But æstheticism does not believe in the real transformation and transfiguration of this world, which lies in deformity, into the true world of beauty, into beauty as essential being. In the religion of æstheticism beauty is contrasted with what is; beauty is outside being. Æstheticism is incapable of creating beauty as the final and truest reality of the world. Æstheticism is not theurgic. In this phantom-like anti-realism, lies the profound tragedy of æstheticism: in this is the seed of its death. Æstheticism goes out into a phantom world, into beauty as something not existent, away from the deformity of that which does exist. If æstheticism could creatively attain the final beauty of being, it would save the world. For beauty saves the world, as Dostoevski says. In the genuine, noble, aristocratic æstheticism there was a religious longing. The longing of Huysmans was not satisfied by the "refined Thebaid" of æstheticism: he passes on from æstheticism to Catholic mysticism, finishes in a monastery and by his life reveals the religious depths of æstheticism. The best of the French æsthetes have entered mystic Catholicism, men foreign to bourgeois modernism and self-satisfied decadentism. But if on the one hand æstheticism approaches religious depths, on the other hand it degenerates into bourgeois modernism and æsthetic gourmandism, into parlour-academicism. This road smells of decay. By this way of spiritual death men are trying to save art by a return to classic-canonic ideals, to academicism, parnassism, to pure Apollonism. Only that æstheticism retains world significance and creative significance which has led to the final depths of religion.

Æstheticism intensified to the extreme, a dissatisfaction with the deformity of life, the impossibility of living longer in this deformity. And no matter how æstheticism degenerated, producing the new baseness and new deformity of bourgeois modernism, it radically altered something in the sense of life and cut off all return to the earlier adaptations to life's deformity. The autonomy of beauty has been forever confirmed, its distinction from both good and truth, its independent place in divine life. The everyday prose of life is not only the result of sin, it is sin: submission to it is evil. The holiday poesy of life is man's duty, and for the sake of it man should sacrifice everyday life, its goods and its peace of mind. Beauty is not only the aim of art—it is the aim of life. And the final aim is not beauty as cultural value, but beauty as being itself, that is the transformation of the chaotic deformity of the world into the beauty of the cosmos. With hitherto unheard-of clarity, symbolism and æstheticism set this aim of transforming life into beauty. And if the purpose of transforming life into art is illusory, the purpose of transforming the life of this world into essential beauty, into beauty of being, of the cosmos, this is mystically real. The cosmos is just this: beauty as being. Cosmic beauty is the aim of the world-process: it is another kind of being, a higher being which is in process of creation. The nature of beauty is ontological and cosmic. But all definitions of beauty are formal and partial. Beauty in its final essence is indefinable. Beauty is the great mystery. One must be initiated into the mystery of beauty and without this initiation beauty cannot be truly known. To know beauty, one must live within it. This is why all external definitions of beauty are so terribly disappointing.

But the final reality of beauty is accessible to us in this world only symbolically, only in the form of symbols. The realistic grasp of essential beauty, without the intermediary symbol will be the beginning of the transfiguration of this world, of a new heaven and a new earth. Then there will be no art, or æsthetic experience either, in the strict sense of the word, æsthetic experience in which final being is made evident by means of symbols. The way to beauty as being, to the cosmos, to the new heaven and the new earth, is a religious-creative way. This is entrance into a new life of the world. To live in beauty is the commandment of the new creative epoch. The creator expects from the creation of

246

beauty nothing less than good. Failure to obey the commandments of beauty may be punished by hellish torment. The imperative to create beauty in all things and everywhere, in every act of life, opens the new world-epoch, the epoch of spirit, the epoch of love and liberty. In this imperative there is a heavenly aristocracy, a genuine hierarchism, not the bourgeois hierarchism of this world. And every creative act is a transition beyond this world, the conquest of the world's deformation. But in the religious-creative epoch this will mean the production of a new cosmos. Herein lies the religious meaning of the present crisis of art and of culture. The negative, uncreative revolt against the beautiful, old, pure art is powerless and fruitless: this revolt can easily turn into barbarian nihilism. Revolt produces only anarchy. And just as powerless and fruitless is the revolt against pure science. Art, like all the rest of culture, must be lived out by man. The creative crisis of art should be immanent and super-cultural rather than barbaric and uncultural. Cultural values are sacred, and any nihilistic attitude towards them is godless. In art as in science, the justice of the law and the redemption are still alive. Only an immanent-creative conquest of art and science, as of all culture, rather than an external and nihilistic conquest, is possible for the sake of higher being. This brings us to the problem of theurgy, of theurgic creativeness—the basic problem of our times.

§

Theurgy does not create culture, but new being. Theurgy is super-cultural. Theurgy is art creating another world, another being, another life; creating beauty as essence, as being. Theurgy overcomes the tragedy of creativeness, directs creative energy towards a new life. In theurgy the word becomes flesh. In theurgy art becomes power. The beginning of theurgy is the end of literature, the end of all differentiated art, the end of culture, but an end which takes unto itself the world-meaning of culture and art, a super-cultural end. Theurgy is man working together with God,

God-working; it is divine-human creativeness. In theurgic creativeness the tragic opposition of subject and object is removed, the tragic hiatus between the will to a new world and the attainment of only cultural values. The theurge creates life in beauty. Symbolic art is a bridge, a way to theurgic art. The new art must lead us to theurgy. Theurgy is the banner of the art of the last times, the art of the end.

Now it may be that we are not yet sufficiently mature for theurgic art and hence should not mechanically misuse this sacred slogan. But we have at least matured to the place where we are conscious of the inevitable transfer of all art over to theurgy. We are conscious of the theurgic longing of every true artist. Theurgy corresponds to the religious epoch of creativeness. Theurgy is immanently religious art. The religious tendency in art is just as fatal to art as a social or moral tendency. Artistic creation cannot and should not be specifically and intentionally religious. And the effort to restore religious art in the medieval sense of the word is fruitless. This dead restoration we feel in the religious art of Vasnetzoff, for instance. Lay, non-religious, free art must go on to the limits of the religious. In this sense the art of Ibsen and of Baudelaire is religious. The antique classic ideal of art is wrong not because art should not be pure, free of any aims forced upon it from without. Art is absolutely free. Art is freedom, not necessity. But the academic-classic ideal of art is a middle-of-the-road, a hindering ideal, which prevents the revelation of the final depths of art. For the final depths of all true art are religious. Art is religious in the depths of the very artistic creative act. Within its own limits, the artist's creation is theurgic action. Theurgy is free creation, liberated from norms of this world which might be imposed upon it. But in the depths of theurgic action there is revealed the religious-ontological, the religious meaning of being. Theurgy cannot be either an imposed norm or a law for art. Theurgy is the final bourne of the artist's inward desire, its action in the world. The man who confuses theurgy with religious tendencies in art does not know what theurgy is.

248

Theurgy is the final liberty of art, the inwardly-attained limit of the artist's creativeness. Theurgy is an action superior to magic, for it is action together with God; it is the continuation of creation with God. The theurge, working together with God, creates the cosmos; creates beauty as being. Theurgy is a challenge to religious creativity. In theurgy Christian transcendence is transformed into immanence and by means of theurgy perfection is attained. It is not art alone, which leads to theurgy, but art is one of the principal ways to it. The way to theurgic creativeness leads through sacrifice and denial. The theurge offers this life as a sacrifice for the sake of another life. The artist-theurge renounces the ordered art of this world for the sake of the pure creative act. At the end of art we find the same self-denial, as at the end of science, the state, the family—at the end of all culture. Theurgic art cannot be differentiated and individualistic. Theurgic art is synthetic and œcumenic—it is a sort of hitherto-unknown, not-yet-revealed pan-art. Wagner strove for that kind of art but never realized it. There is something false in Wagner and something reactionary in his ways, for he is trying to bring about a religious renaissance by means of the theatre, music and drama. Theurgy is universal action. In it all forms of human creativity meet. In theurgy the creation of beauty in art is joined with the creation of beauty in nature. Art must become a new, transfigured nature. Nature itself is a work of art and the beauty in it is creativeness.

§

In our troubled, seeking, transitory epoch, not yet incarnate and not yet finished, the spirit of music lords it over the spirit of the plastic. Our epoch is the least architectural and the least sculptured of all eras of world history. Our life is not plastic: it is formless; our spirit is not incarnate in forms of beauty. In painting we see de-materialization and dis-incarnation. Architecture has perished completely, and sculpture is no longer sculpture. The nineteenth century had great music, but there was no great plastic art. The German genius is musical, and it has overcome the Latin genius, the genius of the plastic. A truly beautiful culture will create great architecture first of all. Our culture is not beautiful. In our epoch the spirit of music has become a bourgeois spirit. Music has become a favourite relaxation and recreation for the *bourgeoisie*, something which lays upon them no obligations, weakens the will and gives illusory transport into another world. In the spirit of music there is prophecy of incarnate beauty yet to be. Beethoven was a prophet. But in our day music has ceased to be prophecy, has adapted itself to bourgeois life. Scriabin prophesies of the new world-epoch, but in him we feel a sense of foreboding and unconquered chaos. The prophetic future does not belong to the German spirit of music, nor to the Latin spirit of plastic, but only to synthetic, theurgic art: it does not belong to Wagnerian art which still remains within culture, but rather to something else which passes out beyond the bounds of culture into new being. The slavic-Russian renaissance can be neither musical nor plastic; it can be only theurgic. This is prophesied in the great Russian literature. The problem of art as theurgy is primarily a Russian problem, the Russian tragedy of creativeness. In the artist-theurge the power of man over nature is realized by means of beauty. For beauty is a great *force* and it will save the world.

# CHAPTER XI

# CREATIVITY AND MORALS: THE NEW ETHIC OF CREATIVITY

Hitherto, the traditional morals of the Christian world have not been creative. Christian morals were either still the Old Testament law which, like the Christian state, denounced sin, or obedience to the results of sin, a redemptive obedience. The creative New Testament morals of evangelic love have not been revealed in the Christian world —they have only been rarely glimpsed, like lightning flashes, in the lives of such chosen spirits as St. Francis. Christianity was oriented towards the world as a religion of obedience rather than a religion of love. The spirit of the Church Fathers is primarily the spirit of obedience or submission rather than the spirit of love. Christian activity consisted in getting rid of sin. Christianity inoculated the world with the morals of obedience and of well-being. Morals in this world are exactly like the state, economics, the family, science: morals are canonic, under the law. Morals are a law of obedience in relation to God and a law of well-ordered being in relation to the world. Even well-ordered being in this world, be it of the state, the family, science or what you will, is morally justified as a weight and a burden of submission to the results of sin. Everyday obedience is given moral priority over the feast-day of love. Morals have turned out to be an expression of the world's heaviness, of man's oppression under sin and its consequences. The traditional morals of the Christian world are terribly burdensome; they are borne on the *pathos* of heaviness. The categorical imperative is terribly heavy; it lacks all sense of lightness. The good news of the Gospel does not know the categorical imperative, but the Christian world knows it, burdened down as it is by the results of sin. This submissive bearing of the burden of the consequence of sin long ago led to a benumbing of Christian morals, and this burden, the opposite of all lightness of flight, itself becomes sin. And the very submission which began as an act of courage is deformed into hypocrisy. Christianity, as the revelation of grace, freedom and love, is something other than a set of morals under the law: in it there is neither utilitarianism nor general validity. But the Christian world is infected with the utilitarian morals of adaptation, with the criteria of usefulness and good order for this overburdened world. The official morals of the Christian world are through and through adapted to this world, to its heaviness, to lowered forms of intercourse in this world. These are the morals of utilitarian fear. They deny the seraphic nature of man, man's natural divinity. And one looks in vain in this moral system for the Gospel of love and freedom from care, so unadapted to the world's heaviness, so unsubmissive to the results of sin. Christian morals are profoundly opportunistic; they are full of the *pathos* of submissive adaptation, the *pathos* of bearing the burden and the heaviness of the world. This moral consciousness goes to the length of justifying evil, for the patient bearing of the results of sin is considered moral worth. The burden of these morals is not sacrificial. And the opportunism of Christian morals finds its highest religious sanction in the mystic of obedience.

Traditional Christian morals are hostile to all heroism, to all heroic upswing of life, to heroic impulse, to heroic sacrifice. There was heroism in the morals of chivalry, which really were creative, but the source of these morals was neither traditionally Christian nor derived from the early Church Fathers. In the patristic, traditionally Christian consciousness, negative virtues—humility, self-denial, abstinence—eclipsed the positive virtues of courage, nobility and honour. It is remarkable that such leading moralists of modern times as Kant and Leo Tolstoy in their moralism

252

confessed the legalism of the Old Testament. Kant and Tolstoy do not know the true mysteries of the Christian religion but they are outstanding exponents of Christian morals of the law, of obedience rather than creativeness. Tolstoy demanded a radical and revolutionary obedience to the moral law of the Lord of life, and for the sake of this obedience, for the sake of passive resistance to evil, he broke with all opportunistic adaptation. To the consciousness of Kant there was revealed the great mystery of the autonomy of personality but he reasoned that creative personality must be submitted to universally valid law. Creative morals are foreign to both Tolstoy and Kant. In the last analysis, Tolstoy took his morals from Orthodoxy, first cleansing it of all adaptation and the accretions of the historic process. But in Tolstoy's morality we find the same utilitarian concern for good order which is in traditional Orthodox morality. True sacrificial spirit is foreign to traditional Christian morality. It rests on the firm guarantee that "this cup will pass". The spirit of utilitarian adaptation to good order permits no sacrifice of security and well-being in this world. Obedience purchases a secure position in the world, a comfortable place in a safe harbour. There is no group in the world less sacrificial, more utilitarian, than the clergy. The clerical class is the most earthy, the most adapted, and knows best how to take care of itself, of all the classes. The so-called spiritual class is least of all spiritual, most of all fleshly. The tragedy of sacrifice—of willingness to sacrifice—is unknown to the cleric hierarchy.* The Christian world purchased, at the price of an already long since moribund submission, physical well-being and spiritual repose. This Christian world has found for itself a comfortable place in life, not only spiritually but materially as well, with no consciousness of danger or of the need for struggle. Traditional morals of the Christian world are bourgeois in the profoundest sense of the word.

* It must be noted that this was written before the Russion revolution.—D.A.L.

The sin of traditional Christian morals with which the
world is also inoculated, a world which has lost its Christian
faith, is not at all in the extremes of asceticism. This sin is
in the opportunistic adaptability to the bourgeois world.
*Under the sign of submission to the world's heaviness, Christian
morals justify the world as it is, a world lying in sin.* This morality
is impregnated with the *pathos* of small acts and modest
situations: it is afraid of great, heroic, broad-winged action.
And the lack of wings has been raised almost to the rank of
religious heroism. A modest moral professionalism is sanctioned: let each sit modestly in his own place and patiently
do his own small job. It is not good to rise too high above the
world's evil and distortion. One should share the general
deformation and the general diminution of values, the
general depression. Here we have the source of inertia and
reaction on the ground of a certain sort of religious democratism. This type of morality has no love for the heights; it is
hostile to any aristocratic spirit. The dominant morality
connected with Christian consciousness is permeated,
through and through, by a bourgeois-democratic adaptation
to the conditions of the world.

"Bourgeoisity" is a basic moral category. Here, of course,
we are speaking in religious and physical, rather than social
or class, terms. "Bourgeoisity" is submission to conditions
and evaluations set up by the inertia and heaviness of the
world. Everything which evaluates a man not by his innate
qualities but rather by his situation or the milieu in which he
lives is bourgeois. And the opposite of this is every creative
conquest of the world's data, every rise above the evaluation
of the world's inertia. The opposite of "bourgeoisity" is
sacrificial renunciation of well-being and security. "Home-
town" morality is bound to a given locality, limited by the
given conditions, fears any break with them. All "practical"
morality is essentially bourgeois—even Christian everyday
morality is bourgeois; while in the pure morality of the

Gospels there is no trace of this practical, everyday morality, no hint of the bourgeois. Was the morality of St. Francis the dominant Christian morality of the time? Men have always held the morality of the Gospels as inadaptable to life, with its concern for a good situation and for security. And the Christian world has accepted a non-Christian, bourgeois morality as useful for living and justified by submission to the consequences of sin. The dominant Christian consciousness accepted and justified all the bourgeois values of worldly position. Christianity has sanctioned all the false hierarchy of "this world". Bishop Feofan, that great hermit and ascetic, bows before all the bourgeois values of worldly position. It is not the hierarchy of heaven which he recognizes, but the earthly hierarchy of rank. And it turns out that the bourgeois values of the mighty of this world are religious values. The ascetic life of Bishop Feofan, in its attitude toward God, is mystic, but his morality, in its attitude toward the world, is coarsely bourgeois. It is a banal "home-town" morality which carries submissiveness to the point of serfdom.

§

In the nineteenth and twentieth centuries the dominant moral consciousness threw off the last remnants of genuine Christian asceticism and Christian sacrifice of this world for the sake of transcendent yearning for another world. Bourgeois morality conquered, the morality of the conditional values of this world's position, values of riches, power, fame, of sexual indulgence, of the enjoyment of comfort and luxury. Christianity itself is becoming more and more bourgeois: the unreconciled attitude toward "this world", the beauty of striving for another world—all this has vanished. Christian consciousness has forgotten that it is the rich, the powerful, the famous of this world who will find it hardest of all to enter the Kingdom of Heaven. The rich and powerful and famous of this world are people spiritually impoverished, people who have failed to rise spiritually, people often despised, more often to be pitied. The powerful of this world are weak before God: the Christian conquest of "this world" is a conquest of all "bourgeoisity"; it is the sacrifice of worldly profit and well-being to nobility and beauty as a way of life. The religion of Christ is incompatible with the recognition of bourgeois values, with obsequiousness before the riches, the power, the fame, the enjoyment of the world. Traditional Christian morality does not spring from the Gospels, from the revelation of Christ, the Absolute Man, but from extra-Christian, pre-Christian sources. Bourgeois morality is basically the morality of the race and of the race's welfare. The whole of Christian history is full of the duality of the pre-Christian morality of the race and the Christian morality of personality. On the Christian morality of personality it would have been impossible to construct any worldly, racial or social order. The whole Christian morality of personality was based on ascetic sacrifice of this world for the sake of another. And all worldly order has rested on the basically bourgeois, extra-Christian morality of the race. Man cannot live in this world and create new life, using only the morality of submission, only the morality of conflict with his own sins. One who lives in constant terror at his own sins is powerless to accomplish anything in the world.

§

Every man must pass through the redemption and commune with its mystery. The moment of redemption from sin in the life of a man is inevitably connected with obedience and humility, with renunciation of self-assertion, with the sacrifice of spiritual pride. He who does not know this inward labour of submission and renunciation can never hope to rise. Every road leading upward is a sacrificial way and predicates inward spiritual effort to strip off the old Adam. By means of humility man frees himself from his own evil and meanness: he who has committed low and evil deeds is not lost; he is purified by the sacrament of repentance to a new life. But it is impossible to construct a whole

256

life-ethic on humility and submission. If they are recognized as the only guides of life, the great moments of humility and submissiveness can easily be turned into slavery, hypocrisy and spiritual death. The Christian morality of humility and submissiveness is insufficient—it does not reveal all the values of life. Spiritual efforts of humility and submission are only moments on the way—the goal is the creation of new life in love. But Christianity as a religion of redemption has not revealed moral creativeness. Nowadays it is more difficult to accept the Christian morality of the Church Fathers than to accept Christian dogmas and sacraments. And we are astounded at the attempts of the modern consciousness to transform the religion of Christ, the religion of the world-mystery of redemption, into Christian morality. How often do we hear it said that all that is left of Christianity which is acceptable to our consciousness is Christian morals! Men say this only because they consider that Christian morals are infinitely adaptable. The creation of life can be justified by Christian morals only through boundless violation of the Gospels. In the moral consciousness of modern humanity there are creative values which were not revealed in Christian morals. These creative values speak of man's uprising, and it is more difficult to renounce them than to renounce the ever-more-empty rationalism which hinders our acceptance of dogmas and sacraments—these values we should not renounce. Nietzsche's protest against Christian morals is immeasurably deeper and more significant than the rationalistic arguments of Harnack against Christian dogmas. The moral side of Christianity contains the eternal and absolute. This eternal and absolute is connected with the ascetic mysticism of overcoming "this world", with the renunciation of the fleeting goods of this world, with an inward experience of the way that leads through Golgotha. And the most valuable and unshakable element in Christian morals is just that which the modern moralizers of Christianity are least inclined to accept—mystical ascetic. But historic Christian morality evidences many-layered accretions of the everyday, many temporary and conditional adaptations. Our commonly-accepted orthodox morality, which has brought the *pathos* of obedience to the point of submission and subjection to sin and deformity, is not the eternal part of Christianity but only something temporary, like everything else of the everyday.

Neither are the moral ideals of the Church Fathers eternal or absolute. The moral ideal of the Church Fathers was that of *"starchestvo"*—the tradition of certain holy elders in the monasteries, like the Elder (Starets) Zosima in Dostoevski's *Brothers Karamazov*—it decries youth, it denies the creative impulse and upsurge; it is afraid of youth. The patristic ideal of the elders seems to be frightened at pagan youth, in which there should have occurred a repulsion from the world; it considers all youth as pagan. In the first, most intense moments of redemption, the elders probably had to be set over against youth. But the institution of elders (*starchestvo*) is not eternal. Through the redemption the world will come to a new creative morality of youth—not pagan youth, but youth in the Spirit of Christ. Christ, the Absolute Man, is eternally young. In the Gospels themselves the institution of elders is not found. The institution of elders is a human, not a divine, institution. It appeared because human youth found it more difficult to accept the venerable mystery of the redemption than did the elders. This is a human weakness. Great is the wisdom of the elders, passing the boundaries of this world's reason. But life built upon the elders' life-morals always speaks of powerlessness. The elders' morality is always one of fear and worry. Only the morals of youth can be morals of creativeness and daring. The morality of the Gospels is care-free and does not permit of worrying. And the most perfect exemplifier of the Gospel morality is still St. Francis, in spirit a youth rather than an elder. The care-burdened morality, the morality of worry, is the bourgeois morality of this world. We read in the Gospels: "Consider the birds in the sky or the lilies of the field", and again: "Sufficient unto the day is the evil thereof."

258

Here we have youthful freedom from care and worry. Of course we must not confuse the institution of elders with age. The elders have attained wisdom: in simple age there is decline. But in life the morals of the elders easily turn into the morals of old age, the morals of constant fear, constant anxiety, constant concern about the troubles of to-morrow, perpetual denial of the divinely care-free birds of the heaven and the lilies of the field, denial of the Gospel truth, of the truth of St. Francis, of youth. Christ is eternally young and eternally young is the androgyne, the virgin-youth. The future creative morality is morality of eternal youth, transfigured, care-free and unworried. As Carlyle truly says, only victory over fear makes man a man. Creative morality cannot be based upon separating and placing opposite each other the human and the divine: creative morality will always reveal the seraphic nature of man.

§

Wherein lies the eternal value of Christian morality? What is its value for the future ethic of life, for creative ethics? Moral evaluations fall into a whole series of antitheses. There is a morality of weakness and a morality of strength: there is a morality of sympathy, of human welfare, of altruism, and a morality of values of creative upward movement: there is a morality of slavish "offendedness" and a morality of free guilt: there is a morality of the aristocratic nobility of the spirit and a morality of the serf-like plebeian spirit. Nietzsche considered Christian morality slavish, plebeian, a morality of weakness, and so he hated it. He contrasted it with a morality of the lordly, the aristocratically-noble morality of power. Nietzsche said many things about Christianity, things notable and moving, valuable for the moral rebirth of man, for he was surely one of the greatest moralists of all time, in the noblest sense of that word. But whatever Nietzsche says about Christianity we must take and turn inside out. The motives of Nietzsche's criticism of Christian morality are profound and valid but

259

the criticism itself is altogether untrue. Nietzsche talks like a religious blind man, one who has not the gift of seeing the final mysteries. The religion of Christ is not at all what Nietzsche took it for. Christian morality is not slavishly-plebeian but rather aristocratically-noble, the morality of the sons of God, with their primogeniture, their high birth and their high calling. Christianity is the religion of the strong in spirit, not the weak. Christian sanctity has always meant a selection of the strong in spirit, an accumulation of spiritual power. The Christian ethic is an ethic of spiritual victory rather than spiritual defeat. Those who have overcome the world, sacrificing this world's goods, are always the strongest, the victors in the truest sense. And in comparison with the power and the victory of the spirit of Christ, every power and victory in this world is illusory and insignificant. The powerful of this world are weaklings, the vanquished in spirit. True Christian morality lays on man, who has become a son of God, free responsibility for his own fate and for the fate of the world, makes it impossible for the sons of God to feel slavish, plebeian, ignoble resentment against fate, against life and against other people. The experience of free guilt is an experience of power; the experience of slavish resentment is an experience of weakness. He who is counted in the kingdom of the sons of God is free. And he who longs to redeem his guilt and his sin longs for power out of power, rather than longing for weakness out of weakness: he will participate in the salvation of the world. Man's powerlessness to redeem from sin by his own natural powers, man's recourse to the aid of the Redeemer—this is the powerlessness of fallen human nature, the powerlessness of separation from God. But in truth the whole worth of man is in his participation in God and in divine life, in his striving upward. When man is aided by the God-man Redeemer, this is not some external help, alien to man's nature, but an inward aid which reveals his own natural likeness to God, his own participation in divine life, man's inward upward-striving. Christ is not outside us but within us. He is the

260

Absolute Man in us. He is our communion with the Holy Trinity.

The religion of Christ is the religion of man's highest powers—it is the very opposite of all weakness or depression in man. Christianity is a way of the revelation in every man of the Man Absolute. But in the world-epoch of the redemption the Absolute Man is revealed in his sacrificial aspect, and Christian morality is sacrificial. Another aspect of the Absolute Man is revealed in creativeness. Hence the way of Christian morality leads through sacrifice to creativeness, through the renunciation of this world with its tempting goods for the creation of a new world and a new life. The true *pathos* of Christian morality is in readiness to sacrifice. Readiness to sacrifice is always noble, always aristocratic. The plebeian spirit is not sacrificial. The Christian sacrifice of "the world" and its goods always means the sacrifice of security, of a secure place in the world; it always means giving up an assured position in the world. This is consenting to follow Christ even through the phase of being forsaken by God. The sacrifice of Christian morality is directly opposed to all "bourgeoisity". Therefore true Christian morality must recognize the virtue of an insecure position (a virtue which Nietzsche recognized to a large degree) and refuse the bourgeois virtues. But in Christianity sacrifice is never for the sake of human well-being, for the sake of the bourgeois virtues, but rather in the name of God and for the sake of creative values, of values that move upward. This is a way that leads upward through fractionization. Christian morality is always something of the heights, something which uplifts, rather than a thing of the valley, something which flattens out. Christian morality is a morality of values, of the creative heightening of life, rather than a morality of altruistic distribution. Christianity is a religion of love rather than of altruism. Christianity does not permit a lowering of quality for the sake of quantity—it is wholly in quality, i.e. in aristocratic value.

§

The world-crisis of culture, so much talked-about, is also a moral crisis, a revolution of moral consciousness. Amoralism is just the same phenomenon of the world's moral crisis as "decadence" is a phenomenon of the world crisis in art. Morality, as a canonic, universally valid cultural value, has cracked: it is just as over-ripe and broken as are all other canonic, universally-valid cultural values, such as science, classically beautiful art, the family, etc. There is a deep abyss between morals and being, and in our day this abyss has opened. This is a partial, but very clear instance of the break between culture and being. By means of morality, higher being, another life, will never be attained. Amoralism is only an unhealthy, often superficial, symptom of the profound crisis of morality as law, of Old Testament canonic morality. In the world-crisis of morals the longing for moral creativeness is struggling forth, the longing for morals as creativeness rather than obedience. The crisis of moralism, the protest against the law of moral submission, is also a foretaste of a new world-epoch, an epoch of creativeness. In moral life, as in intellectual, artistic, sexual life, the new man longs to create new life and not merely give obedience to the consequences of sin, not merely adapt himself to the conditions of this world. Never yet, in any epoch, has there been born out of canonic morality a new community of men. Like every other law, morality has done more to denounce evil than to create higher truth in life. Nowadays morality has already outgrown the law of obedience which denounces evil and is adapting itself to its conditions. Morality wishes to be creativity of higher truth in life and a higher being. Morality, as a differentiated sphere of cultural life, has ceased to inspire; it is declining and degenerating. It is recognized as being a hindrance to the creation of being. "Average" morality, the morality of security, which has held off the beginning of the end, which hides the ultimate limits of being, must itself sooner or later come to an end, and be overcome by the creative effort of the human spirit. In this crisis of the average and hindering "safe" morality, Nietzsche is of immense significance. His creative spirit longed to stand on the other side of the secure middle line of canonic morality. Canonic morality has always been an expression of the average, the general spirit, rather than the spirit of individual heights. Nietzsche was a great denouncer of the average-general spirit of humanism. The morality of humanism is not one of ends and heights: it is a morality of the average, of the plain. The morality of humanism is still a morality of obedience rather than of creativity, of the race, rather than of divine-humanity. Humanistic morality is distributive rather than productive. Nietzsche is the sacrificial forerunner of a new moral epoch. But he himself is altogether transitory: he is forging no new values.

The new creative epoch will be super-moral as well as super-cultural, rather than pre-moral or pre-cultural. Pre-morality or amorality, like all pre-culture, is nihilism, like every negative anarchic protest which does not create culture, but unfetters chaos. The world crisis of morals must go on to its end rather than return to its beginning. Ibsen is also of great significance in the moral crisis. In Ibsen's work there is the same mountain-atmosphere, the same heroic upstriving which we find in *Zarathustra*. There is also the revolt of qualitatively upswinging individuality against the spirit of the average and the general. Nietzsche and Ibsen are the greatest moralists of modern times, but still they are religiously blind men. Important, too, is the ardent hatred of that crazy Catholic, Léon Bloy, for the bourgeois world and bourgeois moral values. In his book *Exègése des Lieux Communs* there are flashes of true genius, and "bourgeoisity" is profoundly revealed as a religious-metaphysical category. In Léon Bloy there trembles in anger everything in Catholicism which is noble—not submissive to the bourgeois world. But in Bloy's flaming anger there is a lack of faith in the victory of nobility over "bourgeoisity". In Bloy, as in all the great French Catholics of the nineteenth century, we feel a creative powerlessness. The inscrutable ways of fate made Nietzsche creatively daring but religiously blind, and Léon Bloy religiously clear-sighted but creatively powerless.

What, then, is the essence of the moral crisis? The essence is above all a revolutionary movement from a consciousness for which morality means submission to a general-average law, over to a consciousness for which *morality is a creative problem of individuality*. This is a liberation from the left-overs of heteronomous morality. The universally-valid morality of the law was only a denunciation of sin and evil and the reduction of all men to a common level. The law must be fulfilled; that is, one must *not* do wrong, one must free himself from sin. But in this overcoming of sin there is nothing individual or creative, while man's highest purpose is the creation of new life. The creation of new life leads through the mystery of individuality. Creative morality is not the fulfilment of law; it is the revelation of man in moral creativeness. And this revelation of man in moral creativeness always individual and qualitative rather than general and average, somewhere unites with the morals of the Gospel, with the morality of St. Francis, with the individual poesy of New Testament life which knows not the law. What is said here is not anomism. The law must inwardly be lived out, rather than be overthrown by a mob. The sinful side of human nature remains oriented towards the law, but its creative side surpasses the law.

§

Traditional Christian morals have been too exclusively constructed on fear and care for the soul's salvation. Creative morals should be built on courage and concern for creative uplift. Panic fear of perishing demeans man and in the last analysis becomes unmoral and unreligious by its very motives. This kind of fear is neither noble nor beautiful. Constant and cowardly trembling for his soul destroys the image of God in man. Because of his fear, man is ready to renounce all creative values if only he is not to perish. This

264

is a special and very unattractive form of religious egoism. Egoism and cowardice are inwardly related. Equally related to each other are courage and the readiness to sacrifice. Fearlessness of spirit, daring before God, are very high, sacrificial virtues of the religious way of living. Egoistic fear of one's own destruction, which can bring man to a denial of honour, should give way to fear of one's own low estate, deformity and lack of nobility. It is a great slander against Christianity to say that the sense of honour is alien to it. A true sense of honour is possible only on the basis of Christianity, since Christianity is a revelation about personality. Honour is not spiritual pride and self-assertion. Honour is holding high the image and likeness of God in man, which must never be lowered. Honour guards a divine value and hence is one of the eternal bases of morality. Self-renunciation destroys the godless nature in man: honour confirms the divine nature in him. Renunciation of godless self-assertion and guarding one's honour are joined in one virtue, in the revelation of the divine Man.

In chivalry there was true moral creativeness. The idea of chivalry was a forecourt of the revelation about man. But the idea of chivalry was never realized. The actual chivalry of the middle ages was far from the idea of chivalry. Chivalry is eternal by the task laid upon it. It brought into the world heroic values: the value of sacrificial honour and sacrificial loyalty. Personality was forged in chivalry. The modern bourgeois world has wished to substitute "bourgeoisity" for chivalry, bourgeois virtues for chivalrous virtues. And the bourgeois world thought that chivalry was buried for ever as a product of the dark middle ages and that it could never know a renaissance. But if chivalry should perish, high moral schooling of personality would perish with it. The spirit of chivalry continues to live, as the eternal contrast to the bourgeois spirit. The morals of chivalry and bourgeois morals will remain for ever, to the end of the ages, the most profoundly conflicting opposites. The categories of chivalry and of bourgeoisity are religious-metaphysical rather than social historic categories: under changing guises and in various times, they continue to exist. Chivalry remains the eternal task of the human spirit, which outlives the old raiment of medieval chivalry. In our bourgeois epoch, the task of creating a spiritual chivalry, a chivalry of the spirit, stands before the elect of mankind with new compulsive power. In our epoch the renaissance of the orders of chivalry in a new spirit is eminently possible. The spirit of chivalry is called to preserve the true, heavenly aristocratism of moral values, the true, heavenly hierarchism, unstained by the bourgeois hierarchism of this world. That every value is aristocratic—this was the revelation of the spirit of chivalry. Chivalry forms a true, mysterious hierarchy, a sacrificial hierarchy, and hence a hierarchy invisible by the bourgeois world, subject as it is to its own visible but spurious hierarchy. The morality of chivalry is a morality of values and therefore it is in profound contrast to all bourgeois-democratic morals of well-being and order, morals of "the last men".

Democratism (in the metaphysical, rather than the social sense of the word) is profoundly bourgeois, for it places man's well-being and good situation above values, quantity above quality, the average above the individual, distribution above creativity. Aristocratic morals (in the metaphysical rather than the social sense of the word) are morals of value, of quality, of individuality, of creativeness. And every degradation of value, of quality, of individuality or creativeness, for the sake of the general-average, the quantitative for the sake of well-being, good order and distribution, is a sin against God and against the divine in man. Christian œcumenicity, Christian universalism has nothing in common with a democratic lowering of values and qualities, with a bourgeois sacrifice of creativeness for the sake of good order and well-being. Christianity is aristocratic, hierarchic; it is oriented towards value, quality, individuality. At the same time Christianity is œcumenical and universal; it is the salvation of the whole world: of each and all, down to the last grain of dust; it summons all men to the messianic banquet.

266

Christianity recognizes the absolute value of every human person but this recognition has nothing in common with the democratic mechanics of quantities. In truth the creative morality which is coming in the world, which means a great moral revolution, is not a democratic, but an aristocratic morality, for creativeness is all in quality rather than quantity, in value rather than in well-being, in the individual rather than the general-average, in upsurge rather than in distribution, in organism rather than in mechanics. Aristocratism is morally revolutionary—democratism is morally conservative. The chivalric morality of aristocratism can never oppress or enslave anyone—it is a service ever-ready for sacrifice, which concerns the whole world. The knight sacrifices himself and his goods but never sacrifices value: to value he remains absolutely true.

§

Not only utilitarianism but altruism as well is a doctrine of bourgeois-democratic morality, of the average morality of well-being, the morality of quantity. The bourgeois-democratic nineteenth century invented altruism and tried to substitute it for Christian love. Men talk of altruism when love has cooled to the point of death. Love is creativeness of the new communion, communion in the Spirit. Love unites organically, satisfies qualitatively. Love means going out of this world, from its heaviness, its fetters and its fractionization, into another world, a world of freedom and unity. Altruism is all in the heaviness, in the bondage and in the tattered condition of "this world"; in altruism there is no new communion, no quality, no individuality. Altruism would establish a mechanics of an "average" union of men. Altruism subjects value to human well-being. Altruism is all too human; in it there is nothing of the divine, no superhuman value. Superhuman value, on which all truly aristocratic and noble morality is based, is something far beyond the vulgar contrast of altruism with egoism. Christian morality is also something beyond the contrast between altruism and egoism, for it derives its idea of the relationship between men from man's relationship to God: not for the sake of one's own interests or those of the other man, but for the sake of divine value and in the name of God. Man is pain and shame: man must be overcome—every man —you and I. The revelation of man will mean the conquest of man as the highest humanistic value: it will mean the revelation of the divine man. The attempt to give Christianity an altruistic utilitarian character was a great decline of the Christian consciousness. In reality all altruism is essentially a disguised utilitarianism: it is a religion of human well-being. Altruism is still the same bourgeois morality, a morality of bourgeois values. Altruism merely transfers the bourgeois values from "I" to "Thou", it is always seeking bourgeois well-being for others and thus already makes it possible for "I" to share in the bourgeois well-being. Christianity recognizes, equally for "I" and for "Thou", quite other than bourgeois values. Now, from the worldly viewpoint every "Thou" is only an "I" in disguise. And whatever is recognized as valuable for "Thou" turns out to be valuable for "I" as well. If riches and well-being are recognized as valuable for my neighbour, then riches and well-being are recognized as valuable for myself. Altruism cannot get outside bourgeois values, out of "this world".

Altruism is in deepest contrast to all creativeness; it even tries to set up moral obstacles to creativeness. The morality of altruism is opposed to the morality of the creative heightening of the qualities of life. Utilitarian-altruistic morality does not permit man to rise; it is against too great an increase of the qualities and values of individuality, as a sin against "my neighbour": it demands that qualities be equated with quantities. This is a morality of mechanical equality, of depersonalization, of devaluation, a morality of the plane. What is important for Christianity is neither "I" nor "Thou" nor their equalization, but rather divine value and divine truth which surpass both "me" and "my neighbour". Altruism bears the stamp of the spiritually-plebeian: it is an ideology of false, mechanical democracy. The value of the individual which is revealed in Christianity with all its intimacy and infinity sinks and perishes in altruistic-democratic morality. This morality does not know the mystic of readiness to sacrifice and yet it demands the sacrifice of quality to quantity, of the individual to the average, of value to well-being, i.e. the sacrifice of that which is of another world to what is of this.

Creative morality sweeps away altruistic-democratic morality—it truly revaluates values. In the Christian consciousness the boundless value of the individual is joined with a moral cosmism and universalism. It is surprising how altruistic morality is alien to all cosmism and universalism, how it fails to comprehend man's connection with the cosmos. Altruism is lost in the human; it is separated from the cosmic; it does not understand how anyone could be concerned for cosmic harmony rather than for Tom, Dick and Harry. In democratic altruism there is the fatal self-satisfaction of human limitations. Altruistic-democratic ideology knows individualism, knows the general-average, but does not know the individual, does not know the cosmos. Only a cosmic morality, which always understands the place of the individual in the world's hierarchy, can ward off that destruction of personality in individualism which Ibsen has so wonderfully pictured in *Peer Gynt*. Creative morality is individual and cosmic; in it the creative energy of the individual is poured out into the cosmos and the cosmos fills itself with the individual. In creative morality the personal is experienced as universal, and the universal as personal. Creative morality ceases to be interested in the banal and elementary question of egoism and altruism. There is divine truth not only in love for one's neighbour but in love for oneself. Christ commanded us to love our neighbour as ourselves, that is to love oneself as the image and likeness of God. Divine love for oneself has nothing in common with egoism. Egoists may regard themselves with revulsion. Lack of true love for oneself is the source of subversion, unhealthy

269

self-love, envy. Creative morality is a morality of a calling, it confirms the moral meaning of a calling; it knows only the individual way, which each must follow for himself and which is unlike any other. And we cannot renounce individuality or the individual way since every renunciation of the individual way, every refusal of individuality, is itself profoundly individual. It is difficult to compare men in the moral relationship for no one knows what real value one man assigns to another. *The moral objective assigned to each man is something individual.* And therefore the problem of moral evaluation is the problem of intuitive penetration into the secret of individuality rather than some question of quantitive moral mechanics. This is why the Gospel says: "Judge not".

§

The mystery of the redemption frees us from moralism and opens the way to the highest morality of creative love. New Testament love lessens the weight of moralism. The mystery of the redemption lightens the burden of the law but it imposes the burden of creativeness. Redemption leads from the law to creativeness. What was begun in the law is finished in creativeness. And in morality we may discover elements of all three: the law, the redemption and creativeness. Man has not yet outlived the law. The role of the law is negative, but it may be turned either against the ancient sinful chaos or against the creation of a new cosmos. In the first case the morality of the law conserves its religious significance. In the second case, it becomes demonic moralism, an evil added burden, the source of world-reaction. Already in the time of Christ, a demonic overburdening of the law by the scribes and Pharisees had taken place. Even the good may become demonic, as in the case of æstheticism. Any good which is hostile to creativity is demonic, it contains demonic heaviness, moribundity. Thorough-going moralistic exaltation may be a sin against the riches of man's creative nature, against the fullness of individual life, against the

270

meaning of multiplicity. Moral perfection and moral exaltation should not quench the Faustian desire for fullness of life. The destruction of creativeness for the sake of the moral law is a terrible reaction which hinders the fulfilment of Divine predestination and delays the arrival of the final solution. The forces which are exclusively attached to the law do not understand or accept that higher truth that creativity is something greater than the original submission to the will of God, do not understand that God himself has desired the revelation of man's will. Creativity is never the revolt of ancient chaos: creativity is the formation of a new cosmos. There is nothing creative in chaotic revolt: this is always religious reaction and deserves denunciation by the law. *Creativity is cosmic, not chaotic, hence it lies outside any denunciation by the law which is always oriented towards the ancient chaos.* Creativity is least of all anarchy. Creative Dionysism is a Dionysism transfigured, Dionysism which has passed through the law and the redemption, and is joined with Apollonism. In creative Dionysism the person is not submerged and does not disappear in the primeval element, individuality is not dissolved—does not disappear. The morality of the law is hostile to all Dionysism, to all ecstasy: in a certain sense of the word it is exclusively Apollonic: it always stands as a warning of the danger that personality may disappear. But the morality of the law knows only the ancient Dionysian element, a chaotic element; it does not know the ecstasies of a transfigured creative Dionysism. Creative morality is Dionysian morality. But this is not at all the Dionysism of old chaos; this is Dionysism which has passed through the religious meaning of culture. Pagan Dionysism, not illuminated by the world Logos, is a hindrance in the way of the dawn of the religious epoch of creativeness. Chaotic Dionysism is still subject to the judgements of the law, while creativity is not. In creativeness the seraphic nature of man is revealed. Man's passionate nature cannot and should not be quenched or suppressed—it must only be creatively transfigured. The moral system of the

Indian yogis carries a valuable appeal for self-discipline of the will, for spiritual concentration, but this also involves the danger of a final suppression of man's Dionysian-passionate nature. This same danger of quenching the Dionysian-passionate sources of creativity is present in the modern theosophical movement.

§

Two moral ways have been opened before us: obedience and creativeness, the ordering of the world and soaring out beyond it. The world religious crisis is also a moral crisis, a transition to the morality of creativeness. The morality of obedience has fulfilled its mission and is still doing so in our day, in so far as sinful chaos still exists in man; but this must be overcome in so far as the creative revelation of the cosmos is to be accomplished in man. We have seen that the ethic of creativeness is not the ethic of humanism. The ethic of humanism, carried to its limits, may lead to an anti-Christian ethic. The ethic of creativeness must be separated from the ways of "man-godliness", for in it the elevation and deifying of man are accomplished through the Absolute Man, Christ, through the God-man. Creative ethic calls forth hostility against itself, for it is a holiday-poetic ethic, rather than everyday-prosaic: it is of the aristocratic rather than the plebeian spirit. The categories of the aristocratic and the plebeian are not sociological categories and are not connected with the bourgeois hierarchism of the world. The ethic of creativeness should liberate man from the burdensome feeling that he is under a yoke, from the self-consciousness which is present alike in the Book of Genesis and in the new books on economic materialism. This liberation from oppression is attained by voluntary sacrifice. The sin in man must not only be negatively condemned by the law and redeemed, but man's creative nature must be positively revealed, his seraphic and sinless nature, his godlike nature. Humanism's denial of sin could never be revelation of the seraphic and sinless nature of man, a nature predestined for creativeness. In this denial there was a new sin which veiled the image of God in man, for it was a falling-away from the divine in man. Only the creative religious epoch will lead to man's positive consciousness of himself, will liberate man from an exclusively negative selfconsciousness. The ethic of creativity will give inspiration towards new and hitherto unknown life. This is life in the Spirit rather than in the world, life spiritually free from reaction to the world and everything worldly. A new evaluation of the social, also, will flow from the ethic of creativeness. The new creative life cannot move to right or left along the lines of "the world", but only upward and downward along the previously-fixed lines of the Spirit.

# CHAPTER XII

# CREATIVITY AND THE STRUCTURE OF SOCIETY

THE NINETEENTH AND twentieth centuries are a period of unprecedented quickening of social consciousness and an unprecedented sharpening of individualism. We live under the sign both of an extreme sociologism (the generally accepted consciousness to-day is sociological consciousness: sociology has replaced theology) and an extreme, individualistic isolation of personality. What are the mutual relationships between these two poles of contemporary consciousness? Sociologism and individualism are closely connected: these are two sides of one and the same situation of division in the world, two expressions of the same cosmic condition of the world. Sociologism is a false sense of community, a community of individualistic disunion, a degraded community of men estranged from each other. Modern sociologism is in profound contrast to all œcumenism in the religious sense of that word. It is false to place individualism and social consciousness over against each other. Individualism and social consciousness can be beautifully united. The ultra-social world-philosophy of Marxism is in essence an atomistic world-view (*Weltanschauung*). Marxism asserts the social consciousness of hostile, disjunct and separating atoms. In the Marxist consciousness there is nothing organic, no recognition of the reality of the general and superpersonal. In it there is not even the recognition of the reality of the personal. Marxist social consciousness is something which arises only after the sin of individualistic disunion. And the extreme sociologism of Marxism is only one of the expressions of extreme individualism. Such sociologism is impossible for those who are inwardly united. Marxism talks about how to unite in a society, in the necessity of life, atoms which are foreign to one another and hate one another. At the bottom of all the "politics" and all the "social construction" of our times there is an individualistic alienation and disunity. We are too social because we are too disunited and estranged one from another. Such disunity and estrangement create the necessity for an acute social sense, an extreme sociologism of consciousness. Sociologism is only an expression of our slavery, our adaptation to natural necessity. This sociologism is neither free nor creative. In this domination of "social sense" over modern consciousness there is something as oppressive as a nightmare. This external "social sense" both conceals and quenches all the true and final realities. False and superficial values of "social construction" are substituted for all the true and final values. The social, sociological world-view and world-philosophy of to-day deny the reality of man and the reality of the cosmos; they reflect the kindling of a fire which would consume man as well as the cosmos. Sociologism is essentially positivism. Sociologism denies the microcosmic in man; it is the result of breaking away from the cosmos, of a false individualism. The limited consciousness of positivism all rests upon the break between man and the cosmos, on the casting away of man and on joining him to the cast-away, on the loss of a sense of the reality of man and the cosmos. Sociological positivism is the extreme expression of the non-cosmic condition of man; it is an expression of the disunion of man and the world and of exclusive concern with the human relationships which result from this disunion. The opposite of metaphysical individualism is universalism, cosmism. This is an organic contrast. Man's consciousness of himself as a microcosm, a consciousness of man's organic appurtenance to the cosmic hierarchy —this is a consciousness which excludes the possibility of any individualism, any disunion.

The social sense is only an individual case of universalism, only an expression of the cosmic commonality of people.

And the crux of the problem of the social sense is not in the question whether we should start with society or with personality, and to which priority should be given. The crux of the problem is rather whether we should accept both society and personality, ontologically and cosmically. The social consciousness now prevailing hides the creative secret of communion because it denies and does not wish to know the cosmic nature of man and of society; it breaks away from organic roots of communion. Man, isolated in the exclusively human, and in exclusively human relationships, cannot know the secret of communion. The man of positive-sociological consciousness does not know himself or his friends: he does not know the world or his connection with the world. The whole "policy" of the social practice of our world does not know its nature at all, considers itself to be either free creativeness or at least a tendency toward free creativeness. But by nature this "policy" of the social practice of this world is anything but creative or free; it rises out of evil necessity and is really obedience to the consequences of evil. The basic falsehood in all "policy" is that it gives itself out to be the creation of a new communion, when actually it is only an expression of the old divisions, of the non-cosmic nature of the world, an adaptation to evil necessity. "Policy" in reality is always looking backward: it is always a reaction of adaptation. And all the politics of this world, reactionary or revolutionary, liberal or radical, is obedience, rather than creativeness. "Politics" is not real, in the final, metaphysical sense of that word, and it is not radical—it does not touch the roots of being. "Politics" remains on the surface and sets up an illusory being. "Politics" forms part of general culture, but it is not the way to a new world, to a new life. And "politics", like culture, is approaching a world-crisis. The world crisis of "politics" is being realized in socialism, in anarchism, in the quest for religious social forms. This is shattering all forms of social sense in this world—social sense out of necessity. But this does not mean, of course, that politics is unnecessary.

276

§

All the basic elements of a social sense, regardless of their evolution in the course of history, are old. All states, all law, all economics are essentially and in reality ancient things, and belong to the realm of the law, submission to necessity: religiously they are all still in the Old Testament and in paganism. The state-legal-economic social sense, be it conservative, liberal or revolutionary, feudal, bourgeois or socialistic—is always a social sense out of necessity rather than out of freedom: it is adaptation rather than creativeness: it is ever and always the ancient social sense. There is this same adaptation to evil necessity in an absolute monarchy and in a socialistic republic; the same absence of communion in the Spirit, creative and free communion; there is always the same submission to the burden of the law which convicts of sin. Anarchism is on the same level: it revolts mechanically against all law which justly denounces sin, and remains in unredeemed sin and in a non-creative epoch. Every legal system is a legalization of man's distrust of man: it is constant fear, constant expectation of a blow in the back. Existence under state-law is the existence of combatants. All economics is a heavy source of care, labour in the sweat of one's brow, the biblical curse. Economic labour, like all labour, is not creativeness; it predicates submission to the consequences of sin. In the care and anxiety and the sweat of economics, of law or of the state, we do not feel the free grace of love. The New Testament does not know the state nor the law nor economics. These ancient elements of the social sense of "this world" have been built up outside the New Testament revelation. And the New Testament did not reveal its own new elements of social consciousness. The New Testament justifies the state, the law and economicism, not as a revelation of the new communion in Spirit but as submission to the consequences of sin, i.e. it justifies the ancient social consciousness in an Old Testament way by saying that the law is still necessary and that men must still be convicted of sin. That "the governor does not carry his sword without reason", is an Old Testament, not a New Testament, truth, but it has been confirmed by the New Testament for this old and sinful world. The Gospel itself preaches freedom from constant anxiety about how one's life should be ordered. The Gospel feeling for life is neither economic nor state: we do not feel in it the heaviness of sin but rather the easement of redemption. Communion in the Spirit of Christ knows no anxiety and worry either state or economic. The life of St. Francis of Assisi was such a revelation of life in the Spirit of Christ, not knowing the burden and the heaviness of the social consciousness of this world. But the way to this new life leads through heroic and sacrificial action. And the way to a new life for mankind, to communion in the Spirit, can lead only through collective, œcumenical sacrificial action, through renunciation of that security and sense of comfortable order which is provided by the ancient social consciousness of this world.

A Christian state is a monstrous impossibility, an attempt to unite the un-unitable. The state is not a revelation of communion: it is rather an expression of the world's want of communion, the world's non-cosmic situation. The state does not create new being: it is only obedience to the law by men sunk in sin and oppressed by sin. But the state is not only the righteous law which denounces sin: like all the elements of this world, it may itself easily be changed into sin. Hence the dual nature of the state. On the one hand the state justly condemns and punishes sin by the law and the governor wears his sword for a purpose. On the other hand, the state itself may be infected by sin and itself do wrong. The element of power in this world is the source of one of the temptations which Christ resisted in the wilderness. The state is always forgetting its negative origins and its negative nature: it claims to be the positive kingdom of this world, an earthly city. This temptation to imperialism lies in wait for every state. In essence not creative, the state claims to be an absolute kingdom and thus becomes the foe of every

278

creative movement, by the law denouncing not sin but creativity. Every condemnation of creativeness itself becomes sin. Submission to the consequences of sin is transformed into hostility towards every creative movement. Submission becomes slavery. In the orthodox idea of the state we find the *pathos* of eternal rest, hostility towards all movement as sin. Even the kingdom of heaven is represented as eternal rest, and the earthly kingdom is supposed to be a copy of that heavenly rest. Any movement is revolt: only absolute submission gives entrance into the kingdom of rest. The holy state should enthrone eternal immobility, even on this sinful and restless earth. Here the psychology of the Church Fathers goes over into petrification and ossification, into spiritual death. Here we find the psychological source of extreme reaction. The New Testament justifies the state which condemns sin but it does not justify the state which condemns creativeness. By no means can we call the orthodox state absolutism, with its measureless burden, a New Testament or a Christian ideology in the true sense of the word. There is also very little New Testament or purely Christian in the papal theocracy. The imperialistic absolutism of a tsar or a pope is wholly incompatible with Christianity: it is outside the religion of redemption. Here a theory of society which is burdened with sin gives itself out to be a Christian theory of society. Every Christian theocracy has resulted in retaining life, falsely and by force, in the outer court of the church: this hindered the free revelation of humanity, its free reunion with God. Therefore the secularization of the theories of the state and of society is of positive religious significance: it brings the falsehoods to light and shows things as they really are. It is too often forgotten that Christians do not have a city here. They seek a city which is to come. This earth had not yet seen the Christian city. The creativeness of the new city cannot be built up on the ancient elements of social order, the state, the law, economics, elements which after all are of the world's pre-creative epoch. The traditional Christian world view makes all struggle against social evil very difficult, because it holds that every evil is the result of original sin. But will the creativity of the new city be born in revolution?

§

All revolutions, both political and social, are directed towards a mechanical external destruction of the law and the redemption, of the state and the church. These revolutions lack the true revolution of the spirit: they are uncreative, reactionary; they look backward instead of forward. Revolutions are hypnotized by a passionate hatred for the old life: they are psychologically reactionary. Revolution is a reaction against the old, without creating something new. Revolutions affirm the non-cosmic condition of the world: they do not connect the new life with an organic rebirth of the world in the cosmos, rebirth into cosmic harmony. Hence revolutions are ill-adapted towards cosmic world order, when this order is seen as forward movement. Revolutions continue in the same plane as reactions and by reaction they are negatively determined. The fateful psychology of revolution, which is a reactionary psychology, is incapable of creative upflight. Revolutions are burdened with accumulated desire for revenge, with negative attachment to the hated past, with the power of mechanical feelings. There is an unhealthy hysteria in revolutionary psychology: the creative mystery of that which is to come is hidden from it. Revolutionary passion is not creative passion. Revolutions are hostile and suspicious of every form of creativity. Men of a creative spirit are not revolutionaries in the social-mechanical sense of that word. Theirs is another sort of revolution, measurelessly more radical, more organic. Revolutions are still in the epochs of the law and the redemption and do not pass over into the epoch of creativeness. All the thinking and all the psychology of the revolutionaries is thinking and psychology of the world-epoch of the law, thinking and psychology of denouncing unredeemed sin.

The revolutionaries want to separate themselves from sin and evil, superficially and mechanically, and by this very attitude they often merely intensify sin and evil. They are not willing to live out the law and the redemption inwardly and organically, in order then to move over into creativity. The law in the state and redemption in the church cannot be destroyed: they must be mystically lived through. In the mechanical revolt against the realm of the law and the realm of redemption there is no creative spirit: this revolt renders man powerless, directs his energies into wrong paths. The law cannot be externally repealed for a world which lies in sin, just as science, for example, and the other pre-creative cultural values cannot be done away. But the law must be inwardly lived out and overcome. The law is done away with by creativity through the redemption. But creativity through the redemption overcomes the world's evil, living it out organically rather than mechanically. The external alternation in history between reaction and revolution, between the will to conserve and the desire to destroy, is eternal deception, illusion, unreality. Reaction and revolution do not reach to the roots of being: these changes remain superficial: they are mechanical and hence unreal. In the unhealthy atmosphere of political reaction and revolutions an illusory being is created, illusory passions and interests grow up. In this illusory "politics", which is presented as the most genuine life, there is no true reality in the metaphysical sense; the true essential is lacking. Reactions and revolutions are sinful nightmares. The way of creative social theory predicates another consciousness, a will turned in another direction. Creativity builds a new man and a new cosmos, new communion of man with man, of man with the cosmos. But creativeness does not destroy anything mechanically, externally, in illusion. The creative epoch in social theory, overcoming the Old Testament elements of social theory, must be freed from illusory "politics", from illusory reactions and illusory revolutions. The creative way does not permit the mechanical casting aside of the burden of a social theory which stands under the law: this must be experienced inwardly, and then overcome.

The two poles—extreme statehood (imperialism) and extreme anarchism—are equally repugnant to Christian consciousness; they are two opposite expressions of the non-cosmic, chaotic condition of the world, of the world's degeneration and dis-unity. Absolute statehood and absolute anarchism are two sides of one and the same defective condition of the world. To create the cosmos out of "this world", to arrive at world harmony and unity, is something which can be done neither by the state nor by anarchy; both are equally mechanical and superficial. State ideology and the ideology of anarchism are falsely-religious, un-Christian. One is just as mechanical as the other. Facing the injustice of a state which passes all bounds, the anarchistic revolt may be relatively just, but absolutely, in the light of a higher divine and cosmic justice, it is always wrong. In its inward dialectic, the state must take the blows of anarchy—they are on the same plane, and one gives rise to the other. Injustice of state excesses is incapable of condemning the excesses of anarchy, for both are born of the same chaos. The state and anarchy are alike alien to the creative spirit: they do not produce a new communion. It is not without reason that authority lifts the sword against the chaos of a world which is falling apart. And not without reason does uncontrolled freedom rise against the sword of authority, thus merely increasing the chaos and disintegration of the world.

Equally repugnant to the Christian consciousness are two other poles: the bourgeois-capitalistic social theory and the socialist theory of society. Both are expressions of the same hostility, the same love-less condition of the world, the same degrading power of necessity over the sons of God. The unity in love of man with man or of man with nature are just as unattainable on the grounds of socialist theory as on the grounds of bourgeois-capitalist theory. The ground of one is the same as that of the other. Socialism is flesh of the flesh and blood of the blood of bourgeois theory—the ideals of socialism are bourgeois ideals. Socialism accepts *in toto* all the bourgeois evaluations of the good things of this world and merely desires to develop them further and distribute them in a new way, making them the inheritance of the whole world. Socialism never doubts the value of worldly wealth and of a good well-satisfied life. It only desires riches and satisfaction in life for all; desires a universal bourgeoisie. It is not so much scorn of the bourgeois, as envy of it, which characterizes socialism. Socialism wants a final bourgeoisie as the kingdom of this world. Socialism is quite alien to the ascetic conquest of the bourgeois of this world for the sake of another world. In socialism we feel the limitless burden of the "bourgeoisity" of this world: there is no freedom from the world, no hint of wings. Socialism merely finishes the bourgeois construction of the world. In socialism there is no creation of new communion, no new and transfigured relationship of man to nature or of man to man—it is still the same old bourgeois relationship. Socialism is just as much Old Testament, just as much under the law, just as burdened with unredeemed sin, as all other old societies. The last words of Marxist socialism coincide with the first words of Genesis. Socialism is all in the pre-creative world epoch and hence is looking backward instead of forward. So is anarchism. Socialism is an expression of man's slavery to natural necessity rather than of man's authority over nature.

But in relation to bourgeois-capitalist social theory, there is a great truth in socialism. The bourgeois world will have to give way to the socialist world, both by necessity and by justice. Socialism is the necessary and just development of the bourgeois, of a bourgeois world-order. All the bourgeois arguments against socialism are hypocritical and vicious. Socialism is the final justice and the final truth of the bourgeois. The Old Testament elements of a social order which does not know creativeness will have to move on to a socialistic bourgeoisie. The relative truth of socialism is indubitable. But just as indubitable, is the absolute untruth of socialism. Willingness to sacrifice is just as alien to socialism as it is to bourgeois capitalism. But the way to all creativity lies through

283

readiness to sacrifice. And the accounts of socialism against disintegrating bourgeois society, like anarchy's accounts against the disintegrating state, are all the same old accounts, kept in the same old world, of elements warring against each other on the same plane with no way out into another world. Socialism is bourgeois because it belongs wholly to the natural realm of necessity rather than to the supernatural realm of freedom. For this very reason socialism is as devoid of the creative spirit. The seal of over-burdened "bourgeoisity" lies on all social ideologies and hence none of these ideologies is Christian.

§

The Christian consciousness and world outlook require an ascetic attitude towards the good things of this world, the renunciation of bourgeois values. The Christian attitude toward society is one of readiness to sacrifice: it turns away from the kingdom of this world, while every state, every law, all economics, are matters of the good order of this world, and presuppose the acceptance of bourgeois values in life. By its nature the state is neither ascetic nor sacrificial; it is always characterized by a tenacious hold on the world's goods, by the protection of worldly well-being. The slavophil conception of autocracy as an ascetic and sacrificing form of the state was a dream, quite unrelated to historic autocracy which is anything but ascetic or sacrificial, and just as bourgeois as any other state in the world. Christianity was never able to formulate any kind of ideal for the state, for the law or for the economy. The positive social ideals of Christianity were always "not of this world", they were a city of the future which Christians never had but were forever seeking. But, as has already been said, Christianity justifies the ancient social theories, the old forms of the state, as submission to the consequences of sin. The Christian attitude towards society was based on the religious experience of submission rather than on creativity. *Christianity demanded submission not to its own social order but to an alien, pagan, bourgeois, even directly evil, order of society.* And this

284

submission was required not for the sake of values of social justice but for the sake of humility in human religious experiences. Christianity taught a real *pathos* of submission to social injustice as just punishment for the sins of men; there was almost a desire that God's justice should not be realized in earthly society, and at any rate there was profound disbelief in the possibility of such realization. This radical paradox represents the Christian attitude towards society right down through history. In this way Christianity realized its ascetic covenants in relation to a non-ascetic society: but the Christian world was flesh and blood of the life of a non-ascetic, Old Testament, pagan, bourgeois society—belonged to it by all its earthly hopes and desires. The Christian world has not yet known collective social sacrificial living, or love expressed in society. What was accomplished in the individual saints has never been realized socially, collectively or historically. But the sacrificial overcoming of bourgeois society, of bourgeois heaviness, of bourgeois anxiety, is already the way towards the creation of a new and unprecedented life, of a new communion of men, hitherto unknown. Social order has never been social creativeness; it has always been a form of submission and adaptation. A truly radical universal revolution in society will only be realized when the Christian world matures to the point of collective readiness to sacrifice, the point of renunciation of the ancient social theories of this world which still guarantee and protect the goods of the bourgeois world. Not only Christian personality but Christian society as well has to pass through the sacrificial truth of St. Francis. This sacrifice is liberation from the disproportionate heaviness of this world, from the power of natural necessity; for, up to now, all social orders, from the most conservative to the most revolutionary, have been obedient to the weight of natural necessity, have never been an outbreaking into another world.

Regarding the kingdom not of this earth, the creative society is subterranean, of the catacombs. It is not a kingdom of this world; it overcomes the world, sacrifices its goods for

285

the sake of another, freer life. Now the move from obedience over to creativeness in the social order is possible here as everywhere, only by sacrificing security and guaranteed well-being. This readiness to sacrifice has nothing in common with anarchy, with chaos; it is always cosmic in quality. Anarchism is not sacrificial; it is only the old state order turned inside out. The state, the law and the economy are all a part of the cultural values of humanity. The liberal social theories would set up the same differentiated values in politics as in other spheres of culture. The world-crisis of culture, discussion of which runs all through this book, is at the same time a crisis of differentiated political values, a crisis of every old social order. In social order just as in philosophy, in art, in sex, in morals and in everything else, there is always present a tendency towards the outer limit, towards the finished and the final. Socialism, anarchism and theocratism have already outpassed the limits of normal canonic social theory in politics: in these ambitions they have passed the boundaries of culture. The research for a coming city, no matter what form it may take, religious or anti-religious, always passes the boundaries of canonic culture, the boundaries of differentiated politics—it is always striving for the ultimate and final. To seek the Kingdom of God on earth is to seek a way out of all adaptation to natural necessity: it is a thirst for liberation from the heaviness of the world. The leap into the realm of freedom, about which even the Marxists talk (without any right to do so) is a revolution-ary break with all the old social orders of "this world", with all politics, all state forms, with all concern for security in this world. The revolutionary transition from religious obedience to religious creativeness will be accomplished through the world-crisis of the average, canonic culture and the average, canonic social order. This is transition to the very end.

§

The creation of a new communion or communality presupposes an anthropological revelation, a revelation of
286

divine humanity, a Christology of humanity. The creative mystery of social order, the mystery of communion both human and cosmic, could not be unveiled before the creative mystery of man and of humanity had been revealed. And we have seen that in Christianity the anthropological revelation has not yet taken place. The final anthropological secret will be revealed not in obedience but in creativeness. In creativeness rather than in obedience will be revealed the mystery of society, the mystery of a new communion in love, communion in the Spirit, communion not only human but cosmic as well. Hitherto, in the precreative epochs, all social order has been submission, the bearing of "the world's" burden in consequence of the curse in Genesis, rather than creativeness. The old social theory of the autocratic state and the new social theory of socialism are alike submission rather than creativeness. All the old social order was the realm of Cæsar and not the kingdom of God. All the tribute which man pays to the economy, the law or the state, to the natural order of this world, is tribute to Cæsar rather than to God. Final escape from the circuit of the realm of Cæsar is possible only by conquest of the natural world, by its transfiguration. Marxist socialism is consistent and reveals the whole nature of the social order as obedience to the consequences of sin and adaptation to the necessity of Cæsar's realm. This is the ultimate in the way of necessity; it is giving over everything to Cæsar; but it is a way which does not reveal the mystery of man. More than any other social theory, materialistic socialism denies communion in love, communion in the Spirit; it recognizes only communion in necessity and in the material. Marxist socialism is the last word in a social order based on the non-cosmic condition of the world and on the want of communion, the lack of cohesion, the alienation of men. Socialism is the final justice and the final truth of people striving to unite and make order for themselves in the realm of Cæsar, according to the laws of natural necessity. Socialism is the ultimate obedience in bearing the world's burdens, in the just

287

distribution of those burdens. In socialism there is always negative truth and positive untruth. Along with elements of justice in socialism other elements are in command, out of which there may develop the social order of Antichrist. For the social order of the Antichrist will be the final result of a godless ordering of earthly kingdoms, of the human ant-hill, the final incarnation of the bourgeois, the final appearance of the slavish way of necessity. Only a creative social order, social order in the spirit of love and liberty, is capable of resistance to the social order of Antichrist. Every social order submissive to the burden of "this world" inclines in both its opposite poles toward the social order of Antichrist—in the poles of imperialism and socialism, of the autocratic state and the social republic.

In the burdened society of Cæsar's world two false elements are mingled and alternating: false hierarchism and false democratism. In false hierarchism a man is evaluated not for his inner self and his real quality but for his external appearance and his bourgeois situation in the world. In false hierarchism, the hierarchism of the realm of Cæsar, a man's qualities and his unique individuality are sacrificed to the hierarchy of bourgeois position. Hence false social hierarchism in reality levels down individuality to match the fictive values of bourgeois position, deprives man of his deepest and truest values; it is in opposition to the genuine metaphysical hierarchies of the world. This is a non-creative hierarchy, a hierarchy of inertia, of the world's stagnation and its bondage. Over against this false hierarchism we have false democratism, the reverse of the medal. Democratism, in the metaphysical sense of the word, rejects not only the false hierarchy of social position, the hierarchy of inert evaluations, but rejects also the real, inward-metaphysical hierarchy of the world on which is based everything of individual quality. Democratism mechanically levels-off all individual qualities, destroys the inward man for the sake of the outward. By the metaphysics of democratism a man's value is determined not according to his inward qualities,

288

always diverse, but according to his mechanically fixed social level. The metaphysic of democratism recognizes positive values in the negative and empty, purely mechanical, idea of quality and ties this up with the *pathos* of justice. But equality just by itself has no value. Equality is an evil when in its name high qualities are destroyed and the greatness of individuality is rejected. A consistent metaphysic of democratism is profoundly hostile to every high calling and to all true greatness. This is a metaphysic of the plain, afraid of anything that is of the heights or of exaltation. The metaphysic of democratism resists all elements of genius and rejects the leadership of greatness. In its view, power in the world should belong to some mechanism of quantity, not to the highly qualified individual but to the average and the ordinary. Democratism exerts itself to make quality subject to quantity, the individual to the general, the great to the average. But every value is qualitative, individual, of the heights. Hence the value of equality in democratic metaphysics is hostile to all true values. Democratism is also hostile to the cosmos and its organic hierarchy, just as is false, bourgeois hierarchism. Individualism, with all its precious qualities, predicates an organic hierarchism of the world rather than levelling mechanism. Vocation and greatness in the world are possible only in the case that there is an organic hierarchy in the world.

Christianity recognizes the equal value of all human souls before God, not only the equal value but the absolute value of all souls. But this absolute value of the soul or of the inner man not only has nothing in common with mechanical, levelling-off equality—it is actually profoundly hostile to it, for such mechanical quality denies the existence of the soul and destroys the inner man for the sake of his external social position. In its mystic sense, Christianity is not at all democratic: it is genuinely inwardly hierarchic and aristocratic. Recognition of the inner man and his unique individual qualities, his unique vocation and place in the world predicates the metaphysical recognition of the aristocratic inward structure of the world, its hierarchic organism. This true metaphysical hierarchism and aristocratism has always been the source of all greatness in the world, all heightening of the quality and the values of human life, all movement in the world. The metaphysic of democratism, with all its revolutionary features, is in essence profoundly conservative, inert, and opposed to heightening qualities or values; it is timid and fearful of all greatness. Only genuine aristocratism, aristocratism of the inner man, rather than his external bourgeois situation, can be a dynamic, creative and revolutionary principle. Aristocracy is the only necessary, desirable, normal, cosmic form of authority in the world, since this is the authority of the inner man, the authority of the great and of those called to authority. This is the aristocracy of sacrificial service. This aristocracy can have no points of contact whatever with the false bourgeois hierarchism of social position, for false hierarchism is just as hostile to the inner man, to individual calling and greatness, as is false democratism. False hierarchism and false democratism are two phases of one and the same disease, just as are state absolutism and anarchism, bourgeois capitalism and socialism, etc.

There is the same antithesis in regard to freedom. Freedom differs from equality in that it is a positive value. But freedom, too, may be negatively empty. The slogans of formal freedom, the freedom to wish whatever I want to wish, are negative and empty. This is childish, slavish freedom: it has nothing organic, no real content, no connection with the purposes of the world. Formal freedom for freedom's sake is without purpose or content, is only the reverse side of despotism and slavery. Political revolutions are too often based on this childish and slavish idea of freedom and those who make them are infected with a psychology which has developed in an atmosphere of despotism. A mature freedom, a freedom with real content, predicates the maturing and uplifting of the inner man, his organic union with other men and with the cosmos. A mature, positive freedom has cosmic

290

content and intention towards the world's goal: it is the opposite of wilfulness. And only that freedom can be creative which reveals the place of man in the cosmic organism. External, slavish, negative freedom always has a fearful eye cocked at its neighbour's freedom and is busied with the attempt to limit the hostile freedoms of its neighbours. Positive, mature, creative freedom cannot have these constant fears and cannot be so interested in these delimitations, for it is related to the organic system of the cosmos. This does not deny the meaning of all law, for you cannot constrain man to the organic, you cannot compel love. Law protects freedom in an epoch of disunion.

§

Spencer contrasted the industrial type of society with the military. With him this contrast had a positive-sociological slant. But the contrast between the military and the bourgeois has a deeper metaphysical meaning. In this our world, burdened with sin, the spirit of the military is least of all bourgeois; to a greater extent it passes the bounds of the world. The Middle Ages are the least bourgeois and the most military historical period. Until there is the final victory over evil, until this world has been transfigured into a new heaven and a new earth, the military spirit cannot and should not be destroyed in the human heart. This undying spirit of chivalry, eternally resisting the final victory of the bourgeois, is the spirit of holy wrath against the evil which passes all boundaries. The idea of an eternal bourgeois peace, is an evil, distorted, ungodly idea. Eternal and divine peace is unattainable by way of the bourgeois world, for true eternal peace means bringing the world into a cosmic condition, into beautiful divine harmony. A bourgeois peace of the bourgeois world is not cosmic; it is an evil and everlasting hostility, limited and brought into control for selfish and all-too-human purposes. The willingness to sacrifice which we find in war places war above the security of a bourgeois peace. Nowadays even war is becoming bourgeois: it is determined by the market and by world-exchange. This tradesman's, bourgeois, kind of war must of course lead to a bourgeois peace, a peace that is evil and false. This bourgeois end to all militant spirit is technically almost inevitable. But a bourgeois peace cannot be lasting, for it covers up deep enmity, discontent: it is not cosmic. The bourgeois peace will again bring us to catastrophic military thinking, which will be apocalyptic.

The triumph of the bourgeois spirit in the nineteenth and twentieth centuries has produced a false and mechanical civilization, profoundly in contrast with all true culture. This mechanical civilization, reducing everything to one level, depersonalizing man and depriving him of value—this diabolically technical civilization now all too closely resembles black magic; it is pseudo-being, illusory being, being turned inside out. Bourgeois civilization is the limit of the world's non-cosmic situation. In it the inner man perishes: he is replaced by the external, automatic man. Civilization has developed gigantic technical forces which ought, by their intention, to prepare man's complete reign over nature. But the technical forces of civilization lord it over man, make him their slave and kill his spirit. Modern man understands only partly the nature of the technical forces of civilization which he is developing. The magic character of these forces remains unknown to modern man. There is created a milieu of magic which bewitches the soul of man, a milieu of human living not without peril for spirit, mind and body. Our colossal technical civilization has released evil demons who are revenging themselves on fallen man for his royal pretensions. The power of electricity over the life of modern man is something suspicious. The more discerning among us now begin to suspect the magic quality of electricity: it kills the soul of man, organizes an impersonal, quality-less reign of the bourgeois. By means of electricity man desired to attain the kingdom of this world, and has arrived at slavery and spiritual death. Man is already unable to manage the technical forces which he has unleashed and put into action. Civilization does not realize man's royal

292

dreams. The highly developed capitalistic economy of the twentieth century is no longer the simple biblical curse: "In the sweat of thy brow shalt thou eat thy bread": in this economy there is the black magic of false and fictive being. The technics and economics of modern civilization do not create a new and imperial life for man. Command over nature cannot be realized by means of hostility and separation from it or by hostility and separation between man and man. And in truth man is called to an imperial and creative role in the world. In truth man should rule over nature by the power of white magic. The developing black magic nature of technical civilization will lead to the opposite pole, white magical technics and economics. This brings us right up against the problem of creating a *cosmic social order*, that is to a transition to another way for the world. I see the positive meaning of futuristic civilization with its frightful automatic and mechanical qualities in this, that in it the fate of the material world is being accomplished, that it means the end of the race. There is justice in the fact that the material organic life of the race should end as an automaton, a mechanism; that is layers must fall apart. This is a tragic move over into a new plane of being. But it would be cowardly and beneath us to fall into pessimism. The human spirit on the way of its liberation must pass through mechanization, through the crucifixion of everything that is organic in mechanism.

§

The new city can never be created out of elements of the old social order. The ways to the new city are neither conservative nor evolutionary nor revolutionary. No sort of social evolution can bring us to the coming kingdom of divine-humanity. The state, the law, economics—none of these can be transformed and made Christian, changed into divine humanity, the City of God. You cannot affirm a Christian state or Christian economics by means of maintaining them because they never were, and you cannot affirm them

293

by evolution or revolution, because they never will be. Every state and every economy is essentially non-Christian and opposed to the Kingdom of God. In order that the City of God should reign in the world, all the old social order must burn up, the state, every law, every economy. *The new social order will not be created from elements of "the world"; it will be created, in the "worldly" sense, out of nothing, from other sources which lie outside the world's social evolution, out of Spirit rather than out of the world.* The new social order is vertical movement, rather than horizontal. And we cannot place our hopes on any social force or class, on any historic force, but only on personality reborn in the Spirit. The radical mistake of all those seeking after a religious social order is just this hope of procuring a new social order out of the old. The conservative doctrines of religious social order and the revolutionary doctrines of religious social order alike undertake to derive the City of God from "the world" and neither will break completely with the principle of revolution, of the transformation of the old into a new social order. The old social order is evolving, but it is still based on the same elements. A great evolution has taken place between the autocratic state and a feudal economy, at one side, and the democratic republic and socialism, at the other, but socialism and the democratic republic still remain in the old social order, in submission to the burden of sin, just as did the feudal economy and the autocratic state. We may recognize both the inevitability and the good of this evolution, but this does not touch the problem of a religious social order. The whole ancient social order and the entire old civilization (fully developed only in the twentieth century) must burn to ashes in order that the New Jerusalem should come down to earth from heaven. The way to the New Jerusalem is a way of sacrifice. It is written that it will come down from heaven, which means that it will not be created out of elements of "the world". We cannot deny the meaning of world social order or world civilization, but this meaning is not to be found in their evolutionary tranfiguration into the Kingdom

294

of God, into the city which is to come. The new city is the church which is to be created, created in Spirit, outside the evolution of the world. It is characteristic of the religious social order, as theocracy, that it remains in the grip of Old Testament consciousness. There is the weight of sin in the very idea of a theocracy. Theocracy is, after all, the transfiguration of the state into a religious social order. Theocratic social order is in "the world" rather than in Spirit. The new creative religious social order is not theocracy, neither is it anarchism nor the order of the state nor socialism: it is inexpressible in the categories of "the world", untranslatable into the language of the physical plane of life. The Kingdom of God will come unperceived by "the world", and man will enter it only in the measure of his growth in Spirit. Insofar as man is still outside the higher achievements of Spirit, insofar as he belongs to the physical body of the world, he must participate in the evolution of the world's social order, he must pay tribute to Cæsar. And all the rationalistic disputations about hiliasm, about the thousand-year reign of Christ, must be cast aside. Will the thousand-year reign of Christ be on earth or in heaven, in this world or in another, in the material or only in Spirit? The kingdom of Christ is something outside the evolution of the world. The Kingdom of God will not be born of the elements of "this world". But this does not mean that the Kingdom of Christ will not be on the earth, for the earth is not only physical, but metaphysical; our earth belongs to another world, it belongs to eternity. In the same way our delicate transfigured body belongs to another world, to eternity. And the religious social order will be born not of the physical but of the spiritual body. The New Jerusalem will appear catastrophically, not by evolution; out of the creation of the spirit of divine humanity, rather than out of "the world", or out of the old social order. But the New Jerusalem will be on earth and revealed in the flesh, though not in the physical but rather in the transfigured flesh.

# CHAPTER XIII

# CREATIVITY AND MYSTICISM: OCCULTISM AND MAGIC

Through all human history, mysticism has revealed the world of the inner man in contrast to the world of the outward man. In various forms these mystical revelations of the inward man have always taught of man's microcosmic quality. The mystical experience has revealed the cosmos within man, the whole immense universe. Mysticism is in profound contrast to every kind of closed-in individualism, isolated from cosmic life: it is in contrast to all psychologism. Mystical submersion in oneself always means going out of oneself, a breaking-through beyond the boundaries. All mysticism teaches that the depths of man are more than human, that in them there lurks a mysterious contact with God and with the world. The true escape from oneself, from one's self-imprisonment and separation from the world, is hidden within one's own self, rather than outside; in the inward, rather than the outward. All mysticism teaches this. The man who is described in psychology is, after all, the outward rather than the inner man. The inward man is spiritual rather than intellectual. The mystical element is spiritual: it is more profound and more primordial than the intellectual element. In the course of history, phenomena which belonged to the spiritual or astral plane of man have also been called mystical: mysticism was not yet sufficiently separated from magic. But in the strict, differentiated, absolute meaning of the word, only that may be called mystical which relates to the spiritual plane. In mysticism there is a spiritual audacity and initiative of the inward man, of the deepest depths of the spirit. Purely mental or astral phenomena cannot truly be called mystical and should more properly be called magical.

Mysticism gives vitality and spirit to the sources and the roots of all religious life. Mysticism is the essential basis of all religious consciousness, the hidden source of religion in the world. Religion carries over into life and consciousness what has been immediately experienced in mysticism. The dogmatic consciousness of the œcumenical councils was only an objectivized translation of what had been immediately perceived in mystical experience. The dogmas recount in a conditional language the story of mystical encounters. The dogmas stiffen and become deformed into external authority when their mystical sources are closed, when they are received by the outward rather than the inward man, when they are experienced physically and mentally rather than spiritually. Everyday historical faith is the faith of the outward man who has not plunged his spirit into the mystical springs. This is mysticism expressed in adaptation to the physical plane of life. This is involution into the material. Everyday religiosity and everyday dogmatism are of enormous historical importance: they educate man at various stages of his development. Of course, there is such a thing as religious life for those who do not know the mystical sources of the dogmas, those who accept them on external authority. But to turn religion entirely into external living and external authority is to cause it to fade and degenerate. Then a mystical revival and re-spiritualizing of religion is necessary. In Christianity two elements are always in conflict: the inward-mystical and the outward-everyday; the aristocratic and the democratic; the spiritual and the intellectual; the intimately-secret and that which is adapted to the average level of human society. We must always remember that Christianity, as a historical world-phenomenon, is not only absolute divine revelation, but also an adaptation to the humanity which accepts this revelation in the degree of its spiritual growth and development: the

297

Christianity which is the mysticism of the inward man, and the Christianity which is an historical adaptation to the outward man. Only thus can we understand the tragic duality of Christianity in history, the lack of religion in the outward history of Christianity. We may say of Christianity that it is the most mystical religion in the world and with equal truth that it is a religion not at all mystical but rather historical and everyday, surprisingly adapted to the average level of men and to sobriety which is conditioned by their daily lives. Mystically, Christianity has followed the line of greatest resistance, the line of foolishness for the wisdom of this world. Historically, Christianity has followed the line of least resistance, the line of adaptation to reason and the reckoning of this world—adaptation to man's pagan nature, to the physical plane of life. This dualism presents a great temptation and it must be recognized and thought out. Any everyday Christian, a true believer and not devoid of religious experience, be he priest or layman, will tell you that in Christianity there is nothing mystical, that mysticism in Christianity was always a sign of abnormality and heresy, that the gnostics and the sectarians were mystics, and that the church is against mysticism. And along with this no one will attempt to deny that the greatest and most authentic saints were mystics; that the depths of church-consciousness are mystical, that the Gospel of John, the Epistles of the Apostle Paul and the Apocalypse are mystical books, that the religion of Christ is a religion of the mystery of redemption and that there is an Orthodox mysticism and a Catholic mysticism, recognized by the Church. In Christianity there is a profound mystical tradition which goes back to the apostles. The church in its world-historical action and its necessary adaptation to the level of humanity has been pre-eminently the church of Peter, from whom the priestly succession derives. From Peter comes the tradition of Judæo-Christianity. The Catholic Church openly recognizes itself as the Church of Peter, but the Orthodox Church also accepts the succession from Peter. Peter was the apostle of the average level of humanity. In him is the spirit of involution, of condescension. But Christ's beloved disciple was John, and from him comes the mystical tradition. The mystical church, which because of man's low estate has not yet been fully revealed, is the Johannine Church. The saints and the mystics have been the living bearers of the Johannine tradition: St. Francis is of the spirit of John rather than Peter. The Church of Peter has been the Church of obedience and adaptation rather than of creativity. Religious creativity can proceed only from the Johannine tradition. Ordinary Christianity knows only Peter and his tradition. But holy tradition is not Petrine alone, but Johannine as well. The fearful torpidity of the church of Peter, the decay of its upper ranks, must bring about a revelation of the church of John, an incarnation of the mystical tradition of Christianity. Here, in the mystical sense, the apostolic succession will not be broken. The Church of Peter and the Church of John are one single Church of Christ, but seen from different sides, directed towards different aims which are subordinate to one sole purpose.

§

Our epoch is witnessing not only a genuine renaissance of mysticism, but a spurious fashion of mysticism. The prevailing attitude towards mysticism has become too easy; mysticism has fallen into the hands of cheap writers and all too easily slips over into mystification. Nowadays to be somewhat mystic is considered to be a mark of refined culture, while only recently this was considered a sign of cultural barbarity. In this mode both the depth and the variations of mysticism disappear. The whole complexity of mystical intentions is lost in general phrases about mysticism. Mysticism has become a synonym for the chaotic state of the modern mind. Nowadays men want to see in mysticism a renewed source of creativity. But modern people have a very sketchy knowledge both of the history and the psychology of mysticism: they do not study it from original sources but rather from modernist literature and from their own chaotic intellectual situation (intellectual, not spiritual). Hence it is not clear to the worshippers at the shrine of mysticism to-day that not all mysticism may be a source of creativity and that some types of mysticism are hostile to all creativeness. Not every type of mysticism should be imitated: we must learn to distinguish and to evaluate in mysticism. The modern enthusiasm for mysticism is superficial: we cannot approve of all the forms of this vast wave of interest in mysticism. Even in the best and most noble phases of this renaissance of mysticism there is a large dose of archæology, literature and romantic æsthetics. Men forget that true mysticism necessarily requires ascetic purification. In modern mysticism one may distinguish not only creative initiative but spiritual reaction and spiritual passivity. We must remember that historical mysticism has been a very complex and many-sided phenomenon. In the religious meaning we have given to the word here, the old mysticism, on which the modern chaotic mind gazes with such desire, cannot be called creative. Mysticism contains a foretaste of the creative religious epoch, just as was the case in other phases of world-culture, but man has carried into mysticism, as well as into those other phases, his obedience to the consequences of sin. Mysticism, too, like the cult of the Church, had its temporary side. Now mysticism should become the transfigured life of the world.

In ancient mysticism a pantheistic sense of the world and of God prevailed. But pantheistic mysticism bears the stamp of the oppression of human personality. Sinful man desires to be dissolved in Divinity and, in complete abnegation of everything human and personal, to quench his sin and its bitter consequences. While ordinary religiosity adapted itself to the average level of sinful human nature, pantheistic mysticism renounced human nature altogether and dissolved man in divine being. We find no truly creative effort on the part of man in either ordinary religiosity or pantheistic mysticism. Pantheistic mysticism does not know the original

300

creative energy of man; it is not anthropological; for this type of mysticism man's individuality is a sin and a falling away and every human attainment is the action of Divinity itself, in renunciation of everything human. This type of mysticism has no place for man's originality or his uniqueness; there is no justification for the plurality of being. This ancient mysticism did not recognize man as himself, as an image of the divine, or man's creativity as a divine process; it knows only One Divinity. This is a mysticism without form or face. Mysticism did contain some freedom and inward initiative which was unknown to ordinary religiosity, but still this does not mean that it contained creative anthropologism. Mysticism, too, adapted itself to man's fallen state. While ordinary religious feeling carried the burden of submission by means of adaptation to the average little human existence, mysticism bore the burden of submission by means of renunciation of human existence through man's extinction in God. Neither here nor there do we find the higher, creative *human* existence. In the experience of the mystics the prevailing type is one of passivity, of divine passivity, in which human nature becomes quiet and inactive, completely renounces itself for the sake of life in God. Quietism developed on Catholic soil, although the Catholic is the most anthropological of all types of mysticism. The old mysticism corresponded to the moment of sacrifice, the moment of Golgotha in the life of the inward man. It was as though the resurrection had taken place not for man but rather for Divinity itself, in which man disappears. But pantheistic mysticism contained one undying truth: that the Creator and creativeness are very intimately near each other, that God is in creativeness and creativeness is in God, that everything which takes place in the world and in man takes place in God; also, that God's energy overflows into the world. Jakob Boehme and Angelus Silesius in their power of perceiving man, through and through, represent the highest flight of mysticism.

301

§

We must look more closely at certain different types of mysticism. First we must glance at the mysticism of the non-Christian east, of India, which nowadays has invaded Christian Europe. In all its forms, this mysticism denies man, his "I" and his creativeness. This is the mysticism of the One, hostile to man and rejecting the mystical meaning of the plurality of being which is accepted by western Christian culture. What is Yogism and what is its religious basis? In the religious consciousness of Yoga man is a fallen creature; divine life derives no profit from man; and man must be completely absorbed in Divinity. The mysticism of India is a forerunner of the revelation of the Persons of God and the persons of men; it is submerged in the original undifferentiated divinity in which neither God nor man are visible. By means of concentration, man becomes the possessor of world-power (*Prana*) and may rule the world, but he himself ceases to exist as an individual—there remains only divine world-power. To quote the Swami Vivekananda, who acquainted Europe with the philosophy of Yoga: "All forces are concentrated in *Prana*, and he who has possessed himself of *Prana* has captured all the forces of nature, spiritual and physical. He who has subjected himself to *Prana* has subjected his own consciousness and all the consciousness which exists in the world. He who has subjected himself to *Prana* has brought under his control his own body and all other bodies which exist, because *Prana* is a concentrated manifestation of power." "The man who receives an answer to his prayers does not know that the fulfilment of his prayers proceeds from out of his own nature, that he has succeeded, by means of his mental mood of prayer, in awakening the purity of that endless force which slumbered in him. Thus, according to the teaching of the Yogis, that which men, burdened by fear and poverty, have ignorantly worshipped under various names is in reality the force stored up in every being, the mother of all eternal

302

happiness." "In his essence man is God, and will become God again." "*The sooner we get out of this condition, which we call 'man', the better for us*" [italics mine]. "Limitless knowledge the Yogis call God." In Yoga the pantheistic assertion of unity goes so far as to deny both man and God. Hence, in the Yogi mysticism, the question of man's creative calling cannot arise. The Yogi consciousness knows no person, neither of God nor of man. This consciousness does not know the cosmos, either. "There is only one single way to attain freedom, which is the purpose of all humanity—the way of renunciation, renounce this little life, this little world, this earth, the heavens, the body, earthly sensations—it is the way of renunciation of all things." For Yoga the whole cosmos, with the earth and the sky, is a little world of little sensations. There is a formal and methodological similarity between Yoga and eastern Christian asceticism. But Yoga does not know the grace of love, the overflowing love of God's heart for man and the world, and the answering love towards God in the heart of man and the world. The mysticism of India is all impersonal: it does not perceive human personality in its metaphysical individuality and its value to the very life of God himself: it is all something before the revelation of Man in God, the revelation of personality through the Son of God.

We find the same denial of man in neoplatonic mysticism. Plotinus is the most brilliant and talented expression of the mysticism of the One. For Plotinus neither plurality nor individuality have metaphysical reality. Man disappears in Divinity. Plotinus' thought follows the same line as that of India. "The one, the principle of all things," says Plotinus, "is quite simple." "The one cannot be the same thing as the all, for then it would not be the one: the one cannot be the spirit, for the spirit, too, is everything; neither can it be being, for being also is everything." Plotinus is the first case in European religious philosophy where we find this brilliant expression of the negative, clear-cut understanding of God the one, of mysticism purified of all trace of the world or of being. The one is nothing. The consciousness of Plotinus is the exact opposite of that antinomic Christian revelation by which the whole plurality of being is not quenched but rather confirmed in the One, and God is not the denial of man and of the cosmos but rather their affirmation. The mysticism of Plotinus is the most rational, the least antinomic, form of mysticism. It recognizes divinity before its antinomic revelation in cosmic plurality.

But neoplatonic mysticism and metaphysics were carried over into Christian metaphysics and mysticism. Thus the negative theology which is connected with the Pseudo-Dionysius the Areopagite, approaches the neoplatonic mysticism of the One. But both Plotinus and negative theology turned inside out give rise to positivism, since they dig an impassable gulf between the plurality of this world and the One of another world. There are no positive ways which lead from our pluralistic and complex being to a being single and simple: there is only the negative way of renunciation. In essence, this affirms the incommensurability of God and man. Man belongs wholly to a pluralistic, imperfect and fallen world, and cannot pass over into the perfect world of the One. Neoplatonic mysticism and the negative theology connected with it by-pass completely the Christian revelation of God-manhood, of the profound relationship and even the merging of human nature and Divine nature, a merging which does not destroy man but rather confirms him in absolute life. Of course this is not to deny the great truth in negative theology: the inapplicability to God of any categories. But this truth in negative mystical theology must be related to the First-God, to the primeval Abyss.

The profound genius of Eckhardt absorbed both neoplatonism and negative theology, and here in the west he arrived at a mysticism akin to that of the spirit of India. He speaks of "the profound silence, since into it neither creature nor image can penetrate; no action, no concept reaches the the spirit, there, and it knows no image, knows neither itself

304

nor any other creature". God is born in the spirit of his Son, without any image. "If there were an image here, it would not be true unity, and in true unity lies all its blessedness." The best that man can do is to "Let God work and speak" in himself. "God does not desire anything more from you than that you should get out of yourself and let God be God, in you." "Get out of yourself, for the love of God, so that for the love of you God may do the same. When both have come out, what remains will be something single and simple." "God is a being whom we may know best through nothing." "I place renunciation higher than love." "Renunciation is so near to 'the naught' that nothing except God is sufficiently secret to find there a place for himself. He is so simple and so fine that he finds place for himself in the soul which has renounced everything else. . . . I put renunciation above all sort of humility." "Renunciation touches 'the nothing' so closely that no difference remains between them. Renunciation would like to be 'the nothing'." "When God created the heaven and the earth and all its creatures, that so little concerned His renunciation as though He had never created anything. . . . I will say more: when the Son in the Divinity desired to become man, and so became, and suffered pain, that so little concerned the immobile renunciation of God, that it was as if He had never been man." In Eckhardt the mystical way of renunciation is near to Plotinus, the Pseudo-Dionysius the Areopagite and the mysticism of India. Eckhardt calls us to liberation from all plurality and individualism, from all being: he calls for the quenching of the ego. He is acosmic, and does not believe in the transfiguration of the world. He wants liberation from creating, from the creature-qualities and also liberation from God, since "before he became creative, God was not God". God became God only for the purpose of creation. Here Eckhardt's thought is lost in bottomless profundity. In the dark abyss of Divinity both God and His creation disappear, God and man; even the oppositeness between them disappears. The way of renunciation plunges into ineffable *nothing*, into

305

super-being. This way returns to that which preceded creation, the appearance of both the creature and the Creator. "The non-existing being is beyond God, beyond all differences. There I was only myself: there I denied only myself and saw only myself as the one who created this man. There I was the first cause of myself, of my temporal and eternal being. Only in this was I born. . . . In view of the eternal essence of my birth, I was from the beginning, am now, and ever shall be. . . . In my birth all things were born; I was the first cause of myself and the first cause of all things. I would wish that neither I myself, nor they, should exist. But if I were not, there would be no God." "If thou still lovest God as a spirit, as a Person, as something having an image, cast that all aside . . . thou shouldst love God as he is: non-God, non-Spirit, non-Person, non-Image, but one pure, light Unity, far from all duality. And we must submerge ourselves forever out of being into this one Nothing." Eckhardt's mystical way leads from a state of being in differentiation between Creator and creature, to a complete Nothing in the Original-Divinity before the creative act. Eckhardt never perceived the positive meaning of the concrete movement of the Trinity, of the Persons in Divinity. Hence he is forced to deny, mystically, the profit-bringing meaning of the world's creation. For him creativity is a falling-away from the First Divinity, an ineffable "Nothing", a being above all being. He denies both man and creativity. Absolute destitution and absolute nothing yield us no profit. All gain in the creative process, due to the multiplicity of created things, is only a falling-away from Divinity. In Eckhardt there is an extraordinary mystical profundity, but he is not looking ahead towards the creative revelation and development of Divinity in the cosmos, in concrete persons in the multitude. Eckhardt has become one of the mystical sources of Protestantism, in which there was some truth, but which was a break with the earth and with the cosmos. The mystical realism of the Church was replaced by mystical idealism. The whole of the peculiar German culture is predetermined

306

in Eckhardt. It already contained Hegel. Only Jakob Boehme holds a special place in German mysticism: he is as super-national as he is super-confessional. Boehme's mysticism is all concrete, pictorial, bound up with the face of Christ and the face of man, all permeated by anthropological conscious-ness. In Boehme's mysticism there is a Semitic ingrafting of the Kabbala, with the exclusive position it accords to man, with its concrete spirit. In the nineteenth century Franz Baader and Vladimir Soloviev were permeated with the anthropological and concrete spirit of the mysticism of the Kabbala and of Jakob Boehme, but were not led astray by the abstract and formless spirit of the negative mysticism of India, of Plotinus and of Eckhardt, which is purely Arian in spirit. The Arian-German spirit expresses itself in the pure monistic religion of the spirit held by Hartmann, for whom the "I" does not exist.

§

Of the two great Churches, Catholic and Orthodox, east and west, each has its own official mysticism. And the difference between the structure of the mystical experience explains the difference between the ways the Orthodox east and the Catholic west have taken in the world. There is a profound difference in the primary attitudes towards God and Christ. For the Catholic west Christ is object: He is the object of all striving, of love and of imitation. Hence the Catholic religious experience is one of man's stretching up towards God. The Catholic spirit is Gothic. In it coldness is joined with ardent passion. The Catholic spirit is intimately close to the concrete Gospel image of Christ, of Christ's passion. The Catholic soul is passionately in love with Christ, imitates His sufferings, receives in its own body the stigmata. Catholic mysticism is through and through sensual: it is filled with languor and longing. In it the anthropological element is put into harness. Thus it happens that Catholic mysticism goes through the *nuit obscure*. The Catholic soul cries out: "My Jesus, my beloved!" In the Catholic

Church it is cold, just as it is in the Catholic soul—it is as though God had not come into the soul or the Church. And the soul strives passionately upward towards the object of its love. Catholic mysticism is romantic, full of romantic longing. Catholic mysticism is hungry, it is ever unsatisfied, it never knows marriage but only being in love. The Catholic attitude toward God as object, as the goal for striving, produces the external dynamic of Catholicism. This is not to deny that at the height of Catholic mysticism, for example in St. John of the Cross, a *unio mystica* is attained. The Catholic experience creates a culture which bears the stamp of being in love with God, of earnest longing for God. In Catholicism energy is poured out in the way of historic action; it is not within, since God is not received within the heart: the heart strives towards God by the ways of world-dynamic. The Catholic experience gives birth to beauty out of spiritual hunger and unsatisfied religious passion. Some achievements of Catholic mysticism reach dizzying heights. Angela de Foligno is an example: *"Dans l'immense ténèbre je vois la Trinité sainte et dans la Trinité, aperçue dans la nuit, je me vois même, debout, au centre."*

For the Orthodox east, Christ is subject: He is within the human soul: the soul receives Christ into itself, into the depths of the heart. Being in love with Christ and imitating his passion is impossible in Orthodox mysticism. Orthodox mysticism is prostration before God, rather than striving up towards him. The Orthodox Church, like the Orthodox soul, is just the opposite of Gothic. Orthodoxy is neither cold nor passionate. Orthodoxy is warm, sometimes even hot. For Orthodox mysticism the concrete Gospel image of Christ is not so close. Orthodox mysticism is not sensual; sensuality is considered an enticement: imagination is refused, as a false way of procedure. In Orthodoxy one cannot say: "My Jesus, my near and dear." Christ comes down into the Orthodox Church and the Orthodox soul and gives them warmth. In Orthodox mysticism there is no yearning passion . . . Orthodoxy is not romantic, it is realistic, sober.

308

Orthodoxy is not hungry—it is spiritually satiated. The mystical experience of Orthodoxy is marriage, not merely being in love. The Orthodox attitude towards God as the subject which is received into the depth of its heart, the inner spirituality of this relationship, does not produce external dynamic: everything is directed towards inward communion with God. The Orthodox mystical experience does not favour culture, does not create beauty. In the Orthodox mystical experience there is a sort of numbness towards the external world. Orthodox energy is not poured out in the ways of history. The satiety of Orthodox experience does not produce outward creativeness: man is neither harnessed nor regimented. In this difference between the ways of Catholicism and of Orthodoxy a great mystery lies hidden. And both ways are genuinely Christian.

There is an official Orthodox and an official Catholic mysticism, but the true nature of mysticism is super-confessional. Mysticism is something deeper than confessional disputes and contrasts. But different types of mysticism may give rise to ecclesiastical divisions. Only a deepening of mysticism can revive the life of the Church, counteract the present-day slowing-down in the life of the visible Church. The vital roots of Church life are in mysticism. Everyday life in the Church is always something on the surface, at the edge of things. The Church as it is incarnate in the plane of history is always peripheral. We must go into the depths of mysticism not only for the revival of religious life but in order to investigate the nature of a mysticism which perhaps should be thrown aside. There is one kind of mysticism which would like to return to the original state of rest in the bosom of God, which refuses all movement, all creative dynamic. This is to refuse the very meaning of divine development in the world. Hitherto mysticism has been the product of separate individuals: it has remained incidental and secret. Now the time has come for a universal, objective mysticism, openly manifest. This manifestation of mysticism

309

is characteristic of our times. And our times lay upon us the obligation of recognizing what kind of mysticism may be oriented towards the creative future.

§

There are age-old, occult traditions—a secret subterranean river in world-culture. Not even its most extreme opponents can deny this fact. But to-day occultism has become popular, is attracting great superficial interest, and is in danger of becoming stylish. It is quite probable that occultism is both the force and the mode of to-morrow. Occultism is in danger of becoming something common and vulgar. A special type of exoteric esoterism seems to be developing. Theosophy, now approaching the wider masses, is popularizing occult doctrines, mostly those of the east. It has been discovered that eastern, Indian occultism, is the most popular and acceptable. Materialistic Europe, having betrayed the faith of Christ, finds it easy to accept eastern spiritualism, and reconciles it with its science. It is a strange and terrible thing to say, but Christianity is becoming more foreign and less acceptable to the modern mind of Christian Europe than Buddhism. The popularization of occult doctrines is of enormous symptomatic significance for our times. The day is at hand when secret mystical doctrines will be manifested and objectivized. The way of positivism and rationalism, along which modern man has travelled, has already shown its terrible fruits, and man now yearns for a return to his secret and pristine sources. This manifestation and rebirth of eternal mysticism with its age-old traditions takes the form of naturalistic evolutionism, at least in its first steps. The modern European man, rationalist and materialist in his modes of thought, can reconcile only evolutionist-naturalistic theosophy with his science—his "scientific" attitudes of mind. Modern theosophy is taking on clearly evolutionary and naturalistic colouring. It transfers the habits of scientific thinking to other planes of being. In his yearning for a return to his lost mystical first-sources,

310

modern man is not willing to sacrifice the reason of "this generation", he is incapable of purifying his consciousness by means of sacrificial absurdity. Modern man recognizes his science and his reason as the necessary and mature fruits of world-evolution. And naturalistic theosophy connives with this belief. Theosophy wishes to bring modern man to mysticism and religion with no sacrifice, no renunciation, along the lines of least resistance, by a way of evolution instead of catastrophe. Theosophy wishes to train and develop man up to a consciousness and sense of other planes of being, imperceptibly oblige man to include other worlds in his ordinary thinking and his everyday life. Theosophy is afraid of frightening modern man, drunk with the spirit of extreme self-assertion and having lost his capacity for sacrifice and renunciation. Hence theosophy has developed a whole scale of tactical approaches to modern man—and has, itself, turned into a tactical approach. Theosophy is symptomatic: it can be very useful. For many, theosophy points the way from materialism and positivism to true spiritual life. But mystical ways cannot be easy and free of sacrifice; they cannot flatter the given nature and consciousness of man. At the very beginning of the Christian religious way is the unreasoning surrender of oneself to Christ, without any reserve, up to the crucifixion of truth itself—the consent to receive everything from Him, and through Him, alone.

Up to now, there is still not much of the creative in theosophy—there is even a danger to all creativeness. Theosophy gives its greatest attention to the tactical and educative moment and is oriented backward, towards acquiring the wisdom of the ancients forgotten by modern man. In eastern theosophy there is something hostile to the Christian tempering of personality, there is no revelation about "I", no revelation of either individual or pluralistic being. Here we are speaking not of the substance of occultism but of its external, popular, exoteric manifestations. The anthropological question is always sharply put in occult doctrines. But the prevailing occult and theosophical consciousness teaches that man is made up of a series of accretions and layers, fragments of planetary evolution. In this composite man we recognize only with great difficulty the unique and integral face of man the creator, the image and likeness of God the Creator which was in God before all worlds and before all being. The question remains—does the prevailing occult and theosophical consciousness recognize the first-man Adam as proceeding from God rather than from the evolution of the world, or does it consider man as only the complex result of world-evolution? The popular theosophical books incline to the second viewpoint: for them, man is not primordial and integral but rather derivative and complex. No one can deny the complexity of man and all theosophy must see in man the accretions of all worlds, of all world-epochs; but behind all man's complexity and all the traces left upon him by world-evolution there still remains the primordial, integral man, the image and likeness of God, derived from nothing else and under no circumstances divisible into parts. Behind the external and evolutionary man is concealed the inner and absolute man. Jakob Boehme knew the first-man Adam, and revealed an anthropology which was a mark of genius. In this, the theosophy of Boehme is infinitely superior to modern and popular theosophies. The first-man Adam precedes the world-process and is not derived from it.

§

To-day, occultism, in its deepest manifestations (for example in Rudolf Steiner) is a grave symptom of the decomposition and atomization of the physical plane of being. Occultism, by a kind of second sight, reflects this dissolution of being: the occult way reveals the corpse-like state of being. A strong cosmic wind is rising, which may carry man away, disseminate him through endless worlds. And we do not know what will stand fast in this atomization and dissolution of man and the world—whether there is any permanent substance, "I", whether there is a *man* who can withstand the assault of the elemental world-hurricane, who will remain after the destruction of whole worlds. In occultism there seems to be neither freedom nor meaning nor light at the beginning of the way. Man must proceed in the dark, climb an endless darkened stairway on which no single merciful ray of light falls. Occult knowledge is somehow not an active process of giving meaning to something but only a second-sight description, a passive acceptance of things into oneself. For Steiner's occult science the question remains finally without an answer—is there a meaning in the world-process, and, if so, what is that meaning? Man does not stand against cosmic forces as a god-like substantial being, bringing meaning into the world-process—man is the passive tool of cosmic forces, of endless worlds, and ought to abandon himself to the atomizing cosmic wind. The Churches, and after them science, have put the secrets of the cosmos under lock and key, and have forbidden all approach to them. In serious occultism the secrets of the cosmos are beginning to be revealed, a clear perception of other planes of being is developing. Occultism knows the mystery of the cosmos, but without the mystery of God or of Christ, without the Logos, without primordial meaningfulness. The Christian occultist Steiner sees Christ Himself as only cast out into the world, into cosmic composition and decomposition, as a cosmic agent: he does not see Christ as in Himself, in the Divine Trinity. This is not a religious attitude towards Christ but rather an evolutionary-perceptive attitude. It is as though Steiner saw Christ in chemistry, and not in God. God is very far off in occultism, more distant, even, than in churchly Christianity. Endless evolution will never lead to God. There is no immediate revelation of God in the soul. The soul's wandering begins without God, without a religious revelation of meaning. There is no religious criterion, no "in the name of". Man is armed, he is given sword and shield, but he is not told for the sake of whom or what he should march into battle: there is no Christ, no Virgin Mary, no Holy

Sepulchre, nor even "*la belle Dame*". Through Christ the Redeemer naturalistic evolution of the soul in darkness is ended; the law of Karma is replaced by the free grace of love. In occultism the soul is still unredeemed, its sufferings are without either grace or light. It is as though the way of occultism was made for some unloved stepchildren of God. And there is no end to the dark corridors and steep dark stairways. Herein lies the horror of the evil infinity of world-evolutions. Occultism knows only potential, mathematical infinity, and does not wish to know actual infinity, in which everything is already given, where God is, before all worlds.

§

In the prevailing forms of both theosophical and occult consciousness there is the same danger of denying creativity. It is as though the purpose of life were reduced to the acquisition of ancient wisdom. The purpose of life is not so much creative as pedagogical. Some thousands of years ago, the initiate, standing on high levels of learning, knew the highest wisdom. And modern man, even on the highest levels, can know no more—he can even know less, since nowadays such wise men do not exist in the world. For modern man the ancient wisdom is the limit of striving. There can be no new revelation in the world, no future epochs which will surpass all the attainments of ancient wisdom and the ancient sages. Even Christianity becomes understandable only in the light of the wisdom of India. Eternal wisdom was given once and for all and enlightened wise men communed with it three thousand years ago, exactly as they do to-day. There is no such thing as creative increase of wisdom in the world. We must recognize this form of occult consciousness, at present being popularized in theosophical teaching, as religiously reactionary, oriented towards the past, and hostile to creativeness. For this consciousness the purpose of life is acquisition rather than creativeness, the passive acceptance into oneself of what was given once and for all in antiquity. As the opposite of this we have the other consciousness,

314

which admits the possibility of a revelation of wisdom unknown to antiquity, surpassing everything which was revealed in previous world-epochs. A new revelation is possible, a new epoch of the world. The wisdom of antiquity did not have a genuine anthropological revelation. The anthropological revelation is the expectation of a new, future world-epoch. The purpose of life is not pedagogical, not acquisitory, but creative, forward-looking. Occultism oriented solely toward the wisdom of antiquity, wants a kind of safe risk, a passive, acquisitory creativeness. But the anthropological revelation can never be freed of danger. In occultism the mystical category of priesthood usually prevails over the mystical category of prophecy. Even the idea of ordination or consecration is derived from the priesthood. Occultism is, as it were, a sort of special form of consecration into "creature-ness". Occultism is always oriented towards the created world rather than towards God the Creator or the divine world. Strictly speaking, occultism is outside religious revelation and religious grace. Occultism remains wholly in the sphere of man's relationship to man and man's relationship to nature. In this creature-sphere occultism establishes its tradition of ordination. To-day we can no longer deny the sphere of the occult in knowledge and in action, the occult in human relationships and in man's relations with nature. But occultism does not touch the higher mysticism of world-epochs of revelation. Inevitably, occultism will have to be reborn at the moment of transition into the world-epoch of creativeness, as knowledge of the mystery of a cosmos shattered in its physical stability. But its role is double: occult knowledge may be necessary at the moment of shock to the physical plane of being, or occultism may turn out to be hostile to all human creativeness. Here religious criteria are needed.

§

We must make a clear distinction between mysticism and magic. Only the modern mind, unclear and inexperienced in such matters, confuses the magic with the mystical. Mysticism is spiritual. Mysticism is communion with God. Magic is almost materialistic: it relates wholly to the astral plane. Magic is communion with nature. Mysticism is in the sphere of freedom: magic is still in the sphere of necessity. Magic is action upon nature and authority over nature, through knowledge of nature's secrets. Magic is closely related to natural science and technics. There was a time when magic was pan-science and pan-technics, the only key to all the secrets of nature. Natural history and technics have forgotten their origins: they originated in magic. The natural sciences and their applied practice, like magic itself, thirst for power over nature. Like magic, modern science longs to discover the philosopher's stone and make gold, discover the elixir of life and by it prolong man's days, and many other similar things. This selfish desire for command over nature and the production from it of that which will give man power is something modern science has inherited from black magic. The whole psychology of natural history and natural technics is akin to black magic. And the terror which modern man feels at the magic power over him of the mechanism of nature is punishment for his selfish and magical attitude towards nature. The old magic has imperceptibly been reborn into modern technics and has released enormous magic forces, the significance of which modern consciousness does not yet see clearly.

Christianity drove out the spirits of nature as evil demons, and mechanized nature. The great god Pan died. Nature was to be shackled for the purpose of redemption. For the spirits of nature had dominated man and had brought nature into a state of chaos. And every sort of magic, always based on communion with the spirits of nature, was labelled "black" by Christian consciousness—all the spirits of nature were called demons. Black magic is a product of Christian consciousness to which was given the world-mission temporarily to fetter the spirits of nature and cut off all communion with them. The magicians of the middle ages tried

316

to enter into contact with the spirits of nature and by their aid obtain power and influence. The Church called these magicians and all their magic "black", for all contact with the spirits of nature had to be severed in the Christian epoch of redemption. And the consciousness of the Christian Church justly branded magic as enslavement to and enchantment by natural necessity. Natural necessity, which is as yet not mystically overcome, is of truly magic character: it smacks of witchcraft. Black magic leaves man under the spell of natural necessity, and would give him power and authority without liberating him. And if Christianity has quite broken off all communion with the spirits of nature, black magic continues this communion with the selfish purpose of dominating over them, while remaining under their sorcerous power. For black magic, the world of nature will for ever remain bewitched. The magician thirsts for power in this bewitched world but he is powerless to release it from the spell.

The great god Pan could not finally depart from nature and perish. He was only temporarily fettered and took his revenge by appearing to men in the form of "dark" natural spirits. Then nature was completely mechanized and appeared to man as dead and spiritless. Pan merely moved deeper into the secret depths of nature. The lifeless and spiritless mechanism of nature was thoroughly studied by science and practically utilized by technics. But man could not have the same scientific and technical authority over a living nature inhabited by demons. Science and technics are two children of the Christian liberation of man from the terrifying power of the demons of nature. However, the final aim of Christianity could not be the death of the great god Pan and the mechanization of nature. Christianity bears within itself powerful forces for the renaissance of Pan and a new spiritualization of nature. The spirits of nature will return to us again and nature will become alive anew. But these spirits will no longer terrify man and dominate him, as chaos. The cosmic hierarchy will be restored and man

317

will take his royal place in living nature. Man will rule over the hierarchy of natural spirits not by selfish disjunction but by loving unification. Magic differs from science and technics in that, for it, nature always has a spirit and that it enters into contact not with mechanical forces but with the forces of nature, be they demons or forces of light. When the great god Pan returns and nature again becomes alive for the Christian world, then magic will inevitably be reborn. Science and technics will be transformed into magic, will know living nature and enter into practical communion with nature's spirits. Magic will be no longer black, but shining.

For a long time there have been signs and symptoms of the renaissance and extension of science and technics in the direction of the magical. Within science itself there is a profound crisis. The mechanical world-outlook, as the ideal of science, is shaken and cracking. Even science refuses to see in nature only a dead mechanism. Technical forces are no longer considered so neutral and harmless in their mechanism and lifelessness. Imperceptibly for modern man, nature is beginning to come alive. Man longs for the return of Pan. But when Pan returns, the attitude towards nature will change: it will no longer be scientific and technical in the sense which was accepted in the nineteenth century, which worked with a dead mechanism of nature. Men will have to hearken to the life of nature, to enter into its life with loving intuition. Selfish black magic, although it recognized the spirits of nature, was still alien to nature's life; it desired external authority over nature and was powerless to create anything within it. The bright magic of the coming world-epoch, for which nature will become a living thing, will be creative communion of man with nature, man's power over nature through his loving union with it. Man's hidden occult forces, always present but suppressed by sin, must be revealed, must be expressed in action towards creativeness in nature. Then it will be seen that man may have magical and not merely mechanical

318

authority over nature. That is to say that he will be able to govern nature inwardly by its spirit, and not merely to direct the external mechanism of nature. The dreams of the magicians, the alchemists and the astrologers will be realized. The philosophers' stone and the elixir of life will be found, not by dark selfishness but by bright readiness to sacrifice, not by the violence of witchcraft, but by the power of love. And in this creative magic of communion with nature man's microcosmic quality will be revealed. The living microcosm will be capable of inward communion with the living macrocosm and hence be able to govern it. In the mechanistic world-outlook the consciousness of man as microcosm has been lost; lost, too, the sense of world powers included in man and the intimate relationship of man's spirit with the spirits of nature. The magical communion with nature will mean the conquest of "the world", passing out beyond our given natural order, now so mechanically inert. And the church will recognize bright magic as man's creative task in nature.

Magic will become creative and active and will remove the spell from nature and lead it out of its torpidity. In the creative world-epoch mysticism, which is communion with God rather than with nature, which is spiritual rather than corporeal, can be only creative and active. The mystical way to God will be transformed into a way to creation, to the plurality of being, to man himself. The passive inhumanity of both the old mysticism and the old magic must be overcome; to them there can be no return.

# CHAPTER XIV

# THREE EPOCHS: CREATIVITY AND CULTURE; CREATIVITY AND THE CHURCH; CREATIVITY AND CHRISTIAN RENAISSANCE

DEITY (ECKHARDT'S *Gottheit* and Boehme's *Ungrund*) is deeper than God the Father, Son and Spirit. But in this world the Triune Deity, God in three persons, is coming to expression. And the whole differentiated, many-sided world is a revelation of Divinity. The Trinity is internal movement within Deity, and the dynamic of the Trinity creates the world. But formally and logically there is no possibility of creative movement in God the Absolute: if there is creative activity in God, then he is not Absolute, since something is lacking in Him, there is an incompleteness. But with equal justice we may affirm that the absence of creative movement in the Absolute would be a lack, a certain poverty of God. The world is passing through three epochs of divine revelation: the revelation of the law (the Father), the revelation of redemption (the Son) and the revelation of creativity (the Spirit). These epochs correspond to certain signs in the heavens. It is not given us to know the definite chronological limits of these three epochs: they are all co-existent. To-day we have not fully lived out the law, and redemption from sin has not yet been completed, although the world is entering a new religious epoch. Even in the epoch of the law the world had a premonition of new religious epochs: not only the prophetic consciousness of the Old Testament but the palpitation of the world-spirit in paganism awaited the advent of Christ the Redeemer. The three epochs of divine revelation in the world are three epochs of the revelation about man. In the first epoch man's sin is brought to light and natural divine force is revealed; in the second epoch man is made a son of God and redemption from sin appears; in the third epoch the divinity of man's creative nature is finally revealed and divine power becomes human power. The revelation about man is the final divine revelation about the Trinity. The final mystery is hidden in this, that the divine mystery and the human mystery are one, that in God there is hidden the mystery of man and in man the mystery of God. God is born in man and man is born in God. The ultimate revelation of man means the revelation of God. Not only is God in man but man is the image of God: in him divine development is realized. Man is a participant in the Divine Trinity. Man is not only a small universe, but a small God. Man bears within himself a double image and likeness: that of the universe and that of God. The final revelation of man is the final revelation of the universe and of God. The anthropological revelation, the revelation of man in the creative religious epoch, is at once a cosmic and a divine revelation. Through man's creativeness God in the world is finally revealed. And in its religious depths the anthropological revelation is only the revelation of Christ as Absolute Man. With the appearance of Christ in the world, man's sonship with God, his likeness to God and his participation in the divine nature are all revealed. But Absolute Man is not completely and finally revealed in the appearing of Christ the Redeemer. Man's creative energy is directed towards the Coming Christ, towards His appearing in glory. The creative revelation of man is a continuing and completing revelation of Christ, the Absolute Man. The anthropological revelation of the creative epoch is at once fully human and fully divine: in it humanity is deepened to the point of divinity and divinity is made visible to the point of humanity. The divine-human nature of revelation must become completely evident and this is possible only in the creative act of the revelation of man himself. The whole meaning of our epoch is in the fact that it is passing over to the revelation of man. But this means passing over into suffering, into a temporary agitation of the human image, into the crisis of humanism.

§

Culture has arrived at a point of profoundest inner crisis. All cultural lines lead to ultimate limits and they lead out of differentiated values. The basic problem of the nineteenth and twentieth centuries is the problem of the relationship of creativeness (culture) to life (being). At the peaks of culture man is tormented by the antithesis between creating something and being something. The geniuses have created, but they *were* less: the saints have *been*, but they created little. Creativity was born out of imperfection and insufficiency. The too-perfect cease to create. There is a tragic antagonism between the perfect man, as a result of God's creativity, and perfect human creativeness, as the work of human activity. Enter the way of Yoga, or Orthodox sainthood, or Tolstoyanism, the way of personal perfectionment, and you will cease to create. A twofold tragedy of creativeness reveals the truth that there has not yet been in our world a religious epoch of creativity. *Creativity is antagonistic, on the one hand to human perfection and on the other to the perfection of culture.* Creativeness is caught as in a vice: it is pressed between opposing tendencies—the desire for perfection of the soul and the desire for perfection of cultural value. Creativity is not self-building and self-perfection in the sense that it is understood by the Yogis, the Tolstoyans or even the Christian saints: it is not the building of cultural values in "science and the arts". Religious creativity leads through the sacrifice of both personal perfection and the perfection of culture for the sake of building new being, the continuation of the work of God's creativity. And it is infinitely important to make clear the threefold antagonism: the antagonism between the building up of cultural values and the achievement of personal perfection, the antagonism between creativity and culture, and the antagonism between creativity and personal perfection. Only the creativity of the religious epoch will

322

overcome all three antagonisms. Creativity will escape from the vice of personal perfection and the perfection of cultural values. Creativity will pass over to cosmic perfection in which man's perfection and the perfection of what he creates will become one. Hitherto the world has known chiefly two ways: either the perfection of one's own soul or the creation of perfect culture. The world crisis of culture will show the way out of this antithesis. In creative experience man will get away from the physical plane of the world and its laws. The whole fullness of man's life must become a creative act. But so long as his nature lies in sin, man must still remain under the law and in redemption.

*In both its most profound essence and its religious meaning, culture is a great failure.* Philosophy and science are failures in the creative knowledge of truth; art and literature are failures in the creation of beauty; the family and sex-life are failures in the creation of love; morals and the law have failed in the creation of human relationships; economics and technics have failed in the creation of man's creative power over nature. Culture has crystallized all man's failures. All the achievements of culture are symbolic rather than realistic. In culture men have achieved not knowledge but symbols of knowledge; not beauty but symbols of beauty, symbols of love rather than love itself, not the union of people but symbols of union, not power over nature but rather symbols of power. Culture is just as symbolic as the cult which gave it birth. The cult is a religious failure—failure to achieve communion with God. The cult was only a symbolic expression of the final mysteries. And the Church, in its visible forms, is cultural in nature and must share the fate of culture with its tragic failures. The cult is the religious source of culture and has shared with culture its symbolism. And everything great in culture has been symbolic and cultural.

Culture is eternally and tragically unsatisfied. The crisis of culture is man's final will to pass over from symbolic and conditional attainments to the attainment of the real and

323

absolute. Man has desired not symbols of truth but truth itself; not symbols of beauty but beauty itself; not symbols of love but love itself; not symbols of power but power itself; not symbols of communion with God but that communion in very truth. Culture's failure and dissatisfaction come from the fact that in everything culture achieves an evil endlessness but never reaches the eternal. Culture only creates an evil endlessness, an endless mediocrity. Hence culture, metaphysically speaking, is bourgeois. The creation of eternity means bringing all culture to the very end, to the ultimate limit, i.e. to the conquest of evil endlessness. And we must admit that in the very nature of science, philosophy, morals, art, the state, economics, and even the visible church, there is latent this very evil endlessness, this poor kind of plurality. The crisis of culture also means that it is no longer possible for the culture of evil endlessness, of bourgeois mediocrity, to exist. The creativeness of the new epoch will overcome culture from within rather than from without. The world-creative epoch can be only super-cultural rather than pre-cultural or extracultural: it accepts the positive religious meaning of culture, recognizes the great truth of every culture as over against all nihilism. Culture is always opposed to anarchy or nihilism, to savagery or barbarism. The very failure of culture is a holy failure, and through this failure lies the way to a higher being. But before culture can be transformed into higher being, it has to pass through secularization. The state, the family, science, and art must all become extra-ecclesiastical: they must not be forcibly retained within the courts of the Church. Indeed, the true Church has no courtyard. Secularization means only the destruction of falsehood and violence. The world's culture must come to a new religious life, freely and immanently. We cannot hold back from Nietzsche—we must experience him and conquer him from within. Coming out of religious guardianship means entrance into religious maturity, the full expression of a free religious life. The creation of culture has involved passing through a period

324

of God-forsakenness, through the splitting asunder of object and subject. Religion itself was division, a break with God, the *pathos* of distance.

§

The tragedy of creativeness and the crisis of culture are sensed with special vividness by Russian genius. There is something in the structure of the Russian soul which resists the sort of creativeness that produces an evil and endless, average-bourgeois culture: there is a thirst for creativeness that will bring about a new life and a new world. It is as though the spirit of Russia did not wish to create culture by separating subject from object. The Russian spirit wants to maintain the integral equality of subject and object in one integral act. On the ground of differentiated culture, Russia can be only a second-rate, little-cultured country, incapable of large culture. The Russian soul has usually subordinated its every creative impulse to something vital and essential—religious, moral, or social truth. The cult of pure values does not come naturally to a Russian. It is hard to find a Russian artist with the cult of pure beauty, just as it is hard to find a Russian philosopher with a cult of pure truth. And this is true of all spheres of culture. The Russian lover of truth desires nothing less than the complete transfiguration of life, the salvation of the world. This is a racial trait. This trait is directly connected with what is greatest and truly original in Russian culture, but it gives rise to heaviness and gloominess in Russian life. The Russian soul takes upon itself the burden of responsibility for the world and hence it cannot create cultural values in the same way as does the Latin or the German soul. The tragedy of creativeness and the crisis of culture attained their final acuity in the great Russian writers, Gogol, Dostoevski and Tolstoy. Every truly Russian soul knows this tragedy and this crisis and this does not permit us to live a happy cultural life. Many people in western Europe foresee that the future belongs to the Slavic race, that it is called to-day to speak a new word to the world,

325

that the old races of Europe have already said their word. This Russian messianism can be recognized by the western man who reveres his own great and holy culture, and it is actually so recognized by some prophetically-minded men of the west. The official Russian messianism, bound up with a dominant church and a dominant state, has decayed and fallen apart. But there lives another messianism, that of the Russian pilgrims and the searchers for the City of God and the truth of God.

Russia has always been, in everything, a land of great contrasts and polar contradictions: vulgarity and servility of the soul contrast with dizzying heights! Russia is least of all a land of average conditions, of average culture. With us, in all things, the average level is always very low. In the strict European sense of the word, there is practically no culture in Russia: there is neither a cultural milieu nor a cultural tradition. At its lower levels Russia is still savage and barbaric; it is in a pre-cultural stage of development; primeval chaos still moves within it. This eastern, Tartar lack of culture and this untamed chaotic tendency represent a great danger for Russia and her future. But at its heights, Russia is super-cultured: there the world-crisis of culture is at its most acute. The great and refined culture of the west does not know what Russia knows. Our national self-consciousness is still unclear and chaotic and hence it does not always distinguish the super-cultural truth of Russia from Russia's pre-cultural chaos. The historic task of Russian self-consciousness is to distinguish and separate Russian super-culture from Russian pre-culture: to make the distinction between the Logos of the culture-crisis on the Russian heights and the wild chaos in the Russian depths. The slavophil conception still confused the Logos with chaos, super-culture with pre-culture, and the restoration of that slavophil idea is neither possible nor desirable. The slavophil philosophy contained a prettiness of spirit, possible only before the crisis of culture: the slavophil consciousness did not go so far as an acute consciousness of the tragedy of

326

knowing. Viewed historically, the world-crisis of culture is just as inevitable in Russia as is its obedience to world-culture. For in Russia the uprising against bourgeois culture can all too easily take the form of nihilism and anarchy. But Russia will never be talented in the matter of bourgeois culture. Her talent lies elsewhere. Russia's mission is to become east-west, to unite two worlds. And it is the vocation of Russia to state in its ultimate acuity the final problem of the relation between religious consciousness on the one hand, and creativeness and culture on the other.

In the west the very volume and finesse of its culture blur the clear placing of that problem. But the west is facing a crisis of creativity and a culture-crisis. The west is bowed beneath the greatness of its ancient culture. Free flight is difficult for the western man. The western man is constantly returning to the riches and values of his great past, and his new quest all too easily takes the form of the restoration and resurrection of the past. In recent Catholic tendencies in France, in French symbolism there was new, creative seeking. But both the French Catholics and the French symbolists were under the pressure of their great and ancient culture, and were romantically concerned with its restoration and resurrection. Quite justly they contrasted the nobility of the old culture with the spirit of modern bourgeois culture. They wished to return from the bourgeois to chivalry. But the ultimate refinement of their great and ancient culture made them powerless to create. The constantly returning romanticism of the west bears the stamp of incapacity to create. It is a convulsive attempt to break away, which has produced that deformation called futurism. A Russian, even highly cultured, is far more free in his searching, and more powerful in his creative impulses.

§

Latin-Catholic culture, that most ancient and most refined in the west, has maintained an inherited connection with antiquity—the eternal source of all human culture.

327

This culture bears the visible marks of its sacred origins in cult. The Latin race, the romance peoples, are cultured in their very blood. For only that is culture which is in blood-relationship with the Græco-Roman world, with the sources of antiquity, and with the Church, whether eastern or western, which has received the heritage from antique culture. In the strict sense of the word, there can be no other culture than Græco-Roman. Orthodox-Catholic culture has direct succession from the Græco-Roman. The appearance of the German race on the arena of European history was the inrush of a current of barbarian blood into the cultured Latin blood-stream of the west. The German race is barbaric, having no blood-succession of cultural connection with the world of antiquity. The individualism of the German reformation was barbaric, in contrast to the cultural individualism of the Italian renaissance. Luther and Kant are great barbarians. The German criticism of thought is a product of barbarism, which does not wish to recognize the racial, organic super-personal fact of the inherited value of all culture and all thought. Protestantism, in the deepest truth of German culture, threw overboard not only the sacred tradition of the church, but the sacred tradition of culture as well. German individualism and German criticism break with all tradition: they begin with a barbaric revolt against all tradition—and all culture is based upon tradition. The barbaric, honest and truly genial daring of the German spirit had a liberating and deepening effect upon European culture with its stagnant Latin blood. It was the German mission to bring a greater spirituality into a culture primarily intellectual and physical. Barbaric German thought, unhampered by the old ways, constructs profound forms of religious and philosophical criticism, in which the objective world, out of its immersion in subject, is re-created in the depths of the spirit. But the natural sunny clarity of the Latin thought is quite alien to murky German thinking. Germanism is the metaphysical north; German culture is being built in sunless shadow. The most genial German

328

philosophizing was born of a breaking away from sun-like clarity, rather than from union with the natural source of light. Great and pure, but still barbaric, German culture remains primarily a culture of abstract spirituality, alien to everything plastic, incarnate, concrete. The German race accepted Christianity, even, only as a religion of pure spirituality, without either religious plasticity or religious tradition. The religious mission of Germanism was to struggle against the falsehood of deformation of Christianity on the moral and physical plane, against the corruption of Catholicism, which one-sidedly emphasized pure spirituality in religious life. We comprehend the greatness and originality of Germanism through the bottomless depths of the mystic Eckhardt. The German spirit is alien to the spirit of antiquity and strangely enough, somehow akin to the spirit of India: there is the same idealism, the same spirituality, the same vast distance from the concrete flesh of being, the same recognition of individuality as sinful aberration. Germanism wants to be purely Aryan, and refuses any Semitic ingrafting. The German spirit attempts to re-construct being, being out of its own depths—being which at the outset is not accepted as reality. German culture has barbaric depth and an original sort of purity (honour and loyalty) but it has neither refinement nor elegance. Even in Goethe, the greatest of great Germans, we find coarseness and a lack of taste. Refinement and elegance are the unique heritage of French culture. But culture is primarily refinement and elegance. The German spirit is building up something great, but not cultural in the strict sense of the word. And Nietzsche is not altogether wrong when he says that there is no culture in Germany, but only in France. The German spirit thinks critically about culture, places the problem of culture acutely in its consciousness, reflects upon culture, but has no culture itself. Culture cannot be critical and individualistic—it is always organic and something held in common, it is œcumenical.

Of course the German race has a great and providential

mission in the western world. Great and providential is the mission of German mysticism, of German music and German philosophy. But this mission does not consist in the creation of the most generally valid and most universal culture, worthy of imitation by all the peoples of the world. The German spirit is not setting up universally-valid norms of all culture, as the German *Kultur-Träger* would have us believe. We can and we may learn much from German philosophy and mysticism, but to imitate German culture is impossible. Final refinement has been attained by universal Latin culture, which is primarily culture: it has arrived at the brink of the abyss. In German culture there is still too much of barbaric and *bürgerlich* health; it would like to remain in the middle of the road, in the middle way of Kant and Goethe. The culture of abstract spirituality lacks a sense of finality, of an outer limit. The Germanic spirit is least of all apocalyptic. Nietzsche is not pure German spirit: there is much of the Slavic in him, and he was educated on French culture. German philosophy is doing a great work in the world: it is helping to resolve the world-crisis of culture but indirectly and from the other end, so to speak. And the great German mysticism, a new word said to the world by the German race, will certainly be the final contribution of the Germans to the task of solving world-history. In the mysticism of the Germans there is eternal truth, either for normal culture, or for a passage out into super-culture.

Besides, we have the sources of the ancient Hebrews and the ancient Greeks, their spirit of concreteness and incarnation. Slavic mysticism is primarily apocalyptic, bound up with the times and seasons of universal history, with concrete incarnation, with eschatology. Slavic culture, in the ordinary sense of the word, is much lower than German culture. But the Slavic race took into its flesh and blood the succession and heritage of Greece and Byzantium. By its very position in history, the Slavic race is antagonistic to the German. It can learn from the German but it can neither imitate nor fuse with the German race.

330

§

In the ultimate and secret depths of its being, creativity is of the Church. In religious creativeness the divine-human body of the world is created. The very passage through God-forsakenness and falling-away from God, through splitting asunder, is the way of divine life. Christ Himself passed through the "My God, my God, why hast thou forsaken me?" And only in creativeness are the cosmology and anthropology of the church finally and wholly revealed. In the historic Church, which corresponds to the early, infant, stages of the development of the new man, there has not as yet been a revelation about man. A creative revelation about man is the only way to a rebirth and new development of the Church's waning life. Christianity has remained an unfinished revelation about the absolute significance and calling of man. The anthropological revelation of the creative epoch will be the finished revelation of God-manhood, the complete disclosure of Christ in the life of the world, of Christ uniting Himself with humanity. Christianity in history has fallen into the most terrible sin, sin against the Holy Spirit. Christianity has blasphemed against the Spirit whenever it has recognized the Church as finished, Christianity as complete, creativeness as something forbidden and sinful. For life in the Spirit can be only eternally creative, and every stop or stay in the creative dynamic of the Church is thus a sin against the Spirit. An immovable Church is a Church that is dead, that lacks the Spirit. But Christian men have taken the most holy tradition of the Church, in which man eternally creates in the Spirit, and transformed it into something static, something external to man. The life of the Church has ossified, has cooled, almost to the point of death, and it can be reborn only in man's religious creativeness, only in the new world-epoch. Christianity has grown old and wrinkled. Christianity is a gaffer, two thousand years old. But the eternal cannot grow old. And neither can the eternal religion of Christ grow old. In the cosmos the redeeming sacrifice of Golgotha is consummated in all eternity, and in all eternity lives the mystical body of Christ. And the gates of hell shall not prevail against this true Church of Christ, which knows no material signs or boundaries. It is only the temporal in Christianity which has grown old, it is only a certain epoch of Christianity which has been outlived. The infant stage of the first education of man, the epoch of guardianship and religious fear, has grown old and wrinkled, has lost its vivacity. The abnormality in Christianity is just this wrinkled old-age of the infant. The Church of Peter, the Church of religious guardianship of "these little ones", of the religious guidance of children for whom one is always fearful, has done its work in the world and has conserved the Christian shrine for the broad mass of the people down to the times of mankind's maturity. But the immature and childish religious consciousness dug a deep abyss between God and the world, between the Creator and the creature. The Church has been not so much spiritual, as intellectual and physical, expressing itself on the physical plane of being.

The everyday history of the church has been unspiritual, even unreligious. But now man is turning not to the physical but *to the spiritual body* of the Church. The Christian renaissance of a new humanity, matured in the Spirit, moving out of the epoch of fearfulness and guardianship, can take place only under the sign not of the Church of Peter but of John and of the mystic Johannine tradition. The Johannine Church is not a democratic Church of the guardianship of infants, not an adaptation to the sinful weakness and mediocrity of man—this is the mystical and eternal Church of Christ, the visage of the Church itself, revealing itself to man in ascent towards the heights rather than an adaptation to the lower depths of humanity. Man has now matured into readiness for the new religious Church, not because he has become sinless and perfect, not because he has fulfilled all the commandments of the church of Peter, but because man's consciousness at the height of culture has attained mature and final acuteness and man's nature has been laid open to the point where its ultimate, first bases are revealed. The adult is not better than the child but he is mature. Man has finally moved out of his childhood, has become mature in both his vices and his virtues. Modern man has finally lost his childishness in both virtues and vices. And for modern man there can be no return to childish or infantile religiosity, he cannot return to religious tutelage. Not only cultured folk but the popular masses are striving for a higher spiritual life. The historic Church of Peter is unable to satisfy the modern man; it cannot cope with his religious tragedy; it is always answering questions which have not been asked; it soothes the wrong suffering, heals the wrong wounds; it is helping to save men from childish sins, but is powerless to help with the sins of maturity; it does not want to know anything new in man. The gates of hell shall not prevail against the Church but the new torments of the new human spirit will prevail against the temporary, the infantile and the antiquated in the Church. The answer to these new torments can be given only by the revelation of the mystery of the eternal, mystical Johannine Church of Christ. In this form the church opens to mature man, convulsed in religious torment, the boundless, measureless freedom of creativity in the Spirit, the multiplicity of individual ways in God. The secret will be revealed to man, which has been concealed from infants in the period of tutelage—the secret that submission is not the ultimate in religious experience but only a temporary method; that in daring and sacrificial initiative this childish security must be overpassed, that sin will finally be conquered by heroic creativity. The security and cosiness of historic, everyday churchliness must be sacrificed to the heroic daring of creativeness. Churchliness has hidden from man the heroic, sacrificial mountain way of Christ Himself; it has taken from man the burden of responsibility and has assured him a spiritual life, in which "this cup is taken from him". This was purchased at the price of humility and obedience. But in the Christian world humility and obedience have long since been transformed into servitude and opportunism: they no longer give life, but rather death.

To overcome this religious servility, this heteronomic consciousness, is the first task of a Christian renaissance. Man must know himself religiously not as the slave of God but as a free participant in the divine process.

Christianity has not yet been fully revealed as a religion of love. Christianity has been a religion of the salvation of "these little ones" and of tutelage over frightened children. Christian humanity, throughout its history, has not accomplished love, the life of grace in the Spirit; it has lived under the sign of the world of nature, and its great wrestlers of the spirit taught how men must harden their hearts in order to conquer sinful passions. St. Isaac the Syrian says: "He who loves all men equally, in sympathy and without regard for the person, he has attained perfection." The apostle John taught mystical love and St. Francis realized love in his own life. But these are rare mystical blossoms. Democratic, popular and universally-historic Christian religion has been a religion of obedience, of bearing the burden of the consequences of sin. The "elders" are teaching us not love but submission and constant worry about salvation from destruction. Even in the lives of the saints, how rarely do we find the flowers of mystical love, and how extraordinarily powerful is the *pathos* of obedience and the acquisition of personal salvation! In the whole life of the Church, there is no love: there is no love in the typical Christian hierarch; no love in clerical care or in lay obedience; there is no love in the normal structure of the Christian spirit. Constantine Leontieff was right when he saw in Orthodox Christianity not so much a religion of love as a religion of fear. Love has remained the esoteric, unrevealed secret of the religion of Christ, its mystical tradition: love has only been glimpsed in the lives of a few chosen ones. Mystically, love cannot be joined with fear and tutelage. Love has been revealed in the church only symbolically, not really: only liturgically, not in everyday living. The secret of love is revealed in the cult of the Church, but this cult is just as much a failure in mystical love as the whole of culture is a failure in the realization of

334

new being. Rigid ecclesiasticism is hostile to the spirit of love, hostile to the point of hatred, and is ready to consider sinful the very desire for love. In the life of the Church love has been transformed into a dead and deadly word. And the very idea of Christian love justly arouses dissatisfaction and hostility, as something akin to hypocrisy and falsehood. Love is new, creative life, a life of grace in the Spirit. It can never be an object of education or morality. Love is not a law, and no one can be compelled to love. It is shameful to speak and embarrassing to hear of the Christian state, the Christian family, Christian society so guarded and protected. This is a deception which modern man cannot and should not stand. The religion of love will yet come in the world: this is the religion of the measureless freedom of the Spirit. The Church of love is the Johannine Church, the eternal, mystical church, bearing within itself the fullness of truth about Christ and about man.

§

With the third, the creative epoch, there is closely related a sense of the end, an eschatological perspective on life. In the third epoch, the epoch of religious creativeness, all ends and limits of the world's life and culture will be manifest. The creativeness of that epoch will be directed essentially towards the final, rather than the penultimate: all its achievements must be not symbolic but realistic, not merely cultural but of the whole of life. The religious centre of gravity will be transferred from the clerically-protective to the prophetically-creative. Not only Christian priesthood, but Christian prophecy must become life. Not the angelic element (the priesthood) but the human element must have authority. But a prophetic religious experience cannot be an experience of passive expectation—this is an experience of active, creative striving, of great anthropological tension and effort. We cannot merely passively await the coming of Christ, we must be up and go toward Him. The sense of the apocalyptic will lead to a new religious life only if it becomes

335

actively creative instead of passively expectant. The coming of Christ, in which the absolute Man will be fully revealed in all his power and glory, is connected with man's creative act, with an active anthropological revelation. Man's christological nature will be revealed in man's creative act. The Coming Christ will come only to a humanity which courageously accomplishes a Christological self-revelation, that is, reveals in its own nature divine power and glory. Christ will never come in power and glory to men who are not creatively active—they will never see the second face of Christ: He will eternally turn toward them His crucified, tortured and sacrificing face. To see the face of Christ in power and glory, man must reveal power and glory in himself by a creative act. The epoch of redemption where, only the Crucified Christ is visible, will never end for those who do not perform the creative act which completely reveals human nature. They will ever remain in the Church of Golgotha—will never know the Church of the Coming Christ. *Defensive hostility toward religious creativeness is confirmation of an evil endlessness in redemption itself, resistance to the completion and the fullness and the end of redemption.* Religious opposition to the third, creative epoch desires a permanent, endless redemption, resists the final solution of earthly life and the appearance of the Coming Christ, mighty and glorified. The church of Golgotha in which christological truth is not completely revealed, stands over against the church of the integral Christ, where He is revealed completely. The coming of Christ and his full revelation of the whole truth about absolute Man predicates that in creative activity man shall take his glorious and royal place in the world. To transform the Golgothan truth of redemption into a force hostile to creative revelation about man is a sin, a human falling-away, which gives rise to world-religious reaction; it is hindering the all-resolving end of the world, the setting-up of a new heaven and a new earth. N. Fedoroff spoke boldly of the conditionality of the apocalyptic prophecies, and considered the Apocalypse as a warning threat for the immature.

The sum of all the world's life and the world's culture is the problem of creativeness, the problem of the anthropological revelation. All the threads come together at this point, everything comes to a focus here. But we have not yet known true creativity in the final and ultimate religious sense of the word. Our philosophy is as yet only an introduction to the philosophy of creativeness rather than that philosophy itself. And our present life is only a transition to creative life rather than creative life itself. What creativeness is, is inexplicable. But our initiative towards a full realization of the creative life must be bold and our clearing of the way for it must be merciless. And man to-day, hesitating before his creative task and refusing creative initiative from a false sense of humility, cradled in passive obedience as the highest virtue, is not fulfilling his religious duty; he is not fulfilling the will of God. Creative spiritual life is not movement along a plane; it is vertical movement towards the heights and the depths. This movement towards the heights and the depths is projected in the world upon a plane and externally it is accepted as a shifting of the point of intersection of a perpendicular with the plane. A superficial consciousness sees only the movement along the plane, and this consciousness sees the Church itself as a plane. A deeper consciousness sees the vertical movement. To-day at the cosmic turning-point this vertical movement is changing the world so profoundly that a re-ordering of planes is taking place, a division into layers, an atomization of the world, and a transition to another dimension. And in the depths of the cosmic crisis is being accomplished the conquest of procreative sex as a world-principle, i.e. liberation from the material, from racial life, through the revelation of the virginity of man's androgynous image, the creative rather than the procreative life of the anthropos. Truth and beauty can never triumph on the plane of the world, on the broad field of racial life: they will be lifted upon the cross, and only through the mystery of the crucifixion will the rose of the world's life be resurrected.

# INDEX

Chastity, a sexual phenomenon, 182-3
Chivalry and moral creativeness, 265-6
Christ:
  and Boehme's doctrine of the Androgyne, 66-9
  foundation of true anthropology upon, 78-85, 90-3
  impossibility of accepting God without Christ, 136-7
  and continuance of God's work of creation, 137-9
  the Liberator, 151-2
  and solitude, 158
  *Other references under* Christianity.
Christianity:
  and man as microcosm, 64-70
  and the true nature of man, 80-5
  truth of the Gospel, 94
  modern distortion of the Gospel, 94-5
  New Testament C. a religion of redemption, 95-6
  Gospel silence about creativeness, 96-9
  God gives man creative freedom, 99-100
  and man as creator like God the Creator, 100-1
  and economic materialism, 101-3
  and salvation as a step toward creativeness, 104-6
  and man's freedom in revelation of his creativeness, 106-9
  and creativeness as final revelation on the Holy Trinity, 109-12
  impossibility of a Christian culture, 126-7
  and man's birth in God, 130
  and the Divine Trinity, 134
  God's autocracy and divine-human religion, 136-7
  continuation of creation in Christ, 137-9
  science as product of, 140
  and freedom, 147-50, 158-9
  and sectarianism, 156-7
  and solitude, 157-8
  and asceticism, 160-3
  pagan attitude towards the world, 163-4
  and repentance, 165-7
  as a universal organism, 168
  and diminution of saintliness, 168-70

Christianity:—*(cont.)*
  and genius and saintliness, 176-8
  and sex, 181, 183-4, 196-200, 205
  and the family, 208-12
  and love, 222-4
  and art, 227-30
  and the Renaissance, 230-6
  bourgeois concept of morals in, 251-6
  and the eternal and absolute in morals, 257-9
  its morality of creative values, 259-61
  and democratic and aristocratic morality, 164-7
  and utilitarian-altruistic morals, 267-70
  and morals and redemption, 270-1
  and the state, 277-80, 284-6
  not democratic in a mystic sense, 289
  and a new social order, 293-5
  and the two elements of religious consciousness, 297-9
  and magic, 316-19
  and the three epochs of divine revelation, ch. XIV, 320-37
  *See also* Catholic Church; Mysticism; Orthodox Church.
Classicism:
  and romanticism, 118-20
  and art, 227-30
  and the Renaissance, 230-6
Cohen, 21, 23, 26, 31, 32, 49, 50, 56, 59, 125
Community, the. *See* State.
Comte, August, 21, 88
Copernicus, 75, 76, 87
Criticist philosophy, 58
Cubism, 242
Culture:
  philosophy of, and gnosseology, 125-7
  crisis of, and art, 243-4
  crisis of, and morality, 262-4
  crisis of, and political values, 286
  antagonism of creativity to, 322-3
  failure and dissatisfaction of, 323-5
  Russian and French, 325-7
  Latin-Catholic and German, 327-30
  and the creativity of the Church, 331-5
  and Christological self-revelation, 335-6

Materialism:
a philosophy of obedience, 32, 41, 102
Marx's materialistic humanism, 89
a philosophy of sin, 102-3
and being, 132-5, 139-41
and the state, ch. XII, 274-95
*See also* Evolutionism.
Maxim, St., the Confessor, 188
Mechanical civilization, 292-3
Metaphysics:
desire to become scientific, 21-2
and intuition, 40
Michelangelo, 234, 235-6
Militarism, 291
Morals:
Christian bourgeois concept, 251-6
and insufficiency of humility and submission, 256-7
and the eternal and absolute in Christianity, 257-9
Christian morality of creative values, 259-61
world-crisis of, 262-4
democratic and aristocratic, 264-7
utilitarian-altruistic, 267-70
and redemption, 270-1
and creative Dionysism, 271-2
and creativeness, 272-3
Music, 249-50
Mysticism:
and man as microcosm, 64-70
and God's birth in man, 130
panethistic-emanational, 131-2, 300-1
and asceticism, 160-1
and sex, 184-90
essential basis of religious consciousness, 296-9
modern debasement of, 299-300
different forms of, 302-7
Catholic and Orthodox, 307-10
and occultism, 310-15
and magic, 315-19

NATURALISM. *See* Anthropocentrism.
Nature controlled by man, 70-2
Neoplatonism, 304
Newton, 55
Nietzsche, F., 31, 90-1, 106, 121-1, 158, 170, 226, 240, 242, 244, 257, 259-60, 261, 263, 264, 324, 329, 330

OCCULTISM, 310-15
Œcumenicity ("sobornost"), 33, 35, 36, 49, 157-8
Ontology. *See* Being.
Orthodox Church, and mysticism, 307-10

PAN. *See* Magic.
Pantheistic-emanational mysticism, 131-2, 300-1
Paracelsus, 70
Pascal, 60
Paul, St., 64
Phallic cult, 185-6
Philosophy:
desire to become scientific, 21-3
an independent sphere of culture, 23-4
a general orientation to the whole of being, 27-8
as creativeness, or art of knowing, 29-30
duality of its history, 30-2
and universally valid truth, 32-3, 42-5
and creative intuition, 33-6
non-validity of a logic of philosophy, 36-9
pragmatism, Anglo-Saxon and Bergsonian, 39-41
and passivity of the spirit, 41-2
and reflection and dissociation, 45
critical and dogmatic, 45-6
necessity of the erotic in, 46-7
does not require logic of proof, 47-9
and anthropologism, 49-52
and intuition of being, 52-4
freedom and, 54-5
and the thraldom of theosophy to science, 55-6
*See also* Gnosseology.
Picasso, 242
Pico dela Mirandola, 86
Plato, 32, 47, 54, 185, 201
Plotinus, 37, 131, 303-4, 305, 307
Politics, unreality of, 276. *See also* State.
Pollajuolo, 232
Positivism:
a philosophy of obedience, 41, 57, 58
degrades man, 87, 88
Pragmatism, Anglo-Saxon and Bergsonian, 39-41

Proof, logic of, not required in creative philosophy, 47-9
Pseudo-Dionysius the Areopagite, 304, 305
Pushkin, Alexander, 170-3, 177
Pythagoras, 51

QUIETISM, 301

RACE AND SEX, 192-6
Raphael, 233, 234-6
Rationalism, 58
Realism, in art, 237-8
Redemption:
    in New Testament Christianity, 95-6
    and Gospel silence on creativeness, 97-9
    creative freedom given by God to man, 99-100
    and man as creator like God the Creator, 100-1
    and economic materialism, 101-3
    salvation as a step toward creativeness, 104-6
    man's freedom in revelation of his creativeness, 106-9
    and creativeness as final revelation of the Holy Trinity, 109-12
    and art, 236-7
    and moralism, 270-1
    See also Repentance.
Renaissance, the:
    pagan and Christian elements in, 230-4
    failure of, 234-6
Repentance:
    and sin, 165-7
    necessary for creativity, 166
Revelation, divine, three epochs of, 320-37
Revolutions, uncreative and reactionary, 280-1
Rickert, 21, 37, 115-18
Romano, Giulio, 234
Romanticism, and classicism, 118-20
Rozanoff, 195, 210, 222
Russia, culture in, 325-7

SAINTLINESS:
    diminution of, 168-70
    and genius, 170-3, 176-8
Savonarola, 234

Schelling, 31, 63
Scholasticism, 22
Schopenhauer, 31, 192
Science:
    value of, as opposed to the "scientific," 24-5
    as instrument of orientation in the given world, 25-6
    as obedience to necessity, 26-7
    and gnoseology, 123-5
    as product of Christianity, 140
Scriabin, 250
Sculpture, 249, 250
Sectarianism, and freedom, 156-7
Seraphim, St., 170-2, 177
Sex:
    deeper than mere sexual function, 180-1
    and ascetism, 181-2
    determines the whole of man, 182-3
    cosmic categories of, 183-6
    mystical teaching on, 186-90
    man more independent of, than woman, 190-1, 218
    sexual union momentary and illusory, 191-2
    hostile to personality, 192-3
    source of life and death, 193-6
    and Christianity, 196-200, 205
    begetting sex and creative sex, 200-1
    and genius, 201-2
    and hermaphroditism, 202
    crisis of, and the revelation of the new sex, 202-4
    the sexual act and love, 205-7
    and debauchery, 215-17
    and friendship, 222
Simeon, St., the New Theologian, 72, 82, 160
Sin:
    materialism a philosophy of, 102-3
    categories of sinful being, 113-15
    the fall of man and the beginning of creativity, 136
    and freedom, 147-50
    and repentance, 165-7
    and sex, 185-91
    and Christian morals, 251-2
    See also Man; Redemption.
Socialism, 282-4, 287-8. See also Marx; Materialism; State.
Society. See State.
Sociologism, falseness and unreality of, 274-6

343

344

# A BRIEF OVERVIEW OF
# NIKOLAI BERDYAEV'S LIFE AND WORKS

Nikolai Berdyaev (1874–1948) was one of the greatest religious thinkers of the 20<sup>th</sup> century. His adult life, led in Russia and in western European exile, spanned such cataclysmic events as the Great War, the rise of Bolshevism and the Russian Revolution, the upsurge of Nazism, and the Second World War. He produced profound commentaries on many of these events, and had many acute things to say about the role of Russia in the evolution of world history. There was sometimes almost no separation between him and these events: for example, he wrote the book on Dostoevsky while revolutionary gunfire was rattling outside his window.

Berdyaev's thought is primarily a religious metaphysics, influenced not only by philosophers like Kant, Hegel, Schopenhauer, Solovyov, and Nietzsche, but also by religious thinkers and mystics such as Meister Eckhart, Angelus Silesius, Franz van Baader, Jakob Boehme, and Dostoevsky. The most fundamental concept of this metaphysics is that of the *Ungrund* (a term taken from Boehme), which is the pure potentiality of being, the negative ground essential for the realization of the novel, creative aspects of existence. A crucial element of Berdyaev's thought is his philosophical anthropology: A human being is originally an "ego" out which a "person" must develop. Only when an ego freely acts to realize its own concrete essence, rather than abstract or arbitrary goals, does it become a person. A society that furthers the goal of the development of egos into persons is a true community, and the relation then existing among its members is a sobornost.

He showed an interest in philosophy early on, at the age of fourteen reading the works of Kant, Hegel, and Schopenhauer.

While a student at St. Vladimir's University in Kiev, he began to participate in the revolutionary Social-Democratic movement and to study Marxism. In 1898, he was sentenced to one month in a Kiev prison for his participation in an anti-government student demonstration, and was later exiled for two years (1901–02) to Vologda, in the north of Russia.

His first book, *Subjectivism and Individualism in Social Philosophy* (1901), represented the climax of his infatuation with Marxism as a methodology of social analysis, which he attempted to combine with a neo-Kantian ethics. However, as early as 1903, he took the path from "Marxism to idealism," which had already been followed by such former Marxists as Peter Struve, Sergey Bulgakov, and S.L. Frank. In 1904 Berdyaev became a contributor to the philosophical magazine *New Path*. The same year he married Lydia Trushcheva, a daughter of a Petersburg lawyer. In 1905–06, together with Sergey Bulgakov, he edited the magazine *Questions of Life*, attempting to make it the central organ of new tendencies in the domains of socio-political philosophy, religious philosophy, and art. The influence exerted upon him by the writers and philosophers Dmitry Merezhkovsy and Zinaida Gippius, during meetings with them in Paris in the winter of 1907–08, led him to embrace the Russian Orthodox faith. After his return to Russia, he joined the circle of Moscow Orthodox philosophers united around the Path publishing house (notably Bulgakov and Pavel Florensky) and took an active part in organizing the religious-philosophical Association in Memory of V. Solovyov. An important event in his life at this time was the publication of his article "Philosophical Truth and the Truth of the Intelligentsia" in the famous and controversial collection *Landmarks* (1909), which subjected to a critical examination the foundations of the world-outlook of the left-wing Russian intelligentsia. Around this time, Berdyaev published a work which inaugurated his life-long exploration of the concept of freedom in its many varieties and ramifications. In *The Philosophy of Freedom* (1911), a critique of the "pan-gnoseologism" of recent German and Russian philosophy led Berdyaev to a search for an authentically Christian ontology. The end result of this search was a philosophy of freedom, according to which human beings are rooted in a sobornost of being and thus possess true knowledge.

In 1916, Berdyaev published the most important work of his early period: *The Meaning of the Creative Act*. The originality of this work is rooted in the rejection of theodicy as a traditional problem of the Christian consciousness, as well as in a refusal to accept the view that creation and revelation have come to an end and are complete. The central element of the "meaning of the creative act" is the idea that man reveals his true essence in the course of a continuing creation realized jointly with God (a theurgy). Berdyaev's notion of "theurgy" (in contrast to those of Solovyov and Nikolai Fyodorov) is distinguished by the inclusion of the element of freedom: the creative act is a means for the positive self-definition of freedom not as the choice and self-definition of persons in the world but as a "foundationless foundation of being" over which God the creator has no power.

Berdyaev's work from 1914 to 1924 can be viewed as being largely influenced by his inner experience of the Great War and the Russian Revolution. His main themes during this period are the "cosmic collapse of humanity" and the effort to preserve the hierarchical order of being (what he called "hierarchical personalism"). Revolutionary violence and nihilism were seen to be directly opposed to the creatively spiritual transformation of "this world" into a divine "cosmos." In opposing the chaotic nihilism of the first year of the Revolution, Berdyaev looked for support in the holy ontology of the world, i.e., in the divine cosmic order. The principle of hierarchical inequality, which is rooted in this ontology, allowed him to nullify the main argument of the leveling ideology and praxis of Communism—the demand for "social justice." Berdyaev expressed this view in his *Philosophy of Inequality* (1923).

During this period, Berdyaev posed the theme of Russian

messianism in all its acuteness. Torn apart by the extremes of apocalyptic yearning and nihilism, Russia is placed into the world as the "node of universal history" (the "East-West"), in which are focused all the world's problems and the possibility of their resolution, in the eschatological sense. In the fall of the monarchy in February 1917, Berdyaev saw an opportunity to throw off the provincial Russian empire which had nothing in common with Russia's messianic mission. But the Russian people betrayed the "Russian idea" by embracing the falsehood of Bolshevism in the October Revolution. The Russian messianic idea nevertheless remains true in its ontological core despite this betrayal.

In the fall of 1919, Berdyaev organized in Moscow the Free Academy of Spiritual Culture, where he led a seminar on Dostoevsky and conducted courses on the Philosophy of Religion and the Philosophy of History. This latter course became the basis of one of his most important works: *The Meaning of History: An Essay on the Philosophy of Human Destiny* (1923). His attacks against the Bolshevik regime became increasingly intense: he called the Bolsheviks nihilists and annihilators of all spiritual values and culture in Russia. His activities and statements, which made him a notable figure in post-revolutionary Moscow, began to attract the attention of the Soviet authorities. In 1920, he was arrested in connection with the so-called "tactical center" affair, but was freed without any consequences. In 1922, he was arrested again, but this time he was expelled from Russia on the so-called "philosopher's ship" with other ideological opponents of the regime such as Bulgakov, Frank, and Struve.

Having ended up in Berlin, Berdyaev gradually entered the sphere of post-War European philosophy; he met Spengler, von Keyserling, and Scheler. His book *The New Middle Ages: Reflections on the Destiny of Russia and Europe* (1924) (English title: *The End of Our Time*) brought him European celebrity. Asserting that modern history has come to an end, and that it has been a failure, Berdyaev again claimed that Russia (now the post-revolutionary one) had a messianic mission. He wrote that "culture is now not just European; it is becoming universal. Russia, which had stood at the center of East and West, is now—even if by a terrible and catastrophic path—acquiring an increasingly palpable world significance, coming to occupy the center of the world's attention" (*The New Middle Ages*, p. 36). In 1924, Berdyaev moved to Paris, where he became a founder and professor of the Russian Religious-Philosophical Academy. In 1925, he helped to found and became the editor of the Russian religious-philosophical journal *Put'* (*The Path*), arguably the most important Russian religious journal ever published. He organized interconfessional meetings of representatives of Catholic, Protestant, and Orthodox religious-philosophical thought, with the participation of such figures as Maritain, Mounier, Marcel, and Barth.

In the émigré period, his thought was primarily directed toward what can be called a liberation from ontologism. Emigration became for him an existential experience of "rootless" extra-hierarchical existence, which can find a foundation solely in "the kingdom of the Spirit," i.e., in the person or personality. The primacy of "freedom" over "being" became the determining principle of his philosophy, a principle which found profound expression in his book *On the Destiny of Man: An Essay on Paradoxical Ethics* (1931), which he considered his "most perfect" book. This is how he expressed this principle: "creativeness is possible only if one admits freedom that is not determined by being, that is not derivable from being. Freedom is rooted not in being but in 'nothingness'; freedom is foundationless, is not determined by anything, is found outside of causal relations, to which being is subject and without which being cannot be understood" (from his autobiography, the Russian version, *Self-knowledge*, p. 231).

At around the same time, Berdyaev re-evaluated Kant's philosophy, arriving at the conclusion that only this philosophy "contains the foundations of a true metaphysics." In particular, Kant's "recognition that there is a deeper reality hidden behind the world of phenomena" helped Berdyaev formulate a key principle of his personalism: the doctrine of "objectification," which he first systematically developed in *The World of Objects: An Essay on the Philosophy of Solitude and Social Intercourse* (1934) (English title: *Solitude and Society*). This is how Berdyaev explained this doctrine: "Objectification is an epistemological interpretation of the fallenness of the world, of the state of enslavement, necessity, and disunitedness in which the world finds itself. The objectified world is subject to rational knowledge in concepts, but the objectification itself has an irrational source" (*Self-knowledge*, p. 292). Using man's creative powers, it is possible to pierce this layer of objectification, and to see the deeper reality. Man's "ego" (which knows only the objectified world) then regains its status of "person," which lives in the non-objectified, or real, world. Berdyaev had a strong sense of the unreality of the world around him, of his belonging to another—real—world.

After the Second World War, Berdyaev's reflections turned again to the role of Russia in the world. His first post-war book was *The Russian Idea: The Fundamental Problems of Russian Thought of the 19th Century and the Beginning of the 20th Century* (1946), in which he tried to discover the profound meaning of Russian thought and culture. Himself being one of the greatest representatives of this thought and culture, he saw that the meaning of his own activity was to reveal to the western world the distinctive elements of Russian philosophy, such as its existential nature, its eschatalogism, its religious anarchism, and its obsession with the idea of "Divine humanity."

Berdyaev is one of the greatest religious existentialists. His philosophy goes beyond mere thinking, mere rational conceptualization, and tries to attain authentic life itself: the profound layers of existence that touch upon God's world. He directed all of his efforts, philosophical as well as in his personal and public life, at replacing the kingdom of this world with the kingdom of God. According to him, we can all attempt to do this by tapping the divine creative powers which constitute our true nature. Our mission is to be collaborators with God in His continuing creation of the world.

Summing up his thought in one sentence, this is what Berdyaev said about himself: "Man, personality, freedom, creativeness, the eschatological-messianic resolution of the dualism of two worlds—these are my basic themes."

BORIS JAKIM
2009

# BIBLIOGRAPHY OF NIKOLAI BERDYAEV'S
# BOOKS IN ENGLISH TRANSLATION
## (IN ALPHABETICAL ORDER)

*The Beginning and the End.* Russian edition 1947. First English edition 1952.

*The Bourgeois Mind and Other Essays.* English edition 1934.

*Christian Existentialism. A Berdyaev Anthology.* 1965.

*Christianity and Anti-Semitism.* Russian edition 1938. First English edition 1952.

*Christianity and Class War.* Russian edition 1931. First English edition 1933.

*The Destiny of Man.* Russian edition 1931. First English edition 1937.

*The Divine and the Human.* Russian edition 1952. First English edition 1947.

*Dostoevsky: An Interpretation.* Russian edition 1923. First English edition 1934.

*Dream and Reality: An Essay in Autobiography.* Russian edition 1949. First English edition 1950.

*The End of Our Time.* Russian edition 1924. First English edition 1933.

*The Fate of Man in the Modern World.* First Russian edition 1934. English edition 1935.

*Freedom and the Spirit.* Russian edition 1927. First English edition 1935.

*Leontiev.* Russian edition 1926. First English edition 1940.

*The Meaning of History.* Russian edition 1923. First English edition 1936.

*The Meaning of the Creative Act.* Russian edition 1916. First English edition 1955.

*The Origin of Russian Communism.* Russian edition 1937. First English edition 1937.

*The Realm of Spirit and the Realm of Caesar.* Russian edition 1949. First English edition 1952.

*The Russian Idea.* Russian edition 1946. First English edition 1947.

*Slavery and Freedom.* Russian edition 1939. First English edition 1939.

*Solitude and Society.* Russian edition 1934. First English edition 1938.

*Spirit and Reality.* Russian edition 1946. First English edition 1937.

*Towards a New Epoch.* Transl. from the original French edition 1949.

  *Truth and Revelation.* English edition 1954.

352

CPSIA information can be obtained
at www.ICGtesting.com
Printed in the USA
BVHW032128250620
582041BV00001BA/20